The Troul

I recommend our diplomats and ministers read this book; it will provide them with an intellectual backbone. This will be the essential vade mecum if and when a referendum campaign takes place. The part of Bootle's book in which he analyses the pros and cons of British exit from the EU will be the most influential.

On the big calls [Bootle] has a spectacularly good record. He warned about the bubble in US real estate which led to the credit crunch. Earlier, he forecast the collapse of the dotcom boom. Most creditably of all, back in 1992 he identified that the pound would be forced out of the ERM – and that this would be a good thing for the British economy. His latest book is all of a piece with that prescient judgment of more than 20 years ago.

—Dominic Lawson, *The Sunday Times*

Bootle is right on every count.

—Larry Elliott, *The Guardian*

Bootle writes with energetic prose and makes some good points. His discussion of European monetary union is cogent. The enterprise was unnecessary and it was embarked on too early and with insufficient preparation. It was an integration too far and too soon. Bootle is an accomplished economist whose The Trouble with Markets *provided a penetrating analysis of the origins of the financial crisis. In* The Trouble with Europe, *he asks what has gone wrong with the EU, suggests why reforms are unlikely to happen and maps out a fresh start for UK–EU relations.*

—*Financial Times*

This is a credible plan for life outside Europe and deserves to be widely read.

The Week – Business Books of the Year

Roger Bootle's well-informed and rigorously-argued book brutally exposes the problems besetting Europe and Britain's position within – and conceivably outside – the European Union. It should be required reading for all those preparing to vote.

—David Marsh, Co-chairman of OMFIF, and author of

Europe's Deadlock

A timely and balanced analysis of the contradictions inherent in what has become the European Union, driven not by ideology but by rational economic analysis. It provides a chronological context, pursues some historic comparisons and concludes with a variety of options both for the EU generally and the UK specifically. Bootle recognises that the political will of the elites is never sufficient to overcome economic reality and the voice of the people.

—Gisela Stuart, Labour MP for Birmingham Edgbaston

– Bartley Green, Harborne and Quinton

Roger Bootle manages to weave the economic, political and diplomatic aspects of the European Union's current problems into a compulsively readable analysis which should be of engrossing interest to europhiles and eurosceptics alike.

—William Keegan, Senior Economics Editor, *The Observer*, and author of *The Prudence of Mr. Gordon Brown*

[Roger Bootle] has a distinguished (and, for an economist, unusual) record of being right on the main issues – famously predicting in 1990 that the financial climate in Europe and North American would face 'the death of inflation'.

—Andrew Hilton, Director, Centre for the Study of
Financial Innovation

This is an important book. Anyone who wishes to debate this issue seriously will have to read it. Bootle has done the world a service.

—John Llewellyn, Llewellyn Consulting and former
Chef de Cabinet to the Secretary-General, Organisation
for Economic Co-operation and Development

The Trouble with Europe

Why the EU Isn't Working

What Could Take Its Place

How the Referendum Could Change Europe

Third Edition

Roger Bootle

NICHOLAS BREALEY
PUBLISHING

London · Boston

This third edition first published by
Nicholas Brealey Publishing in 2016
An imprint of John Murray Press

An Hachette UK company

A CIP catalogue record for this title is available from the British Library.

ISBN 978-1-85788-655-9
eISBN 978-1-85788-967-3

Printed in the UK by Clays Ltd, St Ives plc.

John Murray Press policy is to use papers that are natural, renewable and
recyclable products and made from wood grown in sustainable forests.
The logging and manufacturing processes are expected to conform to the
environmental regulations of the country of origin.

John Murray Press
Carmelite House
50 Victoria Embankment
London EC4Y 0DZ
Tel: 020 3122 6000

Nicholas Brealey Publishing
Hachette Book Group
Market Place Center, 53 State St
Boston, MA 02109, USA
Tel: (617) 523 3801

www.nicholasbrealey.com

Contents

Acknowledgements

I nevitably, I owe many people debts of gratitude. The book was inspired by David Green of the think tank Civitas, which generously provided a research grant. For both David's inspiration and encouragement and Civitas' grant, I am extremely grateful. It was David who galvanized me into writing the book. Meanwhile, Civitas' grant enabled me to employ research assistants Melanie DeBono, Sam Dickens and Konrad Malinowski, who greatly increased my productivity and allowed me to finish the book that much more quickly. I am also grateful to the think tank Open Europe for permission to use an adapted version of one of its charts as Table 9.1.[1]

I also owe a debt to *The Daily Telegraph*, for which I write a weekly column, published on Mondays, for permission to draw on some of the material that first appeared in those columns and for continuing to give me a platform from which to air my developing views on Europe and other subjects. In many ways this book is the culmination of the 'conversations' I have been having with *Telegraph* readers over a number of years.

My good friend Leonard Lipman provided much-needed encouragement and solace when my general confidence and belief in the book flagged. Without him, I don't think the book would have been completed. Thanks are also due to Joaly Smith, Faith Elliott, Hayley Charlick and Suhayla Egan for organizing the various versions of the typescript and to Ben Blanchard, Alexander Burgess, Rebecca Heywood, Nina Loncar, Alice Major and Helena Patterson for help with the maps and charts included in the book. Special thanks are due to my PA, Sam

Howard-Carr, not only for help with the typescript but also for organizing me and helping to keep Capital Economics going while I was writing the book. Her support for me has been invaluable.

As with my last three books, I received helpful comments, guidance and criticism from the editorial team at Nicholas Brealey. Several other people helped me by reading early drafts and making critical, but helpful, suggestions. I should especially mention David Barchard, Tony Courakis, David Green, Jonathan Lindsell, John Llewellyn, George de Nemeskeri-Kiss, Robert Rowthorn, Christopher Smallwood and Richard Thoburn.

Several colleagues at Capital Economics also read and commented on early drafts: Paul Dales, Mark Harris, Julian Jessop, Jonathan Loynes, Ben May and Mark Pragnell. Sam Tombs was also very helpful in digging out data. I am grateful to them all, not only for their help with the book but also for their hard work at Capital Economics – especially while I was preoccupied with *The Trouble with Europe*.

Last but not least, I must thank my family, who have had to put up with another period of my absorption in writing a book.

As always, none of the above is responsible for any errors of omission or commission. These remain the responsibility of the author alone.

Roger Bootle
London, March 2016

Preface to the Third Edition

Since the second edition of this book was published in 2015, several important aspects of the subject have taken a new turn – although nothing has happened to undermine the book's main thrust.

Most importantly, as I write, the UK is about to hold a referendum on its continued membership of the European Union. When you read this, the poll may still lie in the future. In that case, if you have a vote, I hope that this new edition will serve as a guide to your thinking about which way to cast it. If you do not have a vote, nevertheless the chances are that, pretty much wherever you are, you will be affected by the outcome. Accordingly, for you the book provides a much-needed analysis of the issues surrounding the referendum, and its importance. For those who read this after the result is known, it is intended to be a guide to the likely consequences.

And they will be momentous. Whatever the result, things will never be quite the same again. If the UK votes to leave, then the first issue to be considered is the future relationship with the continuing EU. This is not a straightforward matter. Two years of negotiations would lie ahead between the UK and its soon-to-be-erstwhile partners. Over and above this, a departure by the UK would mark the first really serious retreat for the European project. This would surely have major consequences, not just for the UK, but also for the rest of the EU. Indeed, one could readily imagine that it might lead to the EU's demise.

Meanwhile, many observers reckon that if the UK votes to leave, it will be impossible to resist a second referendum on Scottish independence. For the EU is more popular in Scotland than it is in England and it seems likely that a majority of Scots will vote to stay in the EU. Bearing that in mind, a second poll could easily result in Scotland seceding from the UK. In that case, British voters would have brought about the severing of not one union but two.

These points are not only relevant to readers after they have heard that the vote is to leave. For what sort of arrangements might be possible after a departure – and indeed what the consequences of departure might be for the UK, Europe and the world as a whole – should surely have a bearing on which way people should vote in the first place.

If the outcome of the vote is for the UK to stay, it might seem, by contrast, as though things are plain sailing. Yet there would still be major issues to sort out. As part of his attempt to renegotiate the UK's relationship with the EU – pursued in the hope of persuading the British electorate to vote to stay in – the British Prime Minister, David Cameron, won some concessions from his European partners. Quite how those would work out in practice, and how they would affect the workings of the EU, remains to be seen.

In any case, even if the UK's continued membership is settled by the referendum, the EU's future is far from trouble-free. Across the continent, there are calls for fundamental reform of the Union. Will the Union respond to these or will it, with the UK problem apparently laid to rest, continue with business as usual?

Overshadowing all this is an issue of even greater importance, one that strikes at the very essence of the EU's identity and purpose. Since the second edition of this book was published – just as it envisaged – questions about the mass migration of people have risen sharply up the European agenda. Amid scenes of great suffering and tragedy, large numbers of refugees from Syria and assorted other countries have arrived on European soil. Umpteen millions more apparently want to join them. How should the EU respond? The profound issues raised by these mass movements of humanity play into Europe's economics, politics and the cohesion of its societies.

Already, the resulting strains have been so great that the Schengen regime of passport-free travel across much of Europe has come close to collapse. This is potentially the second major reverse for the European project.

Moreover, although these developments have tended to overshadow the problems of the euro, all the issues about the single currency that I examine in this book are still bubbling away. Indeed, the Greek crisis continues to rumble on, the position of the Italian economy continues to be dire and the French economy, still falling behind Germany, continues to languish.

Meanwhile, in just about all members of the EU, the Union continues to grow more unpopular. In several countries eurosceptic parties are on the rise, many of them sharing the criticisms of the EU that have animated the eurosceptic movement in Britain. With important elections due in France and Germany in 2017, this upsurge of popular resentment risks causing a political earthquake.

So you could readily say that the EU now faces its most serious crisis ever as these four challenges come together at the same time: the possible exit of one of its largest members, the breakdown of the Schengen regime, the continued fragility of the euro and the gathering unpopularity of the Union among European electorates. Furthermore, these threats are related; a shock emanating in any of these four spheres risks setting off a chain reaction involving the other three. Truly, we are living through *The Trouble with Europe*.

In this third edition, I have not only updated facts and figures where necessary, but I have also brought in a large amount of new material to deal with these, and various other, issues in a new final chapter.

I was fortunate to receive a good deal of praise for earlier editions – as well as a few well-argued, and well-deserved, critiques, from which I have tried to learn. But three strands of criticism have riled me. One is that I am wishy-washy in my conclusions. Apparently, I seem to think that there are good points in favour of both staying in and leaving the EU. Not only that, but when it comes to quantifying various costs and benefits, although I quote lots of numbers, I am reluctant to come down on a hard-and-fast figure for the net result. Indeed, I stress that so many of the factors that bear on these issues are uncertain. Heaven forfend. And to think I considered my balanced approach a virtue!

At the polar opposite, another critic complained that although I acknowledge these uncertainties, I nevertheless conclude that the UK could make a success of life outside the EU. Without certainty and precision, they say, this would be a leap in the dark and they are aghast that I could possibly endorse such a thing. Well I never! As though uncertainty does not bedevil our choices and actions if we decide to stay in.

I never cease to be amazed by the difficulties that people get into over uncertainty. I do wonder how they cope with everyday life. I make no apologies for my attempt to be even-handed and to acknowledge the difficulties, dangers and uncertainties – nor for my decided position, despite the imprecision about key magnitudes, on what is the best way forward.

The third strand of criticism I could find hurtful if it were not so ridiculous – and also so revealing. In debates and discussions about the EU I have many times been opposed by people who begin by asserting their difference from me by saying they are 'pro-European'. By extension, I suppose, I am 'anti-European'. That is news to me. On one occasion when I was extolling the virtues of British political institutions and criticizing the EU's equivalents as being essentially undemocratic and brittle, I was even accused of being racist!

It is extraordinary that people have become so brainwashed by the current pro-EU consensus that they cannot distinguish between an identity, culture and civilization on the one hand, and a particular set of political arrangements and institutions on the other. If I needed something to goad me into renewing my critical assessment of the EU and all its works, this has provided it.

As it happens, I didn't need it. The issues that form the subject matter of this book are, if anything, more alive than when I wrote the first edition. In short, Europe is in turmoil and its future lies in the balance.

What is more, you, the reader, will have a key role to play in shaping that future. My purpose in writing this is to help you play that part to the fullest extent – as someone who is well informed on the key issues and fully cognizant of the consequences of the EU's future going one way or the other. An author could not wish for a better incentive.

Roger Bootle
London, March 2016

Introduction: The Trouble with Europe

The European Union is at a decision point. The objectives with which it was launched and the logic of existing relationships are pushing it towards full political union – some sort of United States of Europe, or at least of the eurozone. In other words, more Europe; deeper integration. This is in tune with the thrust of the EU's historical development and of the EU's past success.

But the EU is a malfunctioning construct for today's world – and even more so for tomorrow's. It needs either to undergo fundamental reform or to break up. It was conceived in a world of large blocs, dominated by the Cold War rivalry between the United States and the Soviet Union and before globalization and the rise of the emerging markets. Its agenda of harmonization and integration inevitably leads to excessive regulation and the smothering of competition. This is largely why, in contrast to the prevailing view that the EU has been an economic success, its economic performance has in fact been relatively poor.

What is more, if nothing changes, the EU's share of world GDP is set to fall sharply and, with it, Europe's influence in the world. Yet to the European establishment that is exactly what integration is supposed to prevent. Meanwhile, the EU is becoming more unpopular; most people do not want to press on to a full political union; and increasing numbers of its citizens want to leave the EU altogether. One way or another, Europe faces some extraordinary challenges. It seems clear to me that European integration is the great issue of our day and that so many other issues hang on its outcome. That is why I felt I had to write this book.

My perspective is that of an economist, and a British one at that. As such, I could be criticized for under-emphasizing political issues. Yet I recognize that in this instance politics and economics are closely related – as they often are. In fact, in this book I put politics at the forefront. This is a case of economics following politics.

The clearest example of my argument that the EU's tortured politics produce poor economic performance is the formation of the euro, which, as I show in Chapter 4, was undertaken for political reasons intrinsic to the European project. It has turned out to be a disaster for the European economy.

As a British citizen, I am bound to be attacked in Europe as being yet another little Englander, harking back to the past and railing against developments on the continent, congenitally predisposed against them – while failing to understand them properly. However, this book is not motivated by any sort of animus against Europe; quite the opposite. Like many British people, I feel both British and European. Indeed, despite the close links between Britain and America, whenever I go to the US I feel more European. The culture I love is European – its food and its wine, its history and its buildings, its literature and its art and, for me, especially its music. It is precisely because I am so much of a European, and because I so desperately want Europe to succeed in the world, that I take issue with the EU as it is currently constituted. For me, the EU is the most important thing that stands between Europe and success.

Naturally, I have written this book hoping that many of my fellow citizens will read it. Nevertheless, it is not written especially for British readers. It tries to take a European perspective and in the process reveals some of the mistakes and foibles of the typical British eurosceptic position.

Different audiences may be shocked by some of what I have to say: eurosceptics in Britain and elsewhere may be appalled by my sympathy and admiration for some of what the EU has achieved; continentals of all persuasions may be surprised and appalled to learn of the EU's poor relative economic performance and disappointing prospects; continental readers especially may also be surprised by my verdict that the EU's prospects would be better if the euro were disbanded; and readers everywhere should be surprised by the emphasis I place on the importance of competition between governments in generating successful political and economic outcomes.

Although, as an economist, I give economic issues full weight, I do not write for professional economists but rather for the general reader. To this end, I have tried to keep the use of technical terms to a minimum. For the reader's convenience, I have included a glossary of terms and acronyms at the back of the book. I have also kept notes on the text to a minimum and also confined these to the back.

The aim of the book is to inform all those who may be called on to contribute to a decision about Europe's future, or their country's part in it, about how Europe stands in the world, how the EU's institutions contribute to that standing and what Europe's prospects are, with or without the EU. When looking for material to help them come to a view, many people find only the ravings of extremists on both sides of the debate, wads of incomprehensible statistics, or oodles of impenetrable Euro-speak.

In contrast, my aim here is to give a balanced and comprehensible account of the EU's development and of the issues now facing it. This is not a polemic. Even so, I cannot claim to be a distanced observer without a view. Indeed, as regards the future, I have a decided position. In an ideal world, I would like the EU to endure and the UK to remain a part of it – but with the Union so fundamentally reformed that it would be almost unrecognizable from its current self.

But after David Cameron's failure to achieve anything substantial in his 'renegotiation', this now seems a pipe dream. So, reluctantly, I have decided that the UK should leave the EU. This book charts my path to that conclusion, culminating in the new Chapter 11.

Part I is about political, institutional and ideological issues. Chapter 1 explains how the EU came to be what it is, the guiding beliefs of those who forged it and the motives of those countries that have wanted, or still want, to join it. It is a remarkable success story of past development.

Chapter 2 explains, however, that what the EU has become makes it ill-suited to current economic and political realities and shows how this tends to lead to bad decisions, which produce poor economic performance.

Part II is devoted to economic issues. Chapter 3 analyses the EU's economic record and shows how and why it has been disappointing, while Chapter 4 analyses one of the EU's worst decisions, namely to launch the euro. Chapter 5 discusses what policies could relieve the EU's economic predicament. In contrasting vein, Chapter 6 looks at the EU's economic prospects if nothing changes and argues that the outlook is for continued relative European decline.

Part III is devoted to change. Chapters 7 and 8 discuss the possibilities for reform. Chapter 9 looks at the issues that should govern the decision of a single country to stay or leave the Union. Chapter 10 considers what institutional structures could take the place of the EU, if it did break up. Finally, Chapter 11 examines the issues surrounding the UK's referendum and other existential threats to the EU.

But the place to start is surely with the origins of the EU – and the ideas that underpinned its development.

Part I

Past History and Present Purpose

1

How the EU Came into Being and Why

We must build a United States of Europe ... The first step in the re-creation of the European family must be a partnership between France and Germany.
—Winston Churchill, 1946

For Germany, Europe is not only indispensable, it is part and parcel of our identity. We've always said German unity, European unity and integration, that's two parts of one and the same coin.
—Angela Merkel, German Chancellor, June 2011

The history of the EU is a story of remarkable development. In this chapter I trace its beginnings in war, before going on to discuss how the EU has changed as regards both its relationship with member states and its geographical reach. I then discuss what has driven the urge towards integration and why countries have wanted to join the Union – and still do.

War and peace

What we now call the European Union was born out of the carnage of the Second World War – and what carnage. It is well known that about 6 million Jews perished at the hands of the Nazis in brutal acts of ethnic cleansing and racial hatred, an astonishing 60% or so of European Jewry. In respect of proportions of a population, or the sheer horror of what took place, nothing can bear comparison with this.

However, umpteen million other people died as well, largely as a consequence of more conventional ways of war. Estimates of Russian dead are particularly unreliable, but it is probably a reasonable approximation that about 20 million Russians (or, more accurately, Soviets) perished during and because of the war – about 10% of the population. Roughly a third of these were civilians.

Less widely known, and still less widely acknowledged, is that about 7 million Germans died in and because of the war, also representing about 10% of the population, rather more than half of them civilians, killed in bombing raids or attacks by the Allied armies or wasted by cold and hunger.

Different people have different views on which episodes were the most traumatic for ordinary German people. Many cite the firestorms unleashed by the bombing of Dresden or Hamburg; and with good reason. But the image that has touched me most deeply is of the wretched rabbles of people, including old men, women and children, trying to flee from the advancing Red Army in the expanses of East Prussia. Taking to the frozen coastal lagoons of the region, in desperation trying to head west, away from the advancing Soviets, the words they most dreaded to hear from their fellow refugees were, 'The ice is cracking.'

German people understandably find it difficult to utter this sentiment in polite company but, as a proud and patriotic citizen of the United Kingdom, I can do it without blushing: some of the greatest suffering during and because of the Second World War was borne by Germans. When you comprehend the scale of the horrors suffered by the German people, as well as their (admittedly well-justified) guilt regarding the horrors they inflicted on others, in addition to the division of their country and its partial occupation by the Red Army, you can readily see why German people have typically been among the most enthusiastic supporters of the European project.

In contrast to these horrors, but still shocking, France lost 'only' about 800,000 people (around 2% of its population). A good deal of these casualties occurred in the German invasion of 1940, but about 50,000 were killed unintentionally by the Allies in the Battle of Normandy after D-Day, about 20,000 in the Calvados department alone. The city of Caen was all but obliterated by the Allies.

By contrast, during the whole war, the British got away with a comparatively modest death toll of just under 400,000 (0.8% of the population), combatants and civilians combined. Thinking of their experience over the whole war and not merely in the Battle of Britain, continental Europeans might readily understand how the British could believe that this was 'their finest hour'.

All of this European slaughter during the Second World War is widely believed to have been exceeded by the carnage of the First. In fact, as regards total losses this is not true: the Second World War was much bloodier. It is true for Britain, though, which lost more than 2% of its population in the First World War; more significantly, it is also true for France. Indeed, in the First World War France lost almost 2 million people, over 4% of its population.[2] Scarce wonder, then, that there was so much reluctance to staging resistance *à l'outrance* during the repeat run in 1940.

With these enormous losses during the First World War behind it, in addition to its not inconsiderable losses during the Second, as well as the humiliation of three times being mauled by German armies (including the defeat by

Prussian-led forces in 1870), it is hardly surprising that in the postwar world, France also sought a European answer to the essential questions about national security.

Indeed, across Europe, after the devastation of 1939–45, both ordinary people and the governing elites inwardly pledged that nothing similar must ever happen again. Many believed that Europe's leaders had to evolve some pan-European entity that would tame and subdue the passions and rivalries of the nation states of Europe. Soon the pledge became explicit. Pledge turned into vision and vision into reality. This vision-inspired reality was a series of institutional structures that evolved into what we now call the European Union.

The founding fathers

One of the earliest supporters of the idea of European union was none other than Winston Churchill, who had talked of some sort of European 'commonality' as early as 1930. In a speech in Zurich in 1946, he uttered the words quoted at the beginning of this chapter: 'We must build a United States of Europe ... The first step in the re-creation of the European family must be a partnership between France and Germany.'

Some people have taken his remarks as an endorsement of the idea of British membership of such a union, but this is clearly not what Churchill had in mind. In the same speech he said: 'Great Britain, the British Commonwealth of Nations, mighty America and I trust Soviet Russia – for then indeed all would be well – must be the friends and sponsors of the new Europe and must champion its right to live and shine.' So he clearly envisaged Britain remaining outside such a European association.

The evolution of the EU owes much to two men who translated Churchill's vision of European union into action: Jean Monnet and Robert Schuman, widely regarded as the EU's founding fathers. Their legacy continues to live on in the EU today, particularly in its vision of the future.

Interestingly, at the beginning of the Second World War, Monnet, a French political economist and diplomat, advocated a full political union between France and Britain to fight Nazism. On 5 August 1943 he said:

> *There will be no peace in Europe, if the states are reconstituted on the basis of national sovereignty ... The countries of Europe are too small to guarantee their peoples the necessary prosperity and social development. The European states must constitute themselves into a federation.*

After the war, Monnet set about work aimed at the creation of a European Community. On 9 May 1950, Robert Schuman, France's Minister of Foreign Affairs, made the 'Schuman Declaration', which had been prepared by Monnet. It proposed to place all French and German production of coal and steel under one central authority. This laid the foundation for the European Coal and Steel Community, the forerunner of the European Economic Community. Indeed, that date is now celebrated as the EU's birthday.

The Schuman Declaration of 1950 laid out the key themes that were to dominate the evolution of European institutions. It said:

> *Europe will not be made all at once, or according to a single plan. It will be built through concrete achievements which first create a de facto solidarity. The coming together of the nations of Europe requires the elimination of the age-old opposition of France and Germany.*

Schuman was a proponent of further European integration. In 1958, he became the first President of the body that may be thought of as the predecessor of the European Parliament. When he left office in 1960, he was acclaimed the 'Father of Europe'.

The European Economic Community (EEC) itself was established by the Treaty of Rome in 1957. (In Britain the EEC was referred to as the Common Market, on membership of which a referendum was held in 1975.) Although its early ambitions may have seemed modestly economic, in the preamble to the founding treaty was enshrined the essential driving force. The signatories to the Treaty of Rome (the heads of state of the six founding members: France, Germany, Italy, Belgium, the Netherlands and Luxembourg) declared that they were 'determined to lay the foundations of an ever closer union among the peoples of Europe'.

Constant change

So, from its very inception, the Community was set up to become something more than it already was. There was a sense that the payoff for current efforts and sacrifices would only come in the future, when full integration was complete. Ever since then, being a member of the Community has amounted, not so much to acceptance of a certain set of conditions in the here and now, as to participation in a process that would lead on to the final destination. This is still the case today – and still the final destination has not been reached.

I will spare readers a detailed account of which treaties did what to whom. The key point, though, is that a succession of treaties has transformed the nature of the Union. In the process, the powers of the EU institutions have radically increased relative to those of the nation states. The major developments were the following:

- In 1957, the Treaty of Rome established the EEC.
- In 1965, the Brussels Treaty streamlined European institutions, laid down the composition of the Council and set out which institutions would be located in the three Community centres – Brussels, Strasbourg and Luxembourg.
- In 1986, the Single European Act marked the watershed, since it extended qualified majority voting in council, making it harder for a single country to veto proposed legislation.
- In 1992, the famous Maastricht Treaty prepared for European Monetary Union and introduced elements of a political union (citizenship, common foreign and internal affairs policies). This is when the EEC dropped one of the *E*s in its abbreviated name and became simply the European Community (EC). This clearly marked the transition from a largely economic association to one with an obvious political dimension.
- In 1995, the Schengen Agreement came into effect, allowing travel without passport control between seven countries (later joined by others): Belgium,

France, Germany, Luxembourg, the Netherlands, Portugal and Spain.

♦ In 1997, the Treaty of Amsterdam saw the UK agreeing to the 'Social Chapter' of the Maastricht Treaty. Moreover, the treaty created a new senior post, a sort of Foreign Minister for the EU, known as the High Representative for Common Foreign and Security Policy.

♦ In 2001, the Treaty of Nice replaced the need for unanimous voting with a qualified majority system in 27 different areas – again diluting the power of a nation state to block measures that it did not like.

♦ In 2007, the Treaty of Lisbon extended qualified majority voting to more areas, established a legal personality for the EU and created a new post: President of the European Council. For the first time in the history of the EU, included in the Lisbon Treaty was a clause making it clear how a state could exit from the Union.

But the story is not over yet. It has been widely mooted that before long, the post of EU President should be filled by the winner of a direct presidential election across the whole EU. The EU, of course, already has a flag and an anthem. Plans for a European army have been discussed. To the ultra-integrationists, the final destination is pretty clear: a United States of Europe.

Even if integration does not go quite that far, given the existence of the euro, matters cannot stay as they are. For, as I make clear in Chapter 5, if the euro is to survive, some sort of fiscal and political union will be necessary. So a United States of the eurozone, if not of Europe, is on the drawing board. Indeed, in January 2014, Viviane

Reding, Vice-President of the European Commission, said: 'We need to build a United States of Europe with the Commission as government and two chambers – the European Parliament and a "Senate" of member States.' So the USE is not a mere pipedream; it is a realistic prospect – or, some would say, even a political necessity.

Geographical expansion

During the process under which the EU's role in each member country's affairs grew steadily greater, so the number of states belonging to the Union also increased dramatically. In her famous Bruges speech of 1988, the then British Prime Minister, Margaret Thatcher, drew a contrast between 'deepening' the Union and 'widening' it; that is, letting in more countries. She wanted less of the former and more of the latter. In the event, the EU delivered more of both.

Figure 1.1 shows the stages of the EU's expansion. The original six signatories to the 1957 Treaty of Rome were joined in 1973 by three more: Denmark, Ireland and the UK. Greece joined in 1981, followed in 1986 by Portugal and Spain. In 1995, Austria, Finland and Sweden joined, making a union of 15 countries.

However, it was in 2004 that the EU was really transformed. This was the largest of all the expansions, bringing in eight former members of the Soviet bloc, plus Malta and Cyprus. In 2007, the accession of Romania and Bulgaria brought the total membership to 27 countries and in 2013 Croatia joined, creating a union of 28 countries – a far cry from the 6 that originally set out on this road in 1957. What is more, as I explain in Chapter 2, there are several other countries in the queue to join.

Figure 1.1 The stages of the EU's expansion

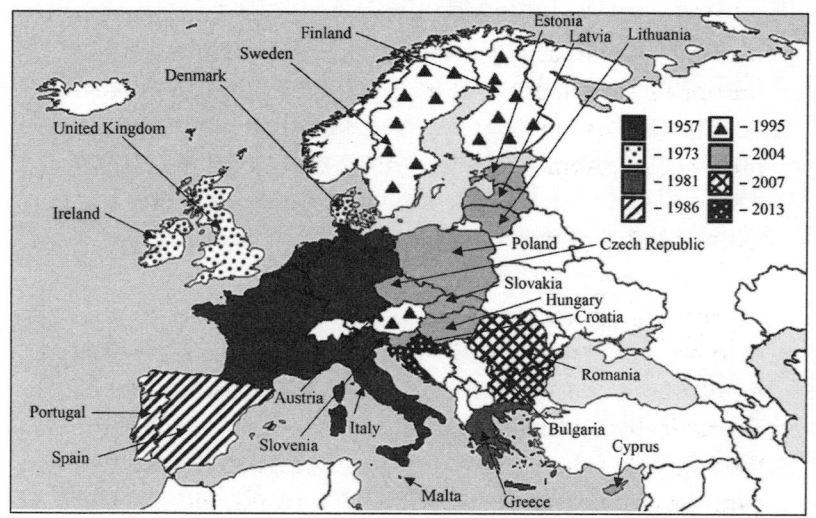

Source: www.europa.eu

Centripetal forces

Why countries wanted to join the EU – and so many others still want to – requires an explanation. One of the reasons is quite simply that as the Union gets larger, remaining outside becomes more and more uncomfortable: diplomatically, politically and economically. Outsiders fear that they will be subject to the EU's overwhelming political power, but also that, if they remain outside it, they will be excluded from its enormous, and still growing, market.

It is almost like the decision facing investors as to whether or not they should stand aside from a great stock-market bubble, like the tech boom, as it continues to inflate. History relates that in the tech boom, as well as in a host of previous bubbles, very few investors did so. Even those who initially avoided it were, by and large, sucked in by the end. The bigger a bubble gets, the more powerful are the forces drawing others in.

Many critics of European integration suggest that as well as this 'sucking in' of new members, there have been some nakedly self-interested motives at work. They have a point – although, as I will show in a moment, this is far from the be-all and end-all of the motives behind integration.

The financial interest

Admittedly, though, several of the countries attracted to membership over recent years have had motives involving a decidedly pecuniary aspect. All of the new joiners have been relatively poor. Accordingly, they have benefited from substantial net injections of EU money, provided by the richer members, which are net contributors.

In 2012, according to the European Commission, the largest net recipient of EU funds was Poland, which received €12 billion, followed by Portugal (€5 billion), Greece (€4.5 billion), Spain (€4 billion), Hungary (€3.3 billion) and the Czech Republic (€3 billion).

You can probably guess who the net contributors were: in ascending order, Cyprus, Luxembourg, Finland, Austria, Denmark, Belgium, Sweden, the Netherlands, Italy, the UK, France and Germany (which paid some €12 billion). The top five *gross* contributors – Germany, France, Italy, the UK and Spain – contributed almost 65% of the total.

Although it is the net rather than the gross figures that measure the true extent of a country's contribution to, or receipts from, the EU, this is not an accurate gauge of the extent of support that may be purchased through flows of money. For when the EU spends money – on regional development aid, for example, or road building – it makes a big thing of the fact that it is the EU that has funded the project, with frequent displays of the blue flag, bedecked with yellow stars.

Yet the funding for all of this is hidden in the national accounts of member countries. The ordinary taxpayer is not made aware of what they are themselves contributing to their countries' benefits, but are instead encouraged to believe that the EU's munificence has descended on them like manna from heaven.

The interests of elites

Moreover, the political elites of those countries that have joined the EU, both the founding members and more recent recruits, have had a clear self-interest in joining; that is, being able to participate in the governance of Europe and enjoying the benefits thereof in terms of interest, power, status and, dare I say it, money. (I comment on the pecuniary attractions of working for the EU in Chapter 2.)

This allure has been particularly strong for small countries, because the EU structure is specifically designed to give them more weight than would be justified on a pure count of GDP or numbers of people. So for many of the political leaders of small European states, the EU has been a wonderful career opportunity. It is as though they have gone from being an ordinary sitting member of the local parish council to Cabinet Minister. Jean-Claude Juncker, for instance, when Prime Minister of tiny Luxembourg, was twice President of the European Council, representing all EU member states. He is now President of the European Commission.

For the elites in the big three countries, Germany, France and the UK, it has been a different story. Nevertheless, each has had its share of benefits and inducements, pecuniary and otherwise. For Germany, to be accepted as an equal rather than a pariah was paramount. In order to secure this, over many years German leaders and officials were happy to take a shrinking violet role in international affairs and, in particular, to play second fiddle to France; at least until recently.

By contrast, for France, the EU represented a way to bolster its power and influence in the world. France called the shots, but they were fired by a much bigger entity. As recently as 2012, the current French President, François Hollande, said: 'To be influential in tomorrow's world, to defend our values and our development model, France needs Europe and Europe needs France.' (The changing attitudes of France and Germany to the EU are taken up in more detail in Chapter 2.)

For British politicians and officials, the postwar world, characterized by loss of empire and pretty much continued relative decline, has been a trying time. While membership of the EU has been a rocky road, it has at least given the UK a forum through which its elites could seek to influence the world – or so they thought. This mattered a lot. For the UK's silky-smooth, Rolls-Royce diplomats and senior officials, groomed to run the world but in danger of being confined to running merely their own little island, it has at least meant that they continued to sit at the top table. This 'top table syndrome', as I call it, has influenced their views ever since.

The guiding beliefs

Yet these cynical explanations are superficial. On the whole, particularly in great enterprises, people have to believe in what they are doing. This is where Anglo-Saxon free market economists so often miss the point completely and in the process greatly under-estimate the strength of the integrationist tendency on the continent. Life is not all about profit or utility maximization – except in the justly notorious, desiccated mathematical models so beloved of American economists.

Human history is dominated by the doings of people who, for good or ill, believe in something other than themselves. Such a belief brings strength, endurance and determination. If necessary, it even enables you to kill. This is why army officers usually place so much importance on the state of their men's morale. And they are right to. In the end, it can make the difference between defeat and victory. Something similar is true in politics.

In Nazi Germany, although some of the perpetrators of its ghastly crimes were merely obeying orders, remarkably, huge numbers did what they did because they believed in the cause. Naturally, far fewer admitted to that subsequently.

For decades, many of the people who fought for the Soviet Union, either against its external enemies or against its supposed enemies within, did so not because they saw some self-interest in so doing, but rather because they believed in Communism. (Admittedly, just as at Stalingrad some troops were forced to fight by the machine guns aimed at their backs by the Soviet security police, so some people who worked for the Soviet interest in peacetime did so because they were made to.)

If the creation of the Soviet Union owed much to the power of belief, its collapse had similar roots. Of course, this was a complex matter, but surely prime among the causes of the Soviet Union's demise is that its people, leaders and led alike, had ceased to believe in its founding myth. Once this had gone, its various failings became insupportable.

The pursuit of European integration was, and still is, sustained by five guiding beliefs: the desire to avoid another European war; the idea that it is natural for Europe to be united; the concept that in economics and politics size really matters; the notion that Europe needs to be united to resist the competitive challenge from Asia; and the idea that European integration is somehow inevitable.

To a greater or lesser extent, these beliefs have been shared by people in all countries that have joined the European Union, both founding members and latecomers. But some countries have also been driven by other factors that need separate attention: the UK, members of the former eastern bloc, plus Finland, Ireland, Spain, Portugal and Greece. I briefly turn to these particular cases, after discussing the all-important guiding beliefs.

The avoidance of war

Avoiding war is surely a most noble motive and it would be quite wrong to be cynical about it. People in Britain in particular under-estimate it at their peril. Whatever you may think of the widely held view that it is NATO, or the Americans, or fear of the nuclear bomb, rather than the European Union, that has kept the peace in Europe, the evolution of the next 60 years was not known in the early 1950s when European integration was being discussed.

And, as always, it would be wrong to read history backwards. Who knows what alternative European histories could have played out if the European Union and its forerunners had not been in place? After all, in the immediate postwar years it looked as though Italy and France were turning Communist. Meanwhile, Spain and Portugal were ruled by dictators.

The original six members of the European Economic Community consisted of three small countries (Belgium, the Netherlands and Luxembourg) and three big ones (France, Italy and Germany), which all had the war monkey firmly attached to their backs. For five of these countries, the primary fear related to Germany. For four of them, it was the fear of being overrun, dominated or humiliated by the Germans. This applied to France, the Netherlands, Belgium and Luxembourg. Given that it was only 20 years from the Versailles Treaty to the outbreak of the Second World War, it was perfectly understandable that after this second war these countries should fear a recrudescence of the same old problem before too long.

The fifth country was also afraid of Germany, for Germany was afraid of itself: afraid of what it would be like if it were left to its own devices and of what consequences would follow, both for itself and for others; as well as being afraid of its own isolation and international pariah status. It craved respectability among nations. During an interview with *Der Spiegel* in 2012, Germany's Finance Minister, Wolfgang Schäuble, was pretty blatant about this: 'Germany would have been prepared to relinquish powers to Brussels, because it was only through Europe that we received a new chance after World War II.'

The sixth country, Italy, was also afraid of itself, but for rather different reasons. It too had experienced a period of fascism, wartime destruction and immense suffering. But in addition, many Italians doubted the ability of the postwar Italian state to deliver prosperity, stability and honesty in public life. Ugo La Malfa, the postwar leader of the Italian Republican Party, famously said about European integration: 'Chain Italy to the Alps, in order not to let it sink into the Mediterranean.' Subsequent developments have confirmed that such fears about the Italian state were well founded – even with Italy chained to the Alps.

Europe reunited

The second key idea was the sense that Europe had been falsely divided for centuries. It was eminently plausible to imagine that Europe's historical destiny was to be reunited. After all, under the Roman Empire, as Figure 1.2 shows, it had been united from the shores of Iberia in the west to the Rhine and Danube in the northeast, and from the Scottish Borders in the north to the southernmost Mediterranean islands.

Mind you, there were a few differences from today's concept of Europe. The Roman Empire was essentially built around the Mediterranean, *Mare Nostrum*. Interestingly, most of Germany and the northern part of what we would call eastern Europe was outside the empire. This was not because the Romans found the Germans too barbarian to stomach (a sentiment felt by some of their descendants today who are resisting German-inspired austerity). Indeed, the Roman historian Tacitus wrote a good deal in appreciation of German life and mores. Rather, they found Germany too difficult to conquer.

However, the southern part of eastern Europe, including some countries that are not yet members of

Figure 1.2 The Roman Empire in 117 CE*

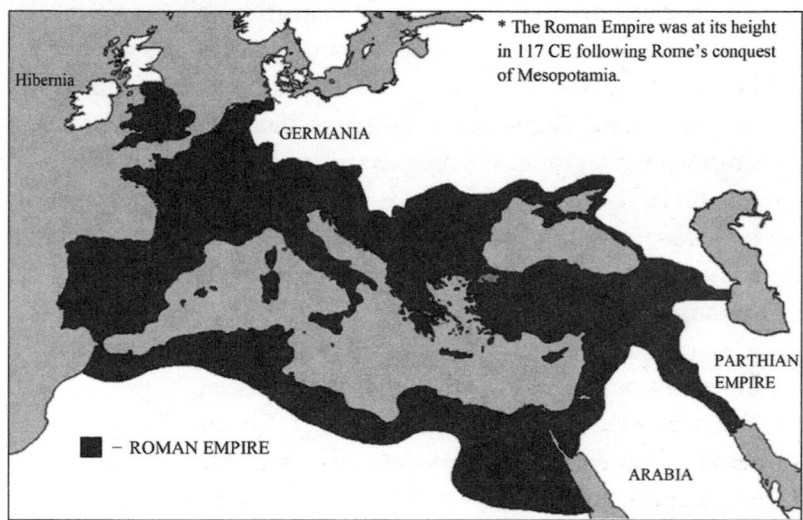

Source: www.ancient.eu.com/Roman_Empire

the EU, was inside the empire, as well as, interestingly, all of Turkey, the north African littoral and much of what we would call the Middle East. Ironically, the successors to those who signed the Treaty of Rome now find these parts too hot to handle.

After the fall of Rome, there were several other attempts to unite Europe, but none matched what Rome had achieved. In the Middle Ages there was the concept of Christendom; that is, the countries under Christian rule. This covered broadly the same territory as the Roman Empire, with a few variations. Unlike the Roman Empire, after the Islamic conquests in the seventh century, the geographical limits did not reach North Africa or the Middle East, but they stretched further into eastern Europe, including not only the various German states, but also parts of Scandinavia,

Ukraine, Bohemia, Poland and Muscovy (subsequently the core of European Russia); see Figure 1.3.

Of course, Christendom was not a political construct, more a description of a territory across which a certain set of presumptions and allegiances loosely held sway. On several occasions, though, the princes of Christendom fought alongside each other in defence of their religion (and the promotion of their own material gain) against the forces of Islam. Even after the Reformation added another split in Christendom, so that it was divided into three (Catholicism, Protestantism and Orthodoxy), something of this loose idea of the association of Christian-governed lands survived.

The notion of a broad supra-national European association survived also in the form of the Holy Roman Empire (depicted in Figure 1.4), even though, in the words of the famous quip, it was neither holy, nor Roman, nor an empire. More concretely, four European leaders sought at different times to establish hegemony across much of Europe: Louis XIV of France, Charles V of Spain, Napoleon and Hitler. Each succeeded for a limited period, but soon afterwards Europe returned to much like its prior constellation of small states and rivalrous empires.

In view of the continent's distant history, it was possible to regard the Europe of nation states that emerged after the end of the Napoleonic wars – and the somewhat different patchwork that emerged at Versailles in 1919, which was largely left intact after 1945 – as inefficient, illogical and dangerous; and even thoroughly un-European. In a speech to the European Parliament in October 1999, Romano Prodi, the ex-President of the European Commission and former Prime Minister of Italy, put it as plainly as could be:

Figure 1.3 **Christendom in 1453***

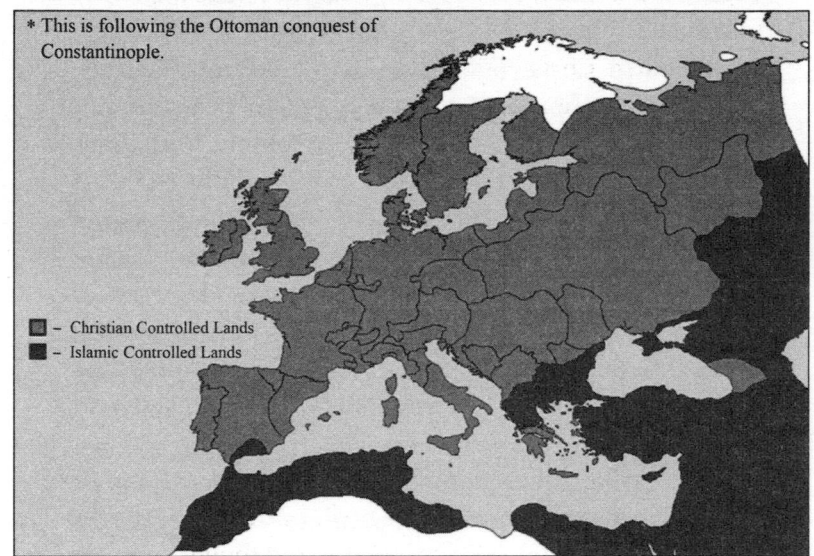

Source: commons.wikimedia.org, www.timemaps.com

Figure 1.4 **The Holy Roman Empire at its peak c.1000**

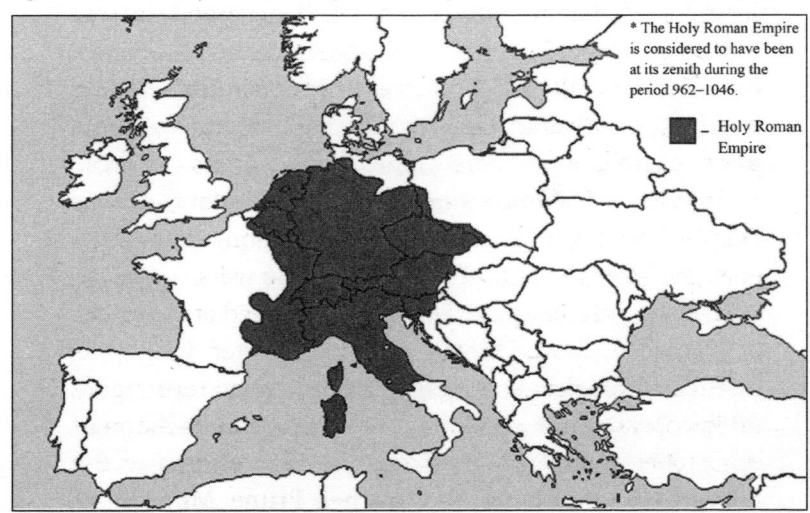

Source: www.britannica.com

We must now face the difficult task of moving towards a single economy, a single political entity ... For the first time since the fall of the Roman Empire we have the opportunity to unite Europe.

Squeezed between giants

This aspiration had a clear link with the third idea behind the impulse towards European integration: the importance of size. The decades immediately after the Second World War were dominated by the Cold War. The world divided into two camps, led by their respective champions, the United States and the Soviet Union. Weakened by the war and now set to shed their empires, in comparison to these behemoths even the former great colonial powers of Europe, Britain and France, appeared shrunken creatures, never mind the lesser lights such as the Netherlands and Belgium.

Of course, the countries of western Europe were part of the American-led 'West', and so they could remain. However, this put them in vassal status to the US, which seemed incompatible with their history and cultural depth. Moreover, to many people the US was far from being a paragon of virtue. If Europe could unite, it could look both the United States and the Soviet Union in the face. The world would also benefit from having a counterweight to these two overbearing giants, imbued with all the European virtues, distilled through the centuries.

Strikingly, even Margaret Thatcher subscribed to this view. Addressing an election meeting in 1966 she said: 'Europe has become a cornerstone of our campaign ... I believe together we could form a block [sic] with as much power as the USA or Russia.'[3]

This idea also had an economic aspect. The prevailing thinking in Europe was that in economics, size really matters. The size of the market determines the scope for economies of scale. Moreover, the size of a country, or a bloc of countries, has a major bearing on its power to negotiate economic relationships with other countries or blocs.

On both counts, opinion was doubtless heavily influenced by the example of the US. There was a strong case to be made that the essential reason for America's economic prowess was the size of its home market. If that was true, why could some combined European entity (whether the United States of Europe or something a little less than a full political union) not enjoy the same benefits? (In fact there are some good reasons why Europe cannot easily ape the US, which I discuss in Chapter 7.)

Interestingly, from an early stage, well before the advent of the euro, there had been an idea that America enjoyed an enormous advantage over Europe by being able to issue the world's currency, thereby greatly reducing its cost of finance. The French President, Charles de Gaulle, referred to this as America's 'exorbitant privilege'. (Having experienced the euro as a rival to the dollar, I doubt that many Europeans have felt 'privileged', but this subject must await the full discussion in Chapter 4.)

So the objective of building up, or belonging to, a large bloc of countries for security or defence reasons went hand in hand with the objective of promoting European prosperity. That in turn would help to promote Europe's influence in the world.

This European thinking about the benefits of integration was mirrored on the other side of the Atlantic. There have always been some members of the

American establishment who have seen the emergence of a united Europe as a potential threat to American hegemony. Even so, from the start, the predominant US attitude to European integration was positive. Again, this was for both political and economic reasons. Politically, in the early decades of the postwar period the US was preoccupied by the Communist threat and saw a more integrated Europe as a bulwark against Communism.

The economic element came into the political equation too. The more economically successful Europe was, the less likely Communism was to spread. Quite apart from this, greater economic success would also help America economically, through trade and investment links and by helping to reduce the US contribution to global defence, aid and international bodies.

As to how to achieve greater prosperity in Europe, to most of the American establishment it would have seemed obvious that bringing down trade barriers and fostering integration would do the trick. In fact, America went further than this. For four years, starting in 1947, the Marshall Plan transferred over 1% of America's GDP each year to the stricken countries of Europe.

Yet once the European project was underway, it never seemed to occur to senior American officials and diplomats that if European institutions were badly constructed, and if the prevailing economic ideology was statist and interventionist, closer integration could actually harm economic growth. To be fair to them, just getting Europe growing again was the immediate priority. Moreover, at the time very few economists recognized the importance of institutions as opposed to 'simple economic forces' for bringing prosperity. It took the fall of Communism and the rise of emerging markets to cause the penny to drop. Perhaps more surprisingly, as a great democracy itself, the US was puzzlingly unaware of the looming democratic deficit at the heart of the EU.

Eastern challenge

Over recent years, with the Soviet Union having disintegrated and even the end of American hegemony now sighted on the horizon, a fourth factor has emerged: fear of the East. Supposedly, the world is going to be dominated by China and India, with perhaps some lesser powers, such as Indonesia, snapping at their heels. If Europe does not unite, then how will it be able to make its voice heard in the world? How will it compete? Indeed, how will it survive?

It is common for defenders of the EU to point out that without the Union, in 20 years' time no single European country, not even Germany, would be able to sit at the table of the decision-makers, and that China would be able to divide and rule by negotiating with each European country individually. As the Italian Prime Minister, Enrico Letta, put it in a joint speech with David Cameron given at Chatham House in July 2013:

> *Today, size matters again. Member states need the collective strength of the European Union to have leverage; otherwise they will be without the power and wealth needed to matter in world politics. Either Europe is a global actor in economic terms and in foreign and defence policy, or each of the member states will struggle to maintain the role that it had in the past century.*

In practice, though, in 20 or 30 years' time the world is likely to be multipolar and with very different institutions, as I argue in Chapter 10. Nevertheless, the fear of European irrelevance and impotence if the EU does not survive has induced more tolerance of the EU's failings than it deserves.

Inevitability

The fifth idea behind the urge towards European integration is really the confluence of the other four; namely, the notion that European integration is simply *inevitable*. Inevitability confers a strange strength on those who are possessed by belief in it. It is strange because, strictly speaking, if you believe that an event or outcome is inevitable, this could be expected to undermine or weaken any impulse to action – since the 'inevitable' event or outcome is going to happen, *inevitably*, whatever you do or do not do. In practice, though, people seem to be goaded into action by the belief that what they are doing is in step with the march of history.

In *War and Peace*, Tolstoy questions why hundreds of thousands of men are moving across Europe towards the great clashes of arms of the Napoleonic wars. He gives all sorts of specific explanations for particular people, but he is clear that they are all simply cogs in a wheel. He sees the whole shifting canvas as the outcome of Fate.

Not that long after Tolstoy wrote his masterpiece, the idea of inevitability came to play a key role in the rise of Communism. Marx developed a theory of the evolution of the economy and society that made Communism 'inevitable'. Many of the revolutionaries who subsequently fought in Russia and elsewhere to bring Communism into being genuinely felt that its eventual triumph was inevitable. This hardened their will and made them prepared to do almost anything to turn the vision into reality.

European integration too has had an air of inevitability about it. It seemed to be the summation and healing of the past and the way of the future. Nation states were on the way out, *passé*. A united Europe would embody the best of European traditions while securing Europe's future in the modern world.

This feeling of inevitability even affected opponents of integration, who so often felt that they were up against a steamroller that would proceed to roll over them come what may. Even objections by the majority of the people were ignored. When referendums on the proposed European Constitution were lost in both France and the Netherlands, the euro elites simply carried on anyway to implement key elements of what had been rejected at the polls. They just refrained from using the C-word.

When Irish voters rejected the Lisbon Treaty in 2008, the question was subsequently put to them again in a second referendum. This time they approved it, but presumably if they had approved the treaty in the first referendum there would not have been a second one. The impression was left that they would be compelled to go on voting until they said yes; once they said yes, they would not be asked again.

Only in the last few years has the halo of inevitability begun to slip, for both supporters and opponents alike. In truth, further European integration was never inevitable, but now that it no longer seems so, it is in fact less likely.

So the European movement has had five guiding ideas, which have sustained the push for continued integration. They have inspired and driven the movement's supporters, filled them with a sense of moral superiority and given them the confidence that history is on their side.

Thinking more broadly, the movement has had not only its ideology, consisting of these five ideas, but also its sacred text (the Treaty of Rome), its patron saints (Monnet and Schuman) and its ultimate goal: the formation of a United States of Europe. In other words, it has had many of the trappings of a religion. This surely helps to explain the strength of mind of the supporters of further European integration and their determination to press on with their objectives even when millions of fellow citizens do not share their views.

Britain's awkward position

The five guiding beliefs – and the integrationist religion – had a major influence in Britain, as well as on the continent. There were also some key economic considerations affecting the UK's decision to join the EEC in 1973, which I defer until Chapter 3. However, there was one peculiarly British aspect to the geopolitics of the case – though it had a decidedly American twist.

Winston Churchill had successfully constructed the narrative of the two great Atlantic democracies, America and Britain, fighting the war together and then together laying the foundations of the postwar world, sustained by fellow feeling, common language and a shared heritage – as well as mutual advantage. There was a substantial element of truth in this, but there was also a darker side to the relationship. During and after the war, America had been keen both to seize commercial advantage over Britain in world markets and, relatedly, to ensure the dismantling of the British Empire.

Most Britons have never understood the tendency of informed Americans to see Britain, with its colonies abroad and the operation of the class system at home, including a hereditary monarch as head of state and the continuation as a political entity of the House of Lords, as not a true democracy. Moreover, the British generally do not recognize the extent to which, towards the end of the war, President Roosevelt sought to make common cause with Stalin, leaving Churchill isolated. For many of those who did know it, or learned it later, this had a profound effect. Even in its early stages, although the 'special relationship' was not a complete delusion and the favours, to some extent, flowed in both directions, it was nowhere near a relationship of equals. Moreover, the US meant to make it more unequal. For America fully intended to reduce Britain's standing in the world – and, of course, it succeeded.

The Suez disaster of 1956, when the US effectively pulled the plug on the joint British/French attempt to seize the Suez Canal back from Egypt's President Nasser, provided the *coup de grâce*. Suez was a profound national humiliation. After that, the choice for Britain appeared to be between becoming an American lapdog or throwing in its lot with Europe.

After Suez, the new British Prime Minister, Harold Macmillan, liked to see Britain's options as much less stark. He fondly envisaged Britain at the centre of three key relationships: with the US, Europe and the Commonwealth, as Britain's former empire now became – a sort of international equivalent of the House of Lords. This triangular situation, he thought, made Britain a crucial country, whose experience and sophistication in world affairs rendered it especially valuable to America.

As he put it, he saw Britain playing Greece to America's Rome.

But as the years went on and European integration deepened, this complacent view seemed increasingly wide of the mark. Did the UK want to sign up to the European project or not? Much of the British establishment now saw throwing Britain's lot in with Europe as 'inevitable'. As it turned out, President de Gaulle of France said 'Non' to British overtures. In the end, though, once De Gaulle had departed, Britain did join the European Economic Community, without most Britons realizing they were signing up to the project of 'ever closer union'. They thought they were merely joining a Common Market. Meanwhile, Britain continued to be an American lapdog just the same.

Escape from Communism

For several of the newer EU members, the centripetal forces drawing them towards membership have been quite different, although their story also involves a relationship with a much larger country. These are the members of the former eastern bloc, which, under Soviet domination, experienced a long period of exclusion and separation from the West. After the Soviet collapse, they now longed to be part of the western club and to be regarded as normal. On a more negative note, they continued to fear that a re-expansionist Russia would at some time seek to gobble them up. In varying degrees, this applies to Poland, the Czech Republic, Hungary, the Baltic states of Latvia, Estonia and Lithuania, Slovakia, Slovenia, Croatia, Bulgaria and Romania.

It also applies to Finland, which was at war with the Soviet Union for most of the period between 1939 and

1944. What is more, Finland had been part of the Russian empire between 1809 and 1917. This, as well as Finland's ethnic and linguistic heritage, marks it out as different from the other Nordic countries that have either stood outside the EU (Norway) or, like Britain, have been in the EU but kept their distance from the euro (Sweden and Denmark).

For all of these countries, membership of the EU was a sign of realignment with the West and appeared to make a clear warning statement and to raise the stakes, if Russia at some future stage turned belligerent. (All of the former members of the eastern bloc, but not Finland, also joined NATO, which provided concrete protection without compromising national sovereignty; see Chapter 10.)

Although it was not originally envisaged that the EU would perform this role – or indeed, that it would be possible – the European Union acted as a receiving house for the countries of the former eastern bloc as they emerged from the nightmare of Soviet domination. Aspiration to membership of the EU provided the drive and political rationale for pushing through painful political and economic reforms. It has also helped to check any tendency towards backsliding since. For this achievement, if for nothing else, the EU can be said to have been a success and to have served humankind well.

Other countries, other motives

For what we now call the Republic of Ireland, anxiety focused not on a bear but rather on a mangy old lion. The southern part of Ireland, Eire, became an independent state in 1922. However, it was not until 1948 that the remaining duties of the British monarch were dropped and the country became a republic. Even then, the UK continued to loom large in its affairs; Ireland did not break the link with sterling until 1979. Membership of the EU represented a real escape from the UK's influence and Ireland's coming of age as a country – not the loss of sovereignty and national identity but rather their clear assertion.

Interestingly, three of the Union's troubled southern members also saw the EU as the giver and guarantor of freedom, although not freedom from outside domination but rather freedom from arbitrary rule and oppression. For these three countries are refugees from dictatorship, albeit not of the Communist variety. In 1974, Greece emerged from a seven-year period of rule by the Colonels. Spain was governed by a fascist dictatorship from 1936 until 1975, for most of the time under General Franco. And Portugal was under a dictatorship from 1926 until 1974.

For these countries, the ceding of power to Brussels did not have the sinister ring that it did to many people in Britain. On the contrary, it represented a sort of liberation and escape, an apparent guarantee of democracy and the rule of law at home, and membership of the club of respectable nations abroad.

A history of achievement

So the EU was forged from a variety of motives, some common to almost all joiners and some specific to individual countries. Some of the motives have had an economic aspect to them, namely that new members thought that they were joining an economic success story – and that their own economic performance would improve as a result. (I will deal with the EU's economic performance separately in Chapter 3.) But many, if not all, countries joining the EU had a decidedly political motivation – in keeping with the political origins of the Union.

In that regard, leaving economics to one side for a moment, in relation to what was hoped for and expected of it, in so many ways the EU can be described as a success:

♦ There has been no European war.
♦ In particular, France and Germany are close allies.
♦ The EU has helped countries from the former Soviet bloc to be reabsorbed into the West.
♦ There is a queue of countries waiting to join.
♦ The EU has leveraged the power and influence of member countries on the world stage.
♦ The institutions of the EU seem to be at the point of transformation so that it, or rather a large part of it, is ready to realize the original dream of a United Europe.

The trouble is that since the original vision of the founding fathers, things have changed. Is the EU really what Europe needs now? Or is it one of Europe's main problems?

2

The Trouble with the EU as a Political Institution

I believe in political union. I believe in political Europe. I believe in the Europe of integration. I believe in a Europe where we have the economy, culture and the politics brought together.
— Nicolas Sarkozy, President of France, 2007

When a cow is born in a horse's stable, it is still a cow.
— Anon.

To an increasing number of contemporary observers, the EU's successes seem to relate to the past. With regard to the present, however, and even more to the future, it has several key defects:

♦ It suffers from a profound identity crisis.
♦ Its institutions are mainly badly structured and badly run.
♦ It is focused on a largely irrelevant agenda, driven by the objectives of harmonization and integration, which produce excessive regulation and smother competition.
♦ It is alienated from its electorates.

One major result of the EU's defects is a tendency for it to come to bad decisions, which then affects, among other things, economic performance. I analyse that in the next chapter. Here, I discuss the political and institutional character of the EU. I start with a discussion of why institutions matter before going on to review the failings of the EU's institutional structure, starting with the essential matter of identity. I then consider the EU's institutions themselves and analyse the changing views of the member countries' electorates.

The importance of governance

For most of our history, human beings have had virtually no say over how they were governed. They were governed the way they were because that was how it had been before – until some other arbitrary power came along and usurped the original one. Dynasties and empires came and went without much of a rationale, except the exercise of brute force, alternating with the passive power of tradition, law and custom.

It should not be forgotten that this long history of arbitrary power also coincides with a long history of next to no economic growth. While the reasons for this, of course, are complex, the point to emphasize here is that governance really matters, not only for human freedom and happiness – surely the most important objectives – but also for economic growth. Accordingly, it is no accident that when growth began to emerge in western Europe in the seventeenth and eighteenth centuries, it was associated with the limitation of arbitrary power, the acknowledged power and sovereignty of the law and the development of a vibrant civil society.

The reasons for the Industrial Revolution happening first in England have been endlessly debated by scholars over the last couple of hundred years and doubtless this will continue. But let me put it this way: it was not all about the availability of coal and water power. Changes in the world of politics and institutions – as well as in the world of finance – played a major role.

Looking back over the last four centuries, three key revolutions were closely associated with disagreements about the legitimacy of the existing sovereign power raising money from the people. The English Civil War, which saw Charles I lose his head and England briefly become a republic, began initially as a result of Parliament's objections to Charles raising taxes to fund his wars. The French Revolution of 1789 was similarly partly inspired by a rejection of punitive taxation. The American Revolution of 1776 was also spurred by the issue of taxation, with the revolutionaries' cry being 'no taxation without representation'. And in the case of both Britain and its then colonial offshoot, the United States, the limitation of sovereign power, specifically the limitation of its economic aspects, played a major role in bringing about subsequent economic success.

Institutions really matter – for both good and ill. In their recent book *Why Nations Fail*, Daron Acemoglu and James Robinson stress the distinction between *inclusive* institutions, which serve the public interest, and *extractive* ones, which essentially serve the interests of the rulers or some special interest group. (This is a similar distinction to the one I draw in *The Trouble with Markets* between *creative* and *distributive* activities.) Societies only progress when inclusive institutions predominate over extractive ones.

The economist and Nobel Laureate Douglass North[4] has stressed that the institutions that matter are not only the formal ones. What matters too are what he calls 'informal institutions', such as sanctions, taboos, customs, traditions and codes of conduct. He points out that after independence, Latin American countries virtually all adopted carbon copies of the US Constitution, although this did not ensure good governance. North says that the reason is that nearly all Latin American countries had been Spanish colonies and were thus infused with Spanish informal institutions, in which 'personalistic' relationships 'are the key to much of the political and economic exchange'. By contrast, the United States had begun life as a British colony and benefited from British informal institutions, which permitted complex impersonal exchange.

So how do the institutions of the EU stack up? Are they well structured? Is there embodied in the EU treaties and the surrounding arrangements a clear limitation on arbitrary power? On what we know, are its institutions likely to operate in a way favourable to the promotion of economic growth? And are the institutions likely to command the loyalty and affection of the people under their sway? The place to start to answer these questions is by looking at the fundamental issue of identity.

What is it to be European?

The EU suffers from a profound identity crisis, which goes right back to the foundation of the Union. Despite the teleological nature of the integrationist project, the founding fathers of the European Union did not have a well-defined idea of the feasible, or desirable, extent of the Union. Because they set about their project during the Cold War, when the Soviet Union loomed large and the idea of eastern Europe being able and willing to join what we now call the EU was a mere pipedream, they probably did not need to consider the issue seriously. But it does need to be considered now.

What is the point of the EU? Is it to link together countries and peoples that are 'European'? Is it to link together countries and peoples that are geographically close together? Is it to link together countries that conduct themselves in a certain way and are prepared and able to obey EU law? Or is it simply to carry on expanding as far as it can, because bigger is better, so that the EU can be regarded as an early progenitor of global government?

Without a clear answer to these questions, it is difficult to see why the EU should not contemplate expansion to nations that are geographically close, such as Israel or the countries of North Africa, even though they are not strictly European. (Interestingly, the remit of the European Bank for Reconstruction and Development (EBRD) does extend into the Middle East and North Africa.) Or if the key concept is cultural, what about countries that are European in character and history but are far distant, such as Canada, Australia or New Zealand?

This question is of existential importance. For if there is no clear answer to the question of how far EU membership should spread, perhaps it should be restricted to a smaller territory – or indeed, perhaps the EU should not exist at all.

Formal criteria

It is clear that EU membership is not open to any old country. According to the Copenhagen criteria (laid out by the European Council in Copenhagen in 1993), to be a candidate for EU membership, a country must:

- have stable institutions guaranteeing democracy, the rule of law, human rights and respect for and protection of minorities;
- have a functioning market economy and the capacity to cope with competition and market forces in the EU;
- have the ability to take on and implement effectively the obligations of membership, including adherence to the aims of political, economic and monetary union;
- adopt the common rules, standards and policies that make up EU law.

This still leaves unclear which countries can, and which cannot, become members. As we shall see in a moment, there are a number of hard cases.

As the European Union developed and the fall of the Soviet Union made it possible to imagine the unification of Europe, the idea gained ground that the EU represented the quintessence of Europe. Accordingly, its extent should be dictated by the extent of Europe itself. That sounds easy enough – until you start to look at these hard cases.

Figure 2.1 shows the extent of further possible expansion. It has already been decided that Europe includes the second wave of former members of the Soviet bloc, Romania and Bulgaria, and Croatia became the 28th member of the European Union in July 2013. In addition, there are five countries that are formally acknowledged to be candidates for EU membership: Iceland, Macedonia, Montenegro, Serbia and Turkey. (Turkey is an important subject in itself, to which I will come in a moment.) There are three others that are not formally acknowledged as applicants but are widely recognized as potential candidates: Albania, Bosnia and Kosovo.

Figure 2.1 Potential expansion of the EU

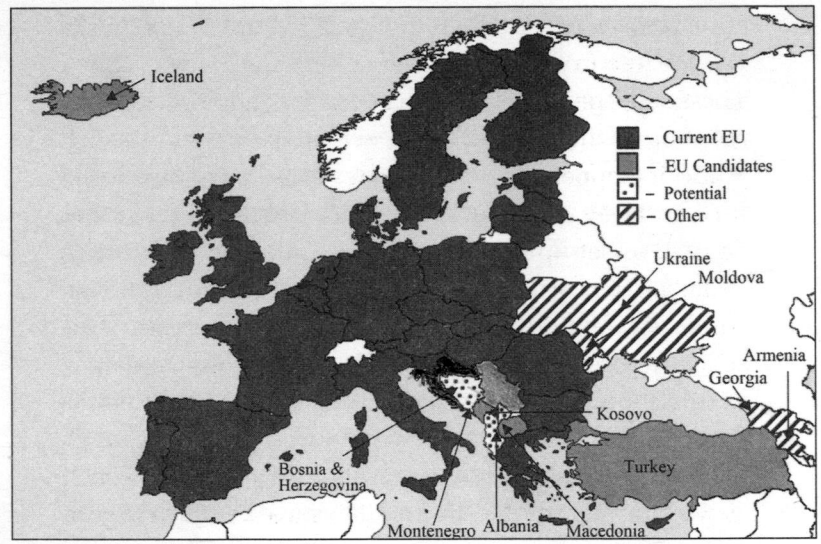

Source: www.europa.eu

More serious issues concern two countries that are not yet even in the line-up of potential candidates, but ultimately could be, namely Ukraine and Russia. These countries can be regarded as part-European, but they have also been outside mainstream European political culture for some time and cannot be regarded as full western democracies governed by the rule of law (although that has not stopped Russia being included in the G-8). Moreover, they are both very large. Ukraine has a population of about 45 million and Russia over 140 million.

Of the two, Ukraine is the more plausible candidate for membership. Its population may be large but it could just about be absorbed, although surely not without even greater angst in the capitals of western Europe than accompanied the accession of Romania and Bulgaria. Even if Ukraine were successfully to complete a reform programme, the combination of very low levels of GDP per capita and a dubious political culture would make Ukrainian entry extremely difficult for the EU to swallow. These same points, plus size, geography and history, surely rule Russia out as a viable proposition.

As it happens, both countries have recently moved further away from possible membership. Russia has decided to set up its own customs union encompassing, so far as is possible, the former republics of the Soviet Union (more about this in Chapter 10). It clearly sees this as a rival organization to the EU and, by establishing it as such, hopes to bed down former Soviet republics in its sphere of influence, to prevent them being drawn towards the EU the way former eastern bloc Soviet satellites such as Hungary and the Czech Republic have been (see Figure 2.2).

Which way Ukraine goes is in the balance. It had been expected to sign a trade deal with the EU in November 2013 at a summit in Vilnius, Lithuania. But at the last minute, under intense economic and political pressure from Russia, Ukraine withdrew. Subsequently it emerged that Russia had offered Ukraine substantial economic aid, including buying its bonds and providing energy supplies at below market price. It was evidently Russia's intention that Ukraine should join its Eurasian Union and that, accordingly, it should be prised away from the EU. This gave rise to considerable unease in Ukraine, with riots and demonstrations in the streets.

In 2014, Russia seized Crimea from Ukraine and incorporated it within Russia, while apparently fomenting unrest in eastern Ukraine, supposedly intending to destabilize that part of the country, possibly leading also to its absorption into Russia. These actions prompted

Figure 2.2 The former Soviet Union and its satellite states

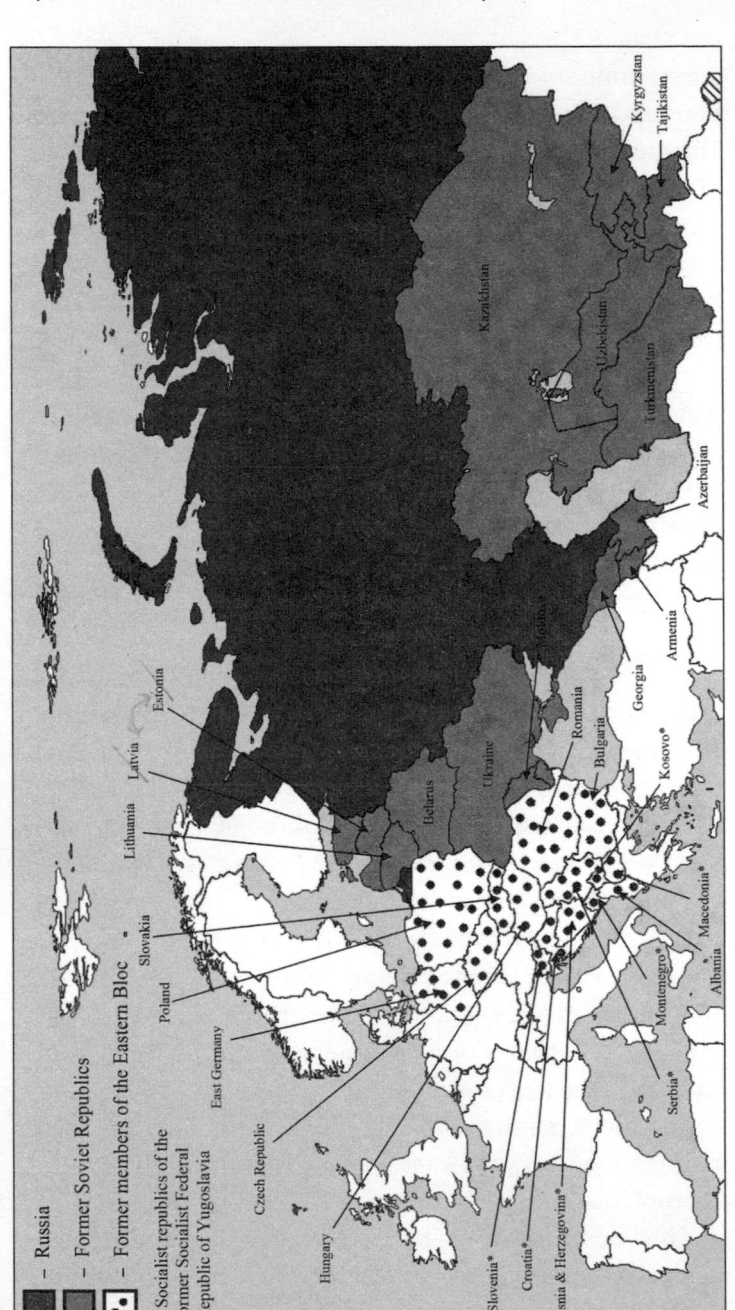

Source: www.britannica.com

major military manoeuvrings on both sides and the imposition of economic sanctions on Russia by the West. This whole episode seemed to mark a clear limit to the EU's eastern expansion.

Russia's intentions may similarly have a big influence over three other former Soviet republics that have established close relationships with the EU but have stopped short of full EU candidate status: Moldova, Georgia and Armenia. Whether the EU will want them in, and indeed whether they themselves would want to join, is being overwhelmed by Russia's evident wish for them not to join.

A different sort of expansion

The size of populations and the attitude of Russia are not the only factors to take into account when thinking about further expansion of the EU. There is also the critical issue of economic development, for which per capita GDP is a reasonable benchmark. It cannot be emphasized enough how large the disparities are in levels of GDP between the current EU and the candidates and potential candidates for EU membership.

Figure 2.3 shows the GDP per capita of the six founder members of the EEC in 1957. Excluding tiny Luxembourg, the richest country was the Netherlands. Its per capita GDP was not quite double the poorest country's, namely Italy. Over the next few decades, the gap gradually closed. Moreover, in the first expansion of membership in 1973, the new members, Denmark, Ireland and the UK, had a per capita GDP broadly in line with existing members.

This was most certainly not the case with the large expansion that took place in 2004, as Figure 2.4 shows.

Figure 2.3 GDP per capita in 1957 of the six founder members of the EEC (excluding Luxembourg, in US$ at PPP, 2011 prices)

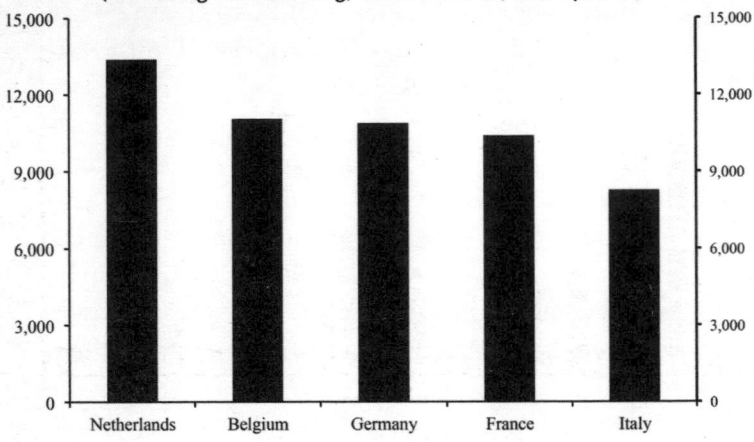

Source: UN, The Economist, Penn World, Datastream, Maddison

Figure 2.4 GDP per capita in the existing 14 members of the EEC in 2004 (excluding Luxembourg) and the new members that joined that year (in US$ at PPP, 2011 prices)

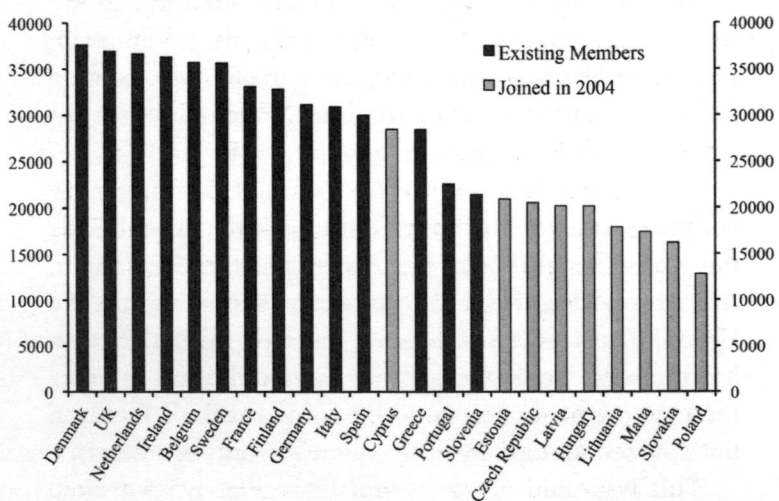

Source: World Bank

Figure 2.5 GDP per capita in 2013 in the existing EU and various possible new members (in US$ at PPP, 2011 prices)

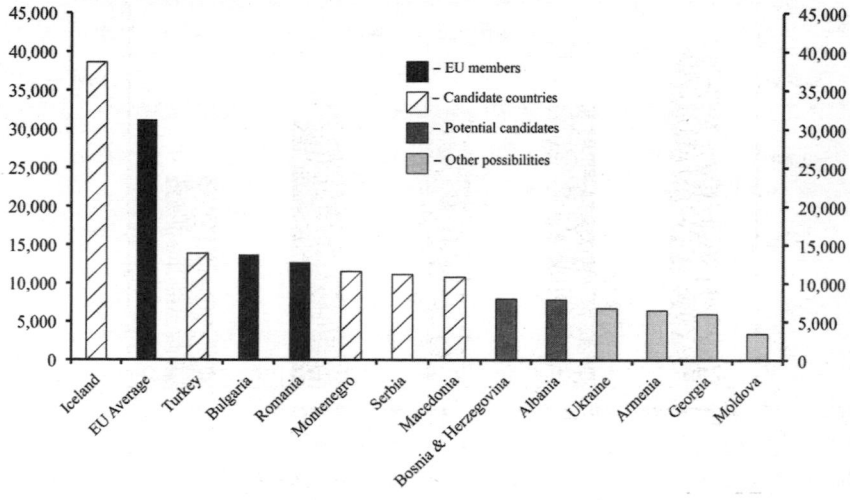

Source: IMF

The per capita GDP of the poorest new member was about a third of the richest (excluding Luxembourg). When Bulgaria and Romania joined in 2007, they were even poorer. Similarly, as Figure 2.5 shows, with the exception of Iceland, present and potential candidates all have a per capita GDP that is a small fraction of the EU average.

As the EU has spread eastward, it has taken in countries at a very different level of development. This has caused significant problems, most notably with the central idea of free movement of people within the Union. The result has been a level of migration that has seriously upset the indigenous populations of older member countries and not only fanned anti-EU feelings, but sparked an ugly upsurge of racism and xenophobia.

This issue did not arise when the EEC was formed, or with the 1973 expansion, since there was a smaller discrepancy in development between the founder members. However, the 2004 and 2007 expansions were different. Future expansions seem set to follow this more recent pattern.

It is almost as though the people generating these two parts of the EU agenda – the free movement of labour and the urge to expand – do not talk to each other.

The Turkish question

The level of development is not the only, or even the main, issue confronting the EU over its most challenging potential entrant: Turkey. The issue of possible Turkish membership goes right to the heart of the EU's identity crisis.

In many ways Turkey belongs naturally in Europe. Unlike Russia, it is a member of NATO and competes in the Eurovision Song Contest and in European football's Champions League and Europa League. Geographically, while most of Turkey is in Asia, part of it is clearly in Europe. Famously straddling both is Istanbul, its major city (although not its capital), one of the cradles of European civilization. Under the name Constantinople, reflecting its foundation by the Roman Emperor Constantine, it was the capital city of the eastern Roman Empire and, under the name Byzantium, capital of that part of the Empire that survived the fall of Rome until the eve of the modern era, succumbing to the Turks in 1453.

On the Asian shores of what we now call Turkey stood the cities of Troy, Ephesus and Halicarnassus, which have figured so large in the European historical imagination. Across the plains of Anatolia (Asiatic Turkey), Alexander the Great fought and defeated the armies of the Persian king Darius, in the process Hellenizing much of the Middle East, in a way that had major consequences, not least for the subsequent spread of the Christian Gospel. It was on the shores of Anatolia that Alexander ordered his Macedonian troops to 'burn their boats' – an expression that has passed down to us in English today. All of that seems pretty European to me.

Moreover, Istanbul is only a few miles further from Brussels than Athens is; and it is not much further distant from Brussels than Helsinki or Lisbon. However, in other matters it is much further apart. When Byzantium fell to the Ottoman armies in 1453, in cultural terms what we now call Istanbul shifted eastwards. Having moved westwards again during the twentieth century, Turkey has recently been moving eastwards once more. Today, it is a predominantly Islamic country. It is still a secular state, but even that does not seem secure. And it has a history of coups d'état and sketchy adherence to the rule of law.

So should Turkey be part of the EU? Several European countries may have large Muslim minorities living within their borders, but that is quite different from admitting to the EU an Islamic country and one with about 76 million people now and, according to the Turkish Statistical Institute, set to have over 90 million people 20 years hence. The EU has reacted to this challenge by dragging its feet on Turkish membership, with the result that the Turks are themselves cooling towards the idea.

Turkey is a litmus test. Is the EU meant to be the modern reincarnation of Christendom? Or is it a union of geographically close states that fulfil certain dry membership criteria? If the EU merely exists to bring together neighbours, how can such a union be close and based on shared values? At its heart, the EU suffers from a profound identity crisis.

The Union's limits

Interestingly, France's former President, Nicolas Sarkozy, recently made some pretty clear statements on the question of European identity and specifically on whether Turkey should be admitted to the EU. He said:

> *What is Europe? Europe is not a sub-region of the United Nations. It's a political project, an integration. We have to constantly give thought to what's happening as regards the enlargement and integration of Europe. I want an integrated Europe, in other words, a Europe that has borders. Turkey is in Asia Minor. Russia is not Europe either, but the Balkan states, they are part of Europe. And what about Ukraine? We would have to take in Ukraine. And then we're going to have a Europe that's so enormous that nobody will be able to do anything in Europe and we've already got the United Nations for that.*

In these remarks, over and above matters of compatibility and shared interests, Sarkozy raised the question of whether there is an upper limit to the size of the Union for it to function properly with an effective democracy and institutions that command the respect (if not the affection) of its citizens. And he was right to do so.

Surely there must be some upper limit to the size and type of union that allows (and indeed requires) the free movement of people within its borders. This alone must rule out Turkish membership, but it must also pose a serious question mark over Ukraine (never mind Russia). Either that, or the Union must change into something utterly different from the dreams of the founding fathers, who were driven by the prospect of 'ever closer union'. (I take up this subject in Chapter 8.) The free movement of people within the EU's borders has been a fundamental principle of the Single Market, but it is incompatible with a membership of countries with huge disparities in income and culture.

The European Union now has a membership whose size and diversity are out of keeping with its institutions, its ambitions and its own sense of what it is and what it is there for. The European Union has stumbled into this position without adequate forethought. It has continued to nurse the idea of ever closer union while expanding its geographical horizons well beyond what the EU's founding fathers could ever have imagined and beyond what has a reasonable hope of being effective.

In many ways, this problem is the result of success: umpteen countries have wanted to join the EU (for a variety of motives) and for the Union it was agreeable to be wanted and to grow larger. Nevertheless, to avoid becoming a horrendous monster, the EU needs to make a choice. It could continue with its current membership or even expand further, but not pursue full integration and ever closer union. Or it could retain this objective but for a smaller group of countries – perhaps those currently belonging to the eurozone. Yet, as we shall see in a moment, to make even that successful will be a tall order.

Institutional structures

The EU is a grouping of countries that is on the verge of becoming a state, but it is not quite there yet. The consequence is that it has emasculated the role of nation states in a number of areas without fully supplanting them. The result is a mess.

There is now a proposal for the eurozone to have its own president. In fact, this would be the EU's fifth president of sorts. There is already the President of the Commission, the President of the European Council, the President of the Council of Ministers (i.e. the rotating Country Presidency) and the President of the European Parliament, not to mention the EU's High Representative (recently the UK's Baroness Ashton). This puts into context Henry Kissinger's quip that since Europe consists of so many nation states, there is not a single telephone number he can call to get something done. Even if he tried to make contact with the EU, as distinct from its member states, it might take four, or even five, calls to do the trick.

The rotating country presidency, which is held for six months before the role is passed on to some other country, is distinctly odd, because countries such as Germany or the UK get treated the same as Luxembourg or Croatia, whose senior civil servants and diplomats are both much less numerous and, in general, less capable and experienced.

On foreign policy, the President of the European Commission, Mr Juncker, attends meetings of the G-7, alongside the Prime Ministers and Presidents of the member countries. However, that does not mean that there is an agreed European policy on any of the issues to be discussed. Indeed, EU members of the G-7 – France,

Germany, the UK and Italy – are at liberty to pursue their own foreign policies, and they often do.

Although the European Commission is the EU's embryo government, its composition is dictated by the multinational nature of the Union. There are 28 Commissioners, one for each member of the EU. The Commissioners are supposed to represent all EU citizens and not simply their own country, but in practice, countries do look to their own Commissioner to argue their case. And the Commission itself is a strange animal. A research document published by the pro-EU think tank the Centre for European Reform describes it as a 'political body that initiates legislation and also brokers compromises among member states; a technical body that evaluates the performance of the member-states' economies; a quasi-judicial authority that polices markets and enforces rules; and a regulator of common policies on behalf of the member states'.[5]

There is also the Council of Ministers, where national leaders meet with each other face to face. In this forum, countries are supposed to be able to protect their national interests, but membership is now so big that even large countries have difficulty in achieving this. For instance, the UK's share of the vote is now down to 8% and its ability to influence, let alone block, measures affecting its interests is decidedly limited. In practice, many key decisions are taken in bilateral meetings between Prime Ministers and Presidents. Given that France and Germany are widely accepted as the motor of the EU, the most important of these meetings concern the French President and the German Chancellor.

The European Parliament is not meant to function in the same way as national parliaments. It can propose or

amend legislation, but its decisions are not binding on the
European Council. European constituencies are very large
and there is little connection between MEPs and ordinary
people back home. The fact that constituencies for the
Parliament are all chunks of one member country, rather
than stretching across countries, reinforces the Parliament's position between the nation states and full union.
And although there are seven cross-country political groupings in Parliament, given the large linguistic and cultural
differences between different country representatives, these
make little impact in the member countries themselves.

Similar problems afflict the European Court of Justice
(ECJ). Each country, regardless of size, supplies a judge.
This scarcely enhances the Court's performance – or its
reputation. Admittedly, some of the Court's judgments
have been widely acclaimed. Perhaps the most celebrated
is the 1979 Cassis de Dijon ruling, which established
the principle of mutual recognition, such that any good
marketed and sold in one state is to be allowed to be
marketed and sold in another. Nevertheless, a raft
of judgments have caused consternation. One of the
most controversial was the 2011 ruling against gender
discrimination in insurance, which *The Economist* called
'pretty bonkers'. Its result was to prevent insurance
companies from discriminating in favour of young female
drivers, who tend to have fewer accidents than young
men. The ruling also forced insurance companies to give
the same annuity rates to male and female pensioners,
even though men and women have markedly different
life expectancies.

More generally, the Court has been criticized, not just
in the UK but in several other member states, for 'judicial
activism'; that is, a tendency to go beyond its remit and

to advance European integration. (Note that the ECJ is not to be confused with the European Court of Human Rights (ECHR), which was set up under the European Convention on Human Rights, which is also referred to as the ECHR and which I briefly discuss in Chapter 9. To distinguish between the two, the European Court, as distinct from the European Convention, is sometimes referred to as the ECtHR.)

The European Central Bank (ECB) is arguably an exception to the list of institutional failures. In technical terms it has worked well. Nevertheless, with its national representatives who are meant to set monetary policy for the eurozone as a whole, it is prone to many of the same difficulties besetting other European institutions. Indeed, many of its policy actions – and more particularly inactions – have been highly questionable. Admittedly, though, it has been saddled with a herculean task in trying to manage the euro. (I discuss the problems of the single currency in Chapters 4 and 5.)

The democratic deficit

The result of these institutional structures is that the electorates of individual countries no longer have the power to exercise the ultimate control over their rulers. Even in a country with a strong democratic tradition such as the UK, democracy has never amounted to an ability to shape, let alone veto, particular laws or governmental practices. Fundamentally, democracy in Britain – as elsewhere – has been about the power to turf out the party of government and its leader when they choose, or are forced, to seek the endorsement of the electorate. Now British people have to accept laws imposed on them as a result of byzantine intrigue between the unelected European Commission and the leaders of the other European member states. This represents a negation of centuries of British history, a central theme of which has been the gradual transfer of powers from the crown to the elected representatives of the people, who can be removed by those people at elections.[6]

Indeed, it is not widely recognized how deep-seated the democratic tradition is in Britain. The Anglo-Saxon kings were elected; not, admittedly, by universal suffrage, but from among the nobility and by the vote of an Advisory Council, the *witenagemot*. After the Norman Conquest in 1066, kings of England were more like dictators and before long they succeeded by primogeniture, not by being elected. But even then, they had to govern with the consent and counsel of the barons, and gradually the authoritarianism of the Normans was moderated by the influences of the Anglo-Saxon tradition and by the increasing authority of parliament.

In 1327 parliament deposed Edward II and in 1399 it deposed Richard II for assuming absolute powers not recognized by the English people. Subsequently, other notable moments occurred with the deposition of Charles I and James II and the establishment of clear parliamentary supremacy under the 'Glorious Revolution' of 1688. The rest, as they say, is history. It is striking that today the European Commission has greater powers to ignore parliament than did most English kings.[7]

Of course, the relative impotence of the British parliament – and indeed, other national parliaments – vis-à-vis the governance of the EU need not be viewed as a fatal flaw if one simply accepts that the size of the political entity that is subject to these democratic constraints has increased. Just as the people of Croydon cannot, by themselves, overturn a British government, so it may seem appropriate that the people of Britain, either directly or through their parliament, cannot, by themselves, overturn a European government.

In fact, this is far too indulgent a conclusion to come to, because even the European electorate as a whole cannot turn out the European Commission, while the European Parliament is a supine and ineffective institution. Moreover, as I argue in Chapter 7, even if the EU's political institutions were radically reshaped, there are good reasons why a European democracy would not work very well.

Administrative failures

Given its evolution and the stresses and strains in its institutional structure, it is hardly surprising that much of the EU does not work efficiently. Admittedly, bad and even chaotic government is not restricted to the EU. Professors King and Crewe have produced a fascinating, though hair-raising, account of blunders made by British governments over the years, including the Thatcher government's programme in the 1980s and early 1990s to encourage people into private pensions, millions of whom were ill-advised to switch out of their existing schemes.[8] Massive compensation payments followed.

The complaint heard particularly strongly in the UK, but also in other member countries, is not so much that the EU is especially incompetent or prone to outright blunder, but rather that it imposes too many regulations without any regard for the cost of enforcing them, or the knock-on effect throughout the system. Moreover, when such regulations are imposed across the EU as a whole, even if they are broadly appropriate and practical in some countries, they may be completely inappropriate in others. What is more, it is widely believed that many of the EU's actual or proposed regulations are extremely petty, so that the irritation factor is much higher than any quantifiable economic cost.

For example, in May 2013 the European Commission proposed a ban on olive oil being served in saucers or jugs in restaurants, for public health reasons. After a reaction of widespread outrage and incredulity across Europe, the Commission President killed off the proposal.

The dispute that emerged in June 2012 over the European Commission's plans to implement reform of data protection laws is an interesting example of the frustrations that European businesses endure. Across the EU, businesses were up in arms about the increased costs they would have to bear if the measure went through. What was so infuriating – and this was just the latest example – was the sense that those who had designed the measure in Brussels were completely out of touch with the real world and were oblivious of the consequences that might flow from the proposed measure.

Irrelevant agendas

The above complaints, frequently heard from eurosceptics, are serious, but not serious enough to make a real difference to economic performance. Yet there is something essentially political that does: the prevailing ethos of the EU pushes it towards interventionism. In the interests of closeness (as in 'ever closer union'), the EU establishment has been keen to harmonize arrangements and outcomes across a broad swathe of economic and social affairs.

Given that the countries of the EU come to this association with substantial differences in histories, structures, circumstances, tastes and preferences, the urge to harmonize naturally implies intervention and the suppression of national differences.

I will discuss the economic implications of this in the next chapter, but it is important to note that this leads the EU into obsessing about various sorts of trivia, while being unable or unwilling to make a meaningful difference to the substantive matters that its citizens care about. The energies and attentions of the European governing elites, which should have been devoted to laying the real foundations for economic growth in the same way as happened in the Asian Tiger economies, were instead diverted onto whatever the pet integrationist scheme was at the time.

To be fair, sometimes the European elites have recognized the need to focus on the real factors underpinning economic success. However, they have never been able to bring the same energy and drive to implementing effective economic measures as they have to the various political projects.

The clearest example of this is the Lisbon Agenda, a set of objectives adopted in 2000:

- Achieving economic growth of 3% p.a.
- Explicit employment targets to be reached by 2010.
- Increasing spending on research and closer links between universities and businesses.
- Support to small and medium-sized enterprises, including reduced regulation and a drive towards liberalization.

♦ Saving energy and promoting environmentally friendly technologies.

This is not a bad set of objectives and the agenda was relaunched in 2005 with a renewed emphasis on growth and jobs. In practice, though, the Lisbon Agenda has proved to be so much hot air. It amounted merely to a wish list, with no substantive actions agreed or implemented. As the French economist Charles Wyplosz put it in January 2010: 'The Lisbon strategy for making the EU the world's most competitive economy is a failure, yet an extension of the failed approach is in the works ("Europe 2020").'

The alienation of voters

One serious problem with the idea of a fully integrated EU is that this notion is increasingly out of touch with what people want. Of course, most major established political parties are europhile, but this is no longer the whole story. Quite apart from the UK, where the eurosceptic party UKIP commands high ratings in the polls, there are now major eurosceptic parties in the Netherlands, Italy, Austria, Greece, Finland, France – and Germany. In some cases their scepticism extends to the euro only, while they continue to support the EU. In other cases, EU membership itself, as well as the euro, is in question.

Naturally, the emergence of these political parties has been both cause and effect of a shift in public opinion. As the euro elite has moved forward to ever closer union, by and large European electorates have been moving in favour of ever looser union – or no union at all. As I document below, this is a massive change from earlier decades, when the EU commanded widespread support and even, in some cases, enthusiasm. This loss of popular support is relevant for two main reasons:

◆ It shows how, either because the EU has changed, or because its citizens have, or both, the EU no longer corresponds to what its citizens broadly want. In a democracy, that ought to give cause for concern.
◆ The lack of popular support for the more integrated, more intrusive EU makes it difficult to function and highlights the danger of creating an alienated citizenry if the EU proceeds to full political union.

Elections provide a measure of voter attitudes. In the latest EU parliamentary elections, average voter turnout across the EU was 43%, down from 62% in 1979. In the UK in 2009, the turnout was less than 35%. In the last two EU parliamentary elections, the turnout in Slovakia was below 20%.

Another way to measure the general support for EU membership is to use the Eurobarometer, a European Commission survey that examines public opinion in the member states. The net support for membership of the European Union is calculated by taking the difference between the percentage of respondents who find EU membership to be a 'good thing' and those who find it to be a 'bad thing'. The question about EU membership was present since the first Eurobarometer was published in 1973, but unfortunately it was removed from the survey at the end of 2011.

In Q3 2011, across the Union as a whole, net support for the EU was at its lowest level since the beginning of the survey: 29%, as compared to a high of 64% recorded in Q1 1991. More recent survey findings by the Pew Research Centre show that support for EU membership and increased integration declined further between 2011 and 2013.

German and French opinion

While there have been some significant differences in popular opinion in different EU member countries, in most countries the degree of support has declined markedly over the years. Given that France and Germany are the two main drivers of the European project, how public opinion towards the EU develops in these countries is critical to the future of the Union. And in both countries opinion has shifted substantially.

The German policy and business elites always have been, and still are, fully aware of the apparent benefits that the EU has brought to their country: new markets for German exports, the ability to act on the world stage and friendly neighbours. Nonetheless, they are increasingly detached from the case for more European integration. Among politicians, the traditional cross-party consensus for more integration is fragmenting. The federalists complain that whenever they want to push for more integration, other EU members are against them.

German public opinion has also shifted significantly. During the Cold War, the German public saw membership of the EU as a barrier to the Soviet threat and a way of integrating into the western world. The majority still believe that membership of the EU is a good thing. However, an increasing number now believe that greater EU integration was a sacrifice made for the benefit of other EU members. During the euro crisis, increasing euroscepticism has been propelled by bitter anti-EU and anti-euro campaigns in the German mass media, something that has never been present before. And now there is a eurosceptic party, AFD, to reflect and stir up anxieties.

Meanwhile, France has been becoming steadily more eurosceptic. The 1992 referendum on the Maastricht Treaty was a turning point. The far right and left political parties opposed the Treaty altogether. In the end, it was voted through with only 51% support. The French public had another shock in store for their leaders when they rejected the European Constitution in a referendum in 2005. Their priorities were focused on national interests, with clear limits to support for the European integration project. Now the eurosceptic National Front is leading in French opinion polls.

Interestingly, French cooling towards European institutions and the objective of further integration is, on the whole, for opposite reasons to the ones that prevail in the rest of northern Europe, especially the UK. Many French voters opposed the draft European Constitution because it was seen as too liberal and insufficiently protectionist!

So it looks as though a split is opening up between the EU's two driving powers, France and Germany. It is not only that French views have changed; they have started to look less like the prevailing attitudes in Germany and more like those in Spain, Italy and Greece. What is more, as I argue in Chapter 4, the French economy is moving in the same direction.

Right from the start there was something profoundly odd about a system in which one country (Germany) punched well below its weight and paid a disproportionate amount of the bills and another (France) punched well above its weight, because of the events that besmirched the European continent some decades ago. Most importantly, there has been an over-arching contradiction at the heart of the EU between a country that, partly because of its history, is prepared to subdue its own national identity into a new Europeanism and another that, partly because of its own weakness but also because of its history, wants to cling on to its identity as a proud nation state.

Changes in Italy

Italy, politicians and people alike, has traditionally been among the strongest supporters of the European Union. Alcide De Gasperi, the founder of the Christian Democrats, said that Italy was 'ready to transfer wide powers to a European Community, provided that it is democratically organized and gives guarantees of life and development'.

Support for deeper European integration underlay the political agenda of all subsequent governments. Even the Italian Communist Party took a pro-European stance in the mid-1960s. In the past, the Italian public has frequently viewed the EU as a provider of democracy and stability, attributes that Italians usually associate with other countries.

The centre-left governments led by Romano Prodi, the former President of the European Commission, have openly supported all major aspects of European integration. By contrast, although the centre-right governments led by Silvio Berlusconi supported EU membership, they also voiced criticism about issues such as immigration and new climate change rules. In April 2013, the Italian government launched an unprecedented critique of the EU, going so far as to question Italy's EU membership.

This followed the refusal by the European Commission to grant temporary protection for migrants from North Africa. Berlusconi was direct: 'Either Europe is something concrete, or it would be best to part ways.'

Among the Italian public, support for the EU has fallen since the early 1990s and especially over the last decade. The present EU, with new and less prosperous member states, is no longer seen as a prerequisite for democracy. More recently, the pressure put on Italy by Germany and other northern countries to reform and enact austerity measures has led to growing resentment and scepticism towards both the euro and the EU. Indeed, all three of Italy's main opposition parties are against the euro.

Even more euroscepticism in Britain

Apart from some members of the establishment, very few British people ever signed up to the political aspect of what is now the EU. Indeed, when the UK joined the EEC on 1 January 1973, the full political import of what membership meant was not properly perceived.

In 1975, there was a referendum on whether the UK should stay in the EU. During the campaign, it was common for both Conservative and Labour supporters of EU membership to focus on the economic aspects, often ignoring the political and constitutional issues. On the 'no' side, by contrast, there was a clear recognition of the questions of identity and the constitution, which foreshadowed developments yet to come.

This united some individuals who on most other issues would have been violently opposed to each other. Both the former Conservative minister the late Enoch Powell and left-wing firebrand Tony Benn, then Secretary of State for Industry, foresaw much of what was to come and strongly opposed it. In a letter to his Bristol constituents in December 1974, Tony Benn said: 'Britain's continuing membership of the Community would mean the end of Britain as a completely self-governing nation and the end of our democratically elected parliament as the supreme law making body in the United Kingdom.'

The feeling of having been misled by their leaders, and in the process being disenfranchised, underlies a good deal of British euroscepticism now. A typical British objection to the EU today is that what member countries, including the UK, have signed up to is not a given set of arrangements, but rather a process in which what they thought they joined or voted for changes before their eyes. As the British judge the late Lord Denning put it in 1974: 'The Treaty of Rome is like an incoming tide. It flows into the estuaries and up the rivers. It cannot be held back.'

In Britain, baiting the EU has now become a national sport. It often goes over the top. In June 2013, Bruno Waterfield and Tim Ross of *The Daily Telegraph* revealed the existence of a colour-in pamphlet for children, published by the European Parliament, entitled 'Mr and Mrs MEP – and their helpers'. They wrote: 'One exercise in "Mr and Mrs MEP – and their helpers" reveals that it takes four people to post a letter and that euro-deputies are greeted with taxpayer funded limousines as they arrive at the airport, before a day that includes dining and shopping.'

The attention given to the colouring-book episode was ridiculous. As Jaume Duch, spokesman for the European Parliament, put it in an interview with the *Huffington Post* on 28 June 2013:

In a week in which the European Parliament secured a deal for solid investments in growth, SMEs, innovation and helping young unemployed people to get jobs – a deal worth 960 billion euros over a seven year period – it got astonishingly attacked over a colouring book for small children costing 7 cents apiece (€1,066 in total).

Yet the British reaction was growing euroscepticism. In the general election of 2015, the UK Independence Party (UKIP) may only have won one seat, but it received almost 4 million votes.

Growing unpopularity in other countries

Among the smaller EU members there have also been significant shifts of opinion compared to when countries first joined. The Netherlands has traditionally been among the most enthusiastic of EU members, but there were always limits to how far people wanted integration to go. The broad political consensus for deeper European integration began to fall apart in the 1990s. Successive governments stated that the Netherlands was contributing too much to the EU budget. The rejection of the European Constitution in a referendum in 2005 highlighted the shift in people's attitudes towards EU integration. While the majority of the government supported the Constitution, 61.6% of people voted against its adoption. What is more, in June 2013, the Dutch government released a list of 54 powers that it wanted to remain at the national rather than European level. This was the most significant step in the country's recent political shift towards a more sceptical stance on European integration.

By contrast, Belgium has always been more inherently europhile. Mark Eyskens, who served as Prime Minister in 1981 and as Foreign Minister during the years leading up to the signing of the Maastricht Treaty, summed up the prevailing Belgian mood as 'Europe is like a fatherland to be loved'. The vast majority of Belgian voters continue to favour their country's membership of the EU and the euro. There are no opinion polls suggesting that the Belgian public's support for the EU has weakened over the last few years. In fact, the Eurobarometer survey, published in May 2013, showed that more Belgians believe that the European Union can solve the economic crisis (32%), compared with only 15% for the national government and 15% for the IMF.

In Spain and Portugal, however, popular opinion towards membership of the European Union has been changing radically. The outbreak of the global economic crisis, the collapse of the housing bubble, the deep recession, rising unemployment and the austerity measures have all soured people's mood, with the EU frequently being blamed. Since 2007, Spanish approval of the EU has almost halved, and in Portugal public support for the EU is among the lowest in the EU, together with the UK and Greece.

In Finland, the eurosceptic and populist True Finns party took almost a fifth of the vote in the 2011 parliamentary elections. In Sweden and Denmark, public euroscepticism has focused mainly on the euro and the common foreign policy, both of which have been opposed by the vast majority of the population since the beginning of the crisis. In Denmark, a poll by Ramboell/Analyse Denmark, released on 25 January 2013, showed that 47.2% of voters surveyed favoured a review of Denmark's relationship with the EU.

During the early 1990s, across the former eastern Europe both politicians and the public displayed a marked willingness to join the European Union. Indeed, many people were ecstatic about EU membership. But the outbreak of the recent economic crisis led to large shifts in public attitudes. The majority of citizens in these countries still favour the EU, partly perhaps because of the large sums received from the EU budget. Nonetheless, support for the EU, and especially the euro, has still diminished significantly.

The Swiss exception

Perhaps the most significant development with regard to public opinion has occurred in a country that is not even a member of the EU: Switzerland. Despite its non-membership, as I discuss in Chapter 9, Switzerland has enjoyed a very close relationship with the EU, while retaining some national freedoms. Many Swiss people, including a good number of business leaders, hoped that Switzerland would proceed to full EU membership in due course. Equally, many eurosceptics, including in Britain, hoped that the Swiss arrangements would provide a model for a new sort of relationship for countries, like the UK, that might decide to leave the EU.

Yet in a referendum in February 2014, the Swiss people voted to restrict immigration into Switzerland, including from the EU, thereby violating the country's treaty with Brussels. This cannot be reconciled with the EU as currently constituted. Either the EU will have to change and reform on the issue of the free movement of labour, or Switzerland is going to move further away from the EU. What is particularly significant is that Swiss voters have expressed a view that is shared pretty much throughout the EU.

A changed world

So what should we make of these shifts in opinion? What we now call the EU, together with the associated process of further integration, has always been a project conceived at the top of European society. It has been the idea of the European elites. Nevertheless, for most of its existence, across nearly all member countries, it has enjoyed a considerable measure of popular support. But not any more. A dangerous divide has opened up between the governing elites and the governed. European history teaches us to be extremely wary of such developments.

Of course, one could assume that popular disillusion with the EU is based on a misapprehension of the situation and of people's own interests. Nevertheless, that would not be a wise, or a well-justified, conclusion. The truth is that when Monnet and Schuman were dreaming their dreams – and putting some of them into action – the world was a very different place. Most important of all, the memory of the Second World War loomed large over everything people thought and did. By contrast, in 2016, it is 71 years since the end of the war. It is remarkable that we are still trying to escape from its shadow.

Yet it was in that shadow that the shape of the EU was cast. Most importantly, after the war Germany was a divided country, with scant hope for reunification. In addition, the Soviet Union dominated European security concerns. The Cold War raged and people lived with the ever-present fear of nuclear annihilation.

At this point, as coming economic and political powers, China and India were nowhere to be seen on the radar, both still mired in poverty. Although Japan had already begun its rise to global success, no other significant Asian countries were following.

From a technological point of view, travel by aircraft was possible, but it was far from being a frequent occurrence for most people. Similarly, there were telephones and televisions, but not many people had them. Most importantly, there were no computers; or, more accurately, none available to ordinary people. And, of course, that meant no internet and no email. Forget the emerging markets or globalization – no one had even heard the expressions. Compared to today's world reality, this was more like the Dark Ages.

Over subsequent decades, during which the world was changing, the EU was also changing – but not in a way that made it more congruent with the changing reality outside. Its membership, of course, greatly increased and became more diverse. Moreover, its pretensions to statehood became more and more obvious and, except in Germany and a few other countries, were widely resented.

At the same time, some of the diverse fears that bolstered initial support for the EU faded: fear of another European war, fear of the Soviet Union, fear of dictatorship. These have largely been supplanted by new ones: fear of recession and unemployment, fear of immigration, fear of crime and disorder, fear of social breakdown and, most importantly, fear of the impotence of government in the face of these threats.

In 2014, the Russian seizure of the Crimea and the apparent attempts to destabilize eastern Ukraine, with a view to absorbing it into Russia, briefly raised a flicker of interest in the EU as the saviour and guarantor of European security.

Nevertheless, this did not last long. It was widely believed that the EU had partially caused, or at least facilitated, President Putin's aggression by cuddling up to Ukraine and dangling the prospect of EU (and possibly, by extension, NATO) membership in front of a country that could legitimately be regarded as part of Russia's 'sphere of influence'. Moreover, it quickly became clear that in relation to the idea of confronting Russia, the leading states of the EU were seriously divided. In particular, with its heavy energy dependence on Russia and its strong trade ties, Germany was decidedly unenthusiastic about taking a tough line.

So even in 2014, when push came to shove, with regard to their security the countries of Europe looked not to the EU, but to NATO. In other words, they were still militarily dependent on America.

The Great Recession and the crisis of the euro obviously increased the disaffection with European elites, but these are not to be regarded as accidents completely outside the responsibility of political leaders. After all, their actions and inactions laid the groundwork for the Great Recession in Europe as well as America; as for the euro, that was completely their doing.

So it is not inappropriate or unfair that European politicians and policies are widely believed to be responsible for the mess that so many Europeans feel they are now in. In this respect, the EU itself is widely regarded as either the source of much of the problem or, even if it is not, as too incompetent or distracted to do anything about it. There is much to be said for both conclusions. The result is that the EU's citizens are increasingly disillusioned and dissatisfied with an institution that, despite its failings, continues to get larger and more intrusive.

From politics to economics

You might readily believe that whatever its political shortcomings, the EU justifies its existence by delivering superior economic performance. That is the subject of the next chapter, so I will not steal its thunder here. Nevertheless, I must say this. However much you, the reader, are surprised by what you glean there about the EU's economic record, you should be ever mindful of the roots of this economic performance – in the politics of the European Union, its institutions and its prevailing ethos, derived from its foundation in the 1950s, in the shadow of a terrible conflict just concluded, and in the foreshadow of a new and more terrible one that might soon commence.

Part II

The Economics of the EU

3

Has the EU Been an Economic Success?

Above all it is important to point out that we can only maintain our prosperity in Europe if we belong to the most innovative regions in the world.
—Angela Merkel, German Chancellor, to the *Financial Times*, July 2005

The EU may have been established primarily for political rather than economic reasons, yet even so, much of its early development was focused on economic integration. Moreover, both for its own citizens and for those abroad, how it performed economically was a prime arbiter of whether or not it was judged to be successful; and it still is. So it is about time that we took stock of whether the EU has been an economic success.

The image of success

To the casual observer, it may seem obvious that the EU has been successful. After all, it is the world's largest economy and trading bloc. It accounts for almost 30% of global output, 15% of trade in goods and about 24% of overall global trade.

What is more, its people are prosperous, with standards of living that their parents and grandparents could only dream about. On the face of it, the average European citizen has all the trappings of material success – as well as generous social benefits and ample leisure to boot.

In fact, this does not prove very much. Size alone is not decisive; after all, the Soviet Union was big. It is on income per capita that the issue turns. On that score, the EU's record is not outstanding. Most countries in the world, including those in Europe that do not belong to the EU, enjoy living standards much higher today than those of 30 or 40 years ago, not to mention umpteen stars of the economic firmament, spread around the world, whose citizens have seen their lives not so much improved as transformed.

Perhaps the very least we can say is that the EU has not been an outright failure. Whatever it has done and not done, it has not produced the sort of abject poverty that exists in parts of Africa today. Nor have its citizens suffered the enforced squeeze of living standards that exists in North Korea, side by side with a prosperous South, nor the juxtaposition of material degradation and advanced science that one can witness in Cuba.

Nevertheless, that is not saying a great deal either. The issue is how much of the success of EU members, and how much of their failure, is down to the EU itself. We will never be able to be sure of the answer, because we lack what economists call the 'counter-factual'; that is, we do not know what would have happened in the absence of the EU. The best we can do here is to look at the performance of EU members compared to non-members and speculate about how the EU's actions and inactions may have contributed to this result. (I briefly review some of the evidence on the benefits of EU membership, and the Single Market in particular, in Chapter 9.)

In what follows, I start by noting the EU's early success and then move on to its more disappointing recent performance. I then briefly review some excuses for the

EU's economic failure, including the idea that it is the policies of national governments, rather than the EU, that are responsible. (I do not discuss the euro as a cause of Europe's woes, since that has a whole chapter devoted to it, straight after this one.)

The core of the current chapter concerns the key areas in which the EU has a major bearing on economic performance. It tries to identify where the EU has gone wrong, including analysing the central idea that the Union should bring benefits to its members as a result of its sheer size. The chapter concludes with a discussion of the importance of competition between governments – which is, of course, the polar opposite of what is achieved through harmonization and integration.

Early success

Early on, the EU certainly showed plenty of signs of success. The first couple of decades of the Community's existence were characterized by very strong economic growth. From 1957 to 1973 (when the UK joined the Community), Germany grew at an average annual rate of 4.7%, France by 5.2%, the Netherlands by 4.6% and Italy by 5.3%. The six countries that formed the European Community in 1957 – that is, the above four plus Belgium and Luxembourg – grew at an annual average rate of 4.9%. By comparison, over the same period the UK grew at an average annual rate of only 2.8%.

Although 2.8% was extremely high by British standards, the fact that the UK was losing ground to the continent was one of the driving forces behind the case for British membership. Implicitly, the British establishment accepted the idea that there were major advantages in being members of a large bloc – or at least this bloc. And they feared that outside it, Britain would be left behind.

In fact, this strong growth among the Six did not establish very much about the benefits of being in the Community. All of these countries were enjoying rapid growth as they made good the effects of war destruction. Several of them also benefited from the one-off surge in productivity that occurs when large numbers of people leave the land and gain employment in cities.

By contrast, the UK had not been that badly damaged in the war, its agriculture was relatively small and efficient and – as countless studies have documented over the years – there were many factors making for relative economic decline that had nothing to do with Britain's exclusion from the Community.

The reasons for the UK's slow growth revolved around the more fundamental, and inherently very tricky, issues of excessive trade union power, weak management, under-investment and poor economic structure. When the UK finally addressed these problems under Prime Minister Thatcher, its relative growth performance improved, not because it was by this stage inside the EU, but rather because it had finally got to grips with many of the real factors that had held the country back.

Indeed, just to prove the point that it was not membership of the then EEC that made all the difference, other countries outside the Community were also growing nicely over the period leading up to the UK's accession (1957–73). Switzerland and Sweden grew at an average annual rate of 4.3%, the United States by 3.8%, Norway by 4.1%, Australia by 4.8% and Canada by 4.6%.

The simple fact is that the main reason for the rapid growth of Community members was not their membership. However, it was typical of some of Thatcher's predecessors, and of some of the languid, often incompetent British establishment, that they thought the solution to the nation's problems was to join a club.

Recent slowdown

By contrast with early apparent success, over the last couple of decades the growth of most EU members has been disappointing. Not only has the growth rate fallen back in comparison to their own past histories, but economic growth has also been low relative to the US and even low relative to their fellow EU member the UK, never mind the rapidly growing countries of Asia. (Some EU members have done well, though: Sweden is a notable example.)

Between 1980 (Thatcher's first full year in power) and 2007 (just before the financial crash), the average annual growth rate was 2.2% for France, 1.9% for Germany, 2.6% for the Netherlands and 1.8% for Italy. These figures compare with 2.5% for the UK and 3% for the US.

If the period is extended to 2015 to include the full impact of the Great Recession (which affected the UK particularly badly) and the subsequent recovery, the UK's lead over the EU average is still there. Over the period, the EU Six, the original signatories to the Treaty of Rome, grew at an annual average of 1.6%, compared with 2.2% for the UK. And by the end of 2015, both the US and the UK were continuing to recover, while some of the eurozone was struggling to emerge from recession. Admittedly, headline growth numbers have to be adjusted for changes in the number of people and the number of hours they work, adjustments that have the effect of making the EU look better compared to the US, but they do not close the gap entirely.

Now it is the EU that is losing ground to the US and the UK. Moreover, as I shall detail in a moment, quite apart from weak economic growth, the EU has become one of the world's unemployment hotspots; hardly the hallmark of an economic success story.

At least by the start of 2016, there had been some sort of economic recovery across Europe, including the eurozone, and on some indicators it seemed as though the peripheral countries were making some much-needed adjustments, prompting some observers to believe that the crisis of the euro was over. However, this is only the superficial picture. In the peripheral countries unemployment remains appallingly high and GDP is flat or falling. Since these countries are continuing to run government budget deficits, this means that the all important debt-to-GDP ratio is still rising. The eurozone crisis is not dead, but merely sleeping. (I take up this subject in more detail in Chapter 4.)

Moreover, the fundamental economic problems besetting Europe remain as serious as ever. Even the German Chancellor, Angela Merkel, recognizes their seriousness. In an interview with the *Financial Times* on 11 December 2012 she said:

> *If Europe today accounts for just over 7 per cent of the world's population, produces around 25 per cent of global GDP and has to finance 50 per cent of global social spending, then it's obvious that it will have to work very hard to maintain its prosperity and way of life.*

Admittedly, the EU is by far the world's most popular destination for Foreign Direct Investment (FDI). Over the past decade, though, the share of global FDI going to the EU (including intra-EU investments) has declined substantially from 45% in 2001 to 23% in 2010, as the share going to emerging markets has risen. Interestingly, two European countries that are not members of the EU, namely Norway and Switzerland, have been just as successful at attracting FDI as most EU members and much more successful than some, such as Italy.

Excuses for economic failure

So much for the facts of relative economic performance. What about the reasons? One excuse for comparatively poor economic performance is the idea that the countries of the EU, or at least many of them, are caught in the equivalent of the so-called middle income trap. Many countries in Latin America are experiencing a growth slowdown and they are not the only ones. All of the BRICs (Brazil, Russia, India and China) have recently experienced decidedly slower growth. Yet this is wholly inadequate as an excuse for disappointing growth in the EU. For a start, EU growth has not slowed down recently but has been poor for a good while. Moreover, when the countries of the EU began to struggle, they were not in a 'middle income' position.

Indeed, sometimes poor European performance is put down to the rather different idea that Europe's standard of living is so high that further advances from this level are not easy to achieve and/or are not avidly desired by the people. In my view this does not stack up either. Living standards are as high as, or higher than, the EU average in Switzerland and Norway and yet GDP there is still increasing at faster rates than in the EU. Singapore has a level of GDP per head that is higher than in the UK, France and Germany, yet over the last four years its economy has still grown by about 5% per annum, well above the average – or even the best – EU rate.

The argument is also sometimes put forward that it is inappropriate to judge the EU by its economic performance because, from the start, European integration has been an overtly political project, designed to achieve peace and stability in Europe. What is more, in that respect it can be regarded as a success.

In Chapter 1, I have already given due weight to the political origins of the EU and to the strength of the political forces holding it together. However, this does not mean that economic performance does not matter. To believe that would be to let the leaders of the EU off much too lightly. Although the original driving force behind the foundation of the EU was political, it was always envisaged that there would be economic advantages too. That was the whole point about market size and the reduction of trade barriers.

There was also a belief that central EU authorities would be bound to make better decisions for Europe as a whole than would competing nation states. The prevailing ethos was that competition between nation states, or at least European nation states, was wasteful.

There was never a time at which the leaders of Europe said to the European people: 'This is a political project that is necessary to preserve peace in Europe, but it will cost you a great deal of money.' On the contrary, they trumpeted the idea of economic advantage – which was easy to sell in the early years because economic growth was so strong.

And that was the whole point about being able to stand tall on the world stage, able to look America in the eye. This would not be possible simply by cobbling together a group of European states. No, the idea was that European integration would make Europe more prosperous and hence able to face America as an equal.

Only in recent years has the idea that there was a price to be paid for European unity come to be widely argued and partly accepted. That case has been argued specifically in relation to the euro, especially in Germany. The idea has been advanced by the elite that preserving the euro may cost money – particularly if you are German – but that the euro is necessary for the survival of the EU itself. Yet that idea was not present before the foundation of the euro, or even in the euro's early years. It has emerged only during the euro crisis of the last few years.

Poor EU economic performance is not the result of a rational choice made by rich, well-provided-for Europeans who have a different set of values from mere material advancement, including the funding of inefficient EU institutions for political reasons. Nor is it the well-anticipated price to be paid for integration and security. It is, quite simply, the result of relative economic failure, brought on by bad policies.

Still, there is massive resistance to acknowledging this, not least among the European elites. It is often argued, for instance, that if laws governing employee protection and macro policies including quantitative easing (QE) are the keys to success, then it is puzzling why the UK has only recently started to recover and why its performance after the crisis of 2008 was so poor. This view puts the cart before the horse. No one is suggesting that UK economic policy has been a paragon of virtue. Indeed, the weaknesses of the UK economy are substantial, particularly regarding the poor level of education and skills attainment. By contrast, in much of continental Europe these aspects of economic policy are more robustly addressed by public policy.

But these aspects of economic performance are deep-seated and difficult to shift. If they cannot be easily shifted, then a critical issue surrounds how economic policy is conducted despite these shortcomings. The point is that in spite of its supply-side inadequacies, the UK has been able to put in a decent macro performance. That is largely due to policy. By contrast, in spite of substantial initial endowments of human and physical capital, the macro performance of much of continental Europe has been disappointing, mainly because of bad policy.

Not everything is down to the EU

Can some of this relative economic failure be explained by factors other than the EU? Yes. In many EU member countries, the factors holding back investment and inhibiting employment and productivity stem from national, rather than EU, legislation. As a consequence, the EU is often wrongly, and unfairly, blamed for economic failures that are national in origin.

This can be seen in the very different levels of unemployment in different EU member countries. In 2015, the Netherlands had an unemployment rate of 7.2% and Germany 4.7%, while the rate in France was 10.2%, that in Greece was 27% and that in Spain 22%. Yet all these countries are subject to the same EU laws and regulations. Admittedly, some of the high unemployment in Spain and Greece is due to a lack of price competitiveness associated with membership of the euro; more on that in the next chapter. Nevertheless, a good deal of it is down to structural factors and different national laws and practices.

Indeed, the differences between various EU members with regard to labour market regulation are startling. The OECD compiles Employment Protection Indicators that attempt to measure how easy (and expensive) it is to dismiss individuals or groups of workers and the procedures involved in hiring workers on fixed-term or temporary work agency contracts. The higher the reading, the greater the difficulties and costs involved. In 2013, for the key indicator covering individual dismissals, the outcomes varied from 3.1 for Portugal down to 1.0 for the UK, with all other EU members scattered in between.

Similarly, the extent of social security spending (including out-of-work benefits) varies enormously across states. The average for the EU 28 is just under 30% of GDP, but that varies between 18% for new member states such as Bulgaria, Latvia and Romania to over 33% for France and Denmark.

So whatever ails European economic performance is not all down to the EU. Much of it is self-inflicted by national governments. Yet some of what holds EU member countries back does derive from the EU, both directly and indirectly.

The indirect role of the EU has been to lull national elites into a false sense of security, making them think that however badly they run their economies, other EU member countries would be running theirs similarly and that in any case, in some sense 'Europe' would bail them out. In practice, poor decisions at the level of individual

nation states have been compounded by more poor decisions in Brussels and Strasbourg.

There are five main areas in which the EU has directly
impinged on economic performance: trade; the movement of capital and people; labour law; competition;
and the raising and spending of considerable amounts of
money. Insofar as the EU has not been a great economic
success, presumably it is because in these five spheres of
competence it has not done a good job and/or because
whatever benefits have accrued have been overwhelmed
by other factors. As I hope you will see after I have exam-
ined each of these factors in turn, both answers are part
of the story.

Trade

The most important of the EU's direct economic contributions concerns trade. Various EU treaties lay down requirements that member countries abstain from imposing tariffs
or other trade restrictions on other member countries.
More than that, external trade with non-member countries
is governed at the EU level. The EU imposes a common
external tariff on imports from the rest of the world. In
2012, the simple average tariff rate was 5.5%, but the range
was huge. Dairy products, for instance, suffered a 52.9%
average tariff, whereas imports of metals and non-electric
machinery were subject to an average tariff of 1.9%.[9]

To the extent that the EU increases trade, this can be
supposed to bring economic benefit through all the usual
channels. Trade increases efficiency by fostering a better
allocation of resources and, by encouraging specialization, it opens up gains through increased economies of
scale (that is, the tendency for average unit costs to fall as
the number of units produced increases).

Yet the promotion of trade within the EU is not an unalloyed blessing. The EU is not merely a free trade area, one within which there are no tariffs, quotas or other restrictions on trade. Rather, the EU is a customs union, an area within which there is internal free trade but which imposes common restrictions on trade with countries outside the union (the common external tariff).

The economics of customs unions are well established and the early debates about British membership featured some of the conclusions. Essentially, customs unions create trade within the union, but they also divert trade from countries outside the union. A priori, it is impossible to tell which is greater, the gains from trade creation or the losses from trade diversion.

The evidence on trade creation within the European Union is mixed. Various academic studies suggest that trade creation has more than offset trade diversion.[10] Nevertheless, the record shows that although trade between EU member countries has greatly increased over the years, this increase has been exceeded by the growth of trade with non-EU members. Consequently, as a share of total exports, EU member countries' exports to other EU members fell from 68% in 2001 to 63% in 2012.

The reason is that the gains from trade creation within the EU have been comparatively minor beside the massive gains occurring from the growth of trade made possible across the world as a whole, first by the GATT agreements on liberalizing trade and later by the process of globalization as China and other emerging markets rapidly developed and enjoyed high rates of GDP growth.

The key point is that the benefits dreamed up by a group of European bureaucrats for members of a

European customs union were overwhelmed by the reality of economic benefits arising naturally on a world scale once the huge, formerly backward and isolated parts of the world were linked into the global market economy.

Capital and people

Similar benefits from EU membership are supposed to derive from the free movement of capital within the EU's borders: a potentially better allocation of resources and enhanced competition. There have been some gains of this sort, as borrowers have been able to draw on a larger pool of capital and investing institutions have had uninhibited choice about where to invest their money.

However, the benefits unleashed by the free movement of capital have probably also been overdone. Insofar as there have been such benefits inside the EU, it must be recognized that capital mobility is occurring simultaneously on a global scale. Being able to reallocate capital across several over-regulated, slow-growing countries, held back by an anti-business culture, is not exactly a game changer compared to investing in only one of these countries.

The free movement of people is a different story. Clearly, this has had a huge effect on some EU members. The UK, for one, has experienced substantial net immigration from eastern Europe. Has this been a good thing? This is a tricky area and there are evidently some significant losers from the process, not least the indigenous workers who now find themselves in keener competition with immigrant labour. (I take up this subject in more detail in Chapter 8.)

Moreover, with some eastern European countries now denuded of much of their local labour force, does the fact that these people are now to be found in the West really represent 'an improved allocation of resources'?

Admittedly, the benefits of the free movement of goods, services, people and capital, in addition to the attractions of being inside the tariff wall, may help to attract FDI into the EU. Nevertheless, as I pointed out earlier, in this regard the EU is less than an overwhelming success.

Labour law

If one of the benefits of the EU is intended to be the freedom of people to move across the Union, other benefits are supposed to flow from its imposition of *restrictions* on freedom in the labour market. Although, as I pointed out above, there are substantial differences between different member countries' labour laws, the EU does impose some Union-wide restrictions. The spheres that it covers comprise gender equality; working time; the Social Charter, which provides guidelines on working conditions and intervention in favour of groups such as minorities and women; and atypical employment contracts, such as contracts affecting part-time, agency and temporary work.

With regard to this area of EU economic competence, how you view the EU's interventions will depend greatly on who you are. Doubtless, plenty of people think they have been helped by the EU's actions. However, speaking as an economist who believes in markets (while acknowledging that not all economists do), I think that the EU's interventions in the labour market have been a disaster. The Commission has implemented a series of regulations that make it more expensive to employ people, more difficult to use them flexibly while they are employed and more expensive to sack them when they perform badly.

The Working Time Directive (WTD) is one of the most debated of EU regulations. It lays down maximum daily and weekly working time (an average of 48 hours per week over a span of 4 months), minimum daily rest, minimum breaks during the working day, minimum paid annual leave and extra protection for night workers.

Employer federations in the UK and the Nordic countries have strongly criticized the WTD. The think tank Open Europe has estimated that EU social policy costs British business and government about £8.6 billion (0.5% of GDP) a year, with WTD being the 'most expensive' of EU social laws. (Having said that, it is open to individual workers to opt out of the WTD, which virtually all City workers and UK doctors now do.)

The Agency Workers Directive, which came into force in October 2011, is also widely criticized. It lays down that temporary staff are entitled to the same salaries, holiday pay and overtime pay as their full-time equivalents. This change has significantly reduced the flexibility of the labour market and, in particular, has placed an extra burden on small firms, many of which especially need flexible arrangements for temporary staff.

Admittedly, EU directives are often exceeded in their anti-business bias by national labour regulations. Moreover, the major variation in unemployment rates and general economic progress across the EU is clear evidence that this is not a problem that can be put down to the EU alone. Still, that is not to excuse the EU dimension.

Furthermore, companies operating in the EU know that its tendency to over-regulate labour markets is deeply embedded and is likely to strengthen over time. So this depresses business confidence and inhibits business investment.

Competition policy

Nevertheless, not all of the EU's interventions operate against the grain of the competitive market ideal. With regard to competition policy, its interventions are designed to ensure a more competitive framework across all member countries.

The EU's involvement in competition policy only arises when trade between member states is affected, so national competition authorities deal with competition issues within member states. Where trade between member states is affected, EU competition policy comes into play across six main areas: restrictive practices; abuse of dominant market position to squeeze out competitors; mergers; market liberalization; state aid; and ensuring that EU competition law is applied equally across member states.

In this area of its activities, the EU has probably, on balance, been beneficial. The European Commission has carried out numerous investigations of anti-competitive practices in industries such as airlines, chemicals, energy and computer games. In 2015, helpfully to coincide with the run-up to the Brexit referendum – surely a coincidence? – it has secured the abolition, to be fully implemented by mid-2017, of the much-hated 'roaming charges' by mobile phone companies. And the EU has been effective in blocking state aid to domestic industry. As an article published in *The Economist* on 18 February 2010 put it:

> *Over several decades the European Commission's competition directorate has evolved into perhaps the most important regulator of its kind in the world. It has been rigorous in the development of antitrust theory and an energetic enforcer of the law.*

Two key failings, however, are that the European Commission has placed too much emphasis on competitors and not enough on consumers, and that it has become too big for its boots. *The Economist* went on to say:

> *Critics, whose concerns have increased with the ferocity of the sanctions imposed, say that by acting simultaneously as investigator, prosecutor, jury and sentencing judge, the Commission is denying defendant firms the basic right to be heard by an impartial tribunal. They are right.*

Spending money

This brings us on to the fifth area of EU economic competence, the raising of a considerable amount of money from member countries and the spending of it in different proportions to national contributions. In 2012, the EU's total expenditure was about €140 billion, or roughly 1% of the EU's GDP, including spending on the Common Agricultural Policy (CAP).

In the wider scheme of things and certainly compared to the size of national budgets, this is pretty small beer. Mind you, 20 years earlier, in 1991, the budget had been only €56 billion. And the direction of travel is clear. If europhiles get what they want, the size of the EU budget will increase consistently over time.

Given the budget's comparatively small size, its contribution to economic performance must all be down to microeconomics. Insofar as the EU successfully identifies deserving causes that would not otherwise receive funding, then, provided that the raising of money does not cause substantial distortions and disincentives, this activity may boost GDP. Well, that might happen in the fairytale version, anyway.

In practice, this is an area in which the EU has been close to a disaster. With about 80% of its money spent on farming and regional aid, the Union's budget does not do much to promote economic growth. Moreover, the EU dishes out money as if it comes from another planet. Due diligence and the careful husbanding of resources are not high on its agenda, with the EU instead being a byword for poor husbandry and extravagance. The British think tank Open Europe has compiled a list of examples of wasteful spending by the EU.[11] Two of its examples will suffice here:

> *In February 2009, Hungarian IT firm Gyrotech Commercial and Supplier Ltd was granted roughly €411,000 from the EU's Regional Development Fund, with another €500,000 coming from other sources, for a project to 'improve the lifestyle and living standards of dogs'. The company, originally an IT business, seems to have requested the money in order to branch out by developing a hydrotherapy system to 'improve dogs' wellbeing'. The company used the funds to build new offices for the centre. However, the offices have remained empty and overrun with weeds and the dog centre has yet to materialise.*

> *A grant of €16,394 was given by the European Agricultural Fund for Rural Development (EAFRD), with an additional €24,119 coming from the Austrian government, towards a project in Austria aimed at raising awareness of the Tyrolean landscape and its diverse features and to 'increase farmers' emotional connection with the landscapes they cultivate'. The main method of achieving these objectives was*

> *interviewing various farmers who were 'expected to reconsider their relationship with the landscape and become more aware of their emotional reactions to it compared to their prevailing rational economic ones'. Other farmers would then be 'influenced' by exhibitions of the work 'by receiving affirmation and taking pride in the distinctive and positive way in which their job is presented'.*

Admittedly, national governments are no strangers to wasteful spending. In Britain, one of the most notorious examples is the project to create fully computerized records for the NHS, which was scrapped in 2011 after it had reportedly cost £10 billion.[12]

Some of the best examples of EU extravagance concern pay and employment policies. The EU is a lavish paymaster for thousands of people who earn salaries – tax free – plus perks and pensions beyond all comparison with what they might earn back home. For instance, in 2013 President Barroso earned a salary of €304,221, plus residence and entertainment allowances taking his income to €366,871. By comparison, the German Chancellor earned a total of €216,456 and the French President was paid €170,280. Spain's Prime Minister earned only €78,000. In the UK, the Prime Minister was paid a basic salary of just under €175,000 and a junior minister about €110,000.

The same point applies to mere parliamentarians: however excruciating the debates may be, sitting in the European Parliament has its compensations. MEPs earn a total of €147,070 a year, plus a staffing allowance of €254,508, plus travel and subsistence allowances. Total annual costs per MEP can top €500,000. By contrast, members of the Italian Parliament earn €140,444 per annum, members of the US Congress the equivalent of about €135,000, while in France, MPs earn a mere €66,176. Given that in a number of western democracies ministers and MPs are severely underpaid, the quality of people going into politics is now widely regarded as low, which gives rise to the counter-argument in favour of high EU salaries that it is necessary to pay good incomes to attract good people. Yet most observers would agree that the average quality of MEPs is not high.

The EU is not only an especially bad spender of public money, it is also bad at accounting for what it does. Between 1994 and 2006, the auditors failed to pass the EU accounts as sound. From the 2007 EU budget until now, the accounts have been counted as 'sound', but the European Court of Auditors has never declared the EU budget free from material error; that is, with an error rate of less than 2%. In the 2011 EU budget the error rate was 3.9% and in 2012 it rose to 4.8%, meaning that out of a budget of €139 billion, nearly €7 billion was in question.

Marta Andreasen, the first person to be employed as the European Commission's Chief Accountant (who was later sacked for 'inappropriate comments' about the accounts), said in November 2012:

This is now the 18th year in a row that the European Court of Auditors have refused to give the EU Budget a clean bill of health. Worse still the 'error rate', shorthand for unaccounted money, is on the rise.

The accounting system is vulnerable to fraud and has not been designed to control payments centrally. There has been a lot of window-dressing

*but essentially the criticism made by the Court (of
Auditors) has not changed.*

The gains from specialization

Thus, in the five areas of intervention and competence
directly related to economic performance, the EU's
record has been less than stellar. Yet one of the key economic ideas behind the integrationist theme was that the
sheer size of the EU would bring benefits. Some of these
ideas were related to trade, which I discussed above, but
there were also other supposed benefits. What has happened to them? Have the gains simply been so small that
they have been overwhelmed by the negative influences
described under the five headings above? Or was there
something wrong with the original analysis? Doesn't
size matter?

The answer is that it all depends. One of the oldest
precepts in economics is the importance of scale. In the
eighteenth century, Adam Smith emphasized the division of labour as the source of prosperity. The more spe-
cialized production was, the more producers would gain
expertise. He also argued that the extent of the division of
labour was limited by the size of the market. Accordingly,
international trade was a huge driver of increased prosperity because it permitted increased specialization.

It is easy to understand this in more homespun terms.
At the most basic level of a one-man subsistence economy, Robinson Crusoe has to do everything himself. He
has no ability to specialize at all. But once Man Friday
appears, he has the ability to specialize and this capability
continues to grow as more and more people appear on
the scene.

If we go to the opposite extreme and imagine the whole world as a single economic unit, the capacity for specialization is enormous. However, for an economic unit as large as the world, with all its complexities, specialization and exchange do not simply happen in a vacuum. At the very least, specialization needs to be conducted across not only distances, but also language barriers and legal systems, and, above and beyond the narrow economic issues, it needs to be governed. In practice, these issues of coordination and governance appear in some shape or form as soon as human beings work together, so the economic benefits of specialization start to interact with, and perhaps conflict with, other considerations.

Part of the case for the EU is that it tears down the barriers to trade within the Union and hence promotes the benefits of specialization. Yet, as the above discussion makes clear, this is not the end of the matter. The EU also represents the suppression of national sovereignty and the assertion of a supra-national authority in umpteen economic and political spheres across a wide territory, which involves a considerable amount of harmonization and regulation. We need to delve deeper to investigate why this is not necessarily optimal.

Size in theory

Governments have a natural tendency to inhibit trade and commerce, because by definition their jurisdiction extends across a certain territory. They assert themselves as entities by affirming their borders with regard to the movement of both things and people. Borders can easily become barriers.

This innate presence of authority at the borders naturally affords the opportunity to raise tax revenues at this point. From the earliest times, governments have obtained a good part of their revenues from taxes on trade; in many cases they still do.

Therefore, a system of many small sovereign states is liable to become a system of sharply divided economies, with tariffs and other trade barriers locking up economic activity within political borders and hence restricting the benefits of trade and specialization.

The removal of such barriers has on several notable occasions throughout history led to the growth of prosperity. This is what happened with the *Zollverein* (customs union) in Germany, established in 1834 under Prussian leadership. And to the American generals and officials worried about Soviet intervention or Communist revolution and concerned to get the European economy going after the Second World War, the biggest economic threat they saw lay in the patchwork of small states across Europe enforcing their own petty sovereignties at the border through the imposition of significant tariffs, quotas and other trade restrictions.

Now suppose that there is open trade between states. In that case, the gains from specialization can be enjoyed by even small political units. Of what advantage is greater size then? There is a considerable academic literature on this subject.[13] The general thrust is to see the increasing size of political entities as potentially bringing economies of scale in the provision of public goods (e.g. defence), but also greater heterogeneity and a tendency to damaging disputes (and bad policies) with regard to the distribution of costs and benefits. Just about everybody, however, recognizes the importance of open trade and economic integration in making it possible for smaller political units to operate successfully. Interestingly, this result, which is confirmed in several academic studies, runs completely counter to the off-the-cuff assumption of many commentators that globalization and economic integration automatically favour the establishment of larger political units.

So, on the face of it, the EU's tendency to transfer powers to itself from nation states operates against the prevailing trend in the rest of the world towards globalization and integration. As authors Alesina, Angeloni and Schuknecht put it in a wonderfully academic way: 'European-level institutions are involved in areas where economies of scale are far from obvious and heterogeneity of preferences among European citizens are high.' In other words, the EU is involved in too many things that it should leave to national governments.

Even so, these academic analyses concerning size do not necessarily point to the superiority of political units consisting of existing nation states, for the self-same arguments can then be advanced for at least the partial break-up of existing states into subregions or nations. Examples include the possible secession of Scotland from the United Kingdom and Catalonia from Spain.

At this point, purely abstract analysis tends to get us nowhere. Much depends on the specifics of the cases in question, on the history and the quality of government. The United Kingdom may or may not be the 'optimum' size for a unit of government according to academic criteria, but these criteria cannot be allowed to be the arbiters of political association. For a start, different assessments of the optimum size may come up with different answers and these answers may change over time. States cannot – and should not – be dissolved and reformed on the basis of such results.

More fundamentally, whether institutions and political associations work is usually the result of non-systematic factors to do with their historical development. Although there is clearly a powerful secessionist tendency in Scotland, by and large the UK and its institutions work well. By contrast, we can have no idea how well new institutions in Scotland and the remainder of the UK would function if the UK did break up. In particular, during the campaign leading up to the referendum on Scottish independence in 2014, it became clear that establishing a satisfactory currency regime for an independent Scotland would be extremely problematic, echoing many of the difficulties of the eurozone that I discuss in Chapter 4. (There is more about this in Chapter 8.)

Subsidiarity

What point marks the best division of sovereignty? It is clearly not the individual, and not the street or local community. At some stage, probably at a point that shifts over time in response to changing attitudes, economic realities and technologies, borders are required to separate one polity from another.

In reality, it is not necessary for all decisions to be taken at one level, whether that is the nation state, a federation of nation states, a region, or a local authority. Different sorts of decisions are best taken at different levels: arrangements for rubbish collection at the local level, defence at the national or supra-national level.

However, there is a host of in-between cases where the answer is not clear. Should the structure and content of school curricula, for instance, be left up to individual state schools, controlled by local authorities, or laid down by central government? The right answer will differ between countries and over time, depending on the effectiveness of local and national authorities and on national objectives for educational attainment.

The EU's approach to the issue of the appropriate level at which to take decisions is in theory very appealing. It is governed by the principle of 'subsidiarity', the idea that a decision should be taken as close to the citizen as possible. Except in the areas that fall within its exclusive competence, the principle is that the Union should not take action unless it is more effective than action taken at the national, regional or local level.

The trouble is that this principle is honoured more in the breach than in the observance. This is for two good, and related, reasons. First, there is a struggle at the heart of the EU between those who want to establish full political union and those who do not and who therefore wish to preserve the powers of nation states. For the former group, any opportunity to wrest powers from nation states tends to be regarded as a step in the right direction. Accordingly, the EU ends up poking its nose into matters that, on a practical and less political analysis, would not be regarded as lying within its proper sphere of competence.

Second, the implementation of subsidiarity runs counter to the objective of harmonization and may lead to competition. Yet harmonization is deeply embedded in the objectives of the EU. Accordingly, the default position of the Union is to resist subsidiarity.

Size in practice

Is there in fact a marked tendency for large economic and political units to do well compared to small ones? The evidence is not conclusive. The chief example of the beneficial effects of size is the United States. From quite early in its history, it achieved a high level of economic success and a high standard of living. Admittedly, it had a huge territory per head of population, giving it a wealth of arable and grazing land per capita, as well as considerable endowments of minerals and oil.

Nevertheless, this is not necessarily decisive. After all, other countries have had these advantages without reaching such high standards of development. The old Soviet Union possessed them and, to a lesser extent, Russia still does. Argentina, Australia and Brazil also enjoy similar advantages. Yet the results have been mixed.

Clearly, how a territory is governed is of major importance. What is necessary for success is a government strong enough to ensure that the law is upheld and a country's wealth is not filched by minority interests, or continually fought over, bringing loss and destruction. However, it also has to be a government that does not inhibit the growth of industry and commerce by excessive taxation or interference. This, and not just the abundance of land, was the secret of America's success.

It is very striking, nevertheless, that many of the world's richest countries are small. By 'small' I mean either small in territory or number of people, or both. According to the IMF, the five countries with the highest GDP per capita in the world are Qatar, Luxembourg, Singapore, Norway and Brunei – all of which have a population of less than 6 million.

Singapore is a particularly interesting example. At independence, the view of the British government was that it should throw in its lot with the much larger Malaysian Federation – which it did. When Singapore was expelled in 1965, it must have seemed that its future was bleak. Now look at it. Never mind Malaysia, Singapore has a higher income per head than the UK. Why? The essential answer is good government – by Singapore for Singapore.

There are several examples of small-country success in the Middle East, but one might argue that their relevance to the rest of the world is limited because their success derives pretty much entirely from oil and natural gas. I refer, of course, to the Gulf states of the UAE, Bahrain, Qatar, Kuwait and Oman. Even in these cases, though, there is a case to be made that their (admittedly non-democratic) governments have managed their affairs rather well. Their oil wealth has not been squandered.

In Europe, successful small states do not have oil at their root – apart from Norway. Switzerland is the best example, but other noteworthy ones are Belgium, the Netherlands, Luxembourg, Denmark, Sweden and Finland. (These last six are, of course, members of the EU, although they were pretty successful before they joined it.)

Democracy and competition

Why might these small political units have done well? In some cases it is largely because they are established as tax havens. Accordingly, their success is distributional; that is, they are in the business of transferring income and wealth from other entities, rather than that of wealth creation. As such, they have little relevance to the question of how the division of sovereignty best promotes overall prosperity.

However, in most cases of small-country success, tax advantage is only a part of what they do and their achievements are much more widespread and broadly based. Even where success is due to them acting as tax havens, this serves the cause of jurisdictional competition. The issue is all about what makes governments behave in the best interests of their countries and their citizens.

Of course, democracy provides a check on what even the governments of large countries can do and it should, in theory, push governments to act in the interests of the majority. By contrast, in a dictatorship where the leaders cannot be ousted at the ballot box, what is there to restrain the government from indulging every pet fantasy project, as well as doling out magnificent incomes and goodies to its cronies? There are plenty of examples of this in Africa today. (Admittedly, not all non-democratic governments behave in that way. The Gulf states, for instance, generally operate with very low or even nil levels of personal taxation. In China, personal taxation is also very low.)

Nevertheless, democracy is not enough to ensure good governance and the promotion of economic success. In western democracies, voters tend to be attracted by proposals for increased spending and the implied consequences for the level of taxes are often left opaque, or it is assumed that 'someone else' will pay. So politicians compete for votes by offering the most tantalizing goodies to voters. Moreover, as I argued in Chapter 2, the larger the political entity, the more difficult it is to make democracy work well.

Competition can provide a more effective restraint on governments. We are used to the idea that competition within economies brings benefits and to the associated idea that preserving competition may require intervention to ensure that no large firms dominate the market. We are also used to the idea that competition between countries brings benefits in the shape of the gains from trade. We are less used to the idea that competition between sovereignties also brings benefits, although it most assuredly can.

The gains concern good governance. Without such competition, governments can carry on with economically destructive policies for ages. Where jurisdictions are in competition, however, the benefits of different policies show up more quickly. The result is to encourage pressure for best practice.

This is closely related to the issue of size. In essence, small countries feel vulnerable and, as a result, their governments are limited in the degree of damage they can do without suffering serious consequences. By contrast, in large countries governments can maintain the trappings of success and power at the international level even if, in per capita terms, their people are seriously poor. This was true of the Soviet Union, for instance.

The benefits of governments realizing that effectively they are in competition with other governments can extend across the gamut of economic policies. Suppose, for instance, that the regulation of the labour market tends to increase unemployment and harm economic growth. In an open economic system, if a small country introduces such policies and it is in close competition with other countries that do not, the consequences will show up smartly as business and trade – and perhaps key people – move to other countries.

By contrast, if the same policies are imposed across a large economic area, let us call it Europe, there may be some loss of economic activity to countries outside the affected area, but it will not be so easy to shift and no part of Europe will lose out to another because it will not be operating worse policies than its neighbours. The larger the economic area in question then, other things equal, the smaller the scope for the loss of business to countries outside the area. Nevertheless, the policies can still be immensely damaging.

The effects of competition can be seen in relation to tax policy. Companies and also certain internationally mobile rich individuals are in a position to locate, and relocate, their residence and economic activity with keen regard to the tax consequences. Clearly, tax is not the only consideration, but if countries with broadly similar attractions have very different tax rates, this will tend to lead to a leaching of companies and rich individuals to the countries with the lower tax rates. For instance, French actor Gerard Depardieu recently relocated himself from France to Belgium in order to reduce his tax liability. To some extent this has always been an issue, but globalization and the related transformation of communications have made it a good deal easier. The result is that governments everywhere are scared stiff of losing a good part of their tax base.

It is widely believed that this competition for tax revenues is a major problem because it results in pressure to keep tax rates down and, relatedly, to keep government spending in check. However, if, like me, you believe that in most western democracies government spends too high a share of national income, then such tax competition is a good thing. It helps to keep in check the government's tendency to gobble up too many resources.

The EU's overwhelming impulse towards integration and harmonization points in exactly the opposite direction. There are already barriers to tax competition within the EU. For example, there are regulations about the permitted range of VAT rates: no country may fall below a minimum of 15% for the standard rate of VAT and 5% for the reduced rate. Moreover, there are moves afoot to curb competition over corporation tax rates. And if and when the countries of the eurozone successfully develop into a full fiscal union, this will involve, if not identical tax rates across the union, at least centrally managed rates. At that point a key constraint on the spending behaviour of governments will have gone.

Europe's golden age

Interestingly, the era when Europe was strongest and most prosperous compared to the rest of the world was a period when it was divided into small states, which competed vigorously with one another. The great explorers set forth not from a united Europe, but from Spain, Portugal, England, the Netherlands, France and the various city states of Italy, including Genoa and Venice. They did so in a spirit of rivalry.

Admittedly, this rivalry sometimes found its expression in war. Revulsion against this form of competition is one of the strongest emotional arguments against the return to a Europe of competing nation states. While the fear is that competition between such entities is bound to be destructive, as it was before, this throws the baby out with the bathwater. It is possible to make institutional arrangements that prevent further European wars while maintaining rivalry in other ways – including in economic competition, just as happens already in everything from football to popular music.

So we have discovered a more fundamental reason for the EU's under-performance that goes beyond the accountants' totting up: the EU has suppressed competition between nation states. More than that, it has smothered them in a suffocating balm of harmonization and convergence. Simply to allude to this or that aspect of bad decision-making or mismanagement misses the point. These defects are systematic. They derive directly from the essential nature of the EU – which is most assuredly not the same as the essential nature of Europe.

The EU's poor economic record

Let us not get this out of perspective. The EU is not an economic disaster – yet. But in economic terms it is a considerable disappointment to many of its supporters. And, internationally, it is an under-achiever. The rapidly growing countries of Asia do not look to the EU as an example; they regard it as showing what they need to avoid.

What explains this under-performance? I have put forward eight reasons:

- The EU's designers put far too much importance on size alone as bringing benefits.
- In the process, they under-estimated the growth of the world economy outside the EU.
- They under-estimated the importance of good governance as the key to economic success.
- The agenda for harmonization and regulation involved too much interference in business.

- ◆ The European social agenda with regard to labour laws and benefits was, and was believed by firms to be, anti-business.
- ◆ Europe's leaders paid insufficient attention to getting the basics of economic success right – unlike so many of their equivalents in Asia.
- ◆ They spent the EU's (admittedly not enormous) funds badly.
- ◆ The very objectives of harmonization and integration hid the consequence of bad economic policies and smothered the natural rivalry between countries that could have produced better economic performance.

Arguably, these failings would not necessarily have held back the European economy if it had already embarked on a dynamic growth path in a relatively stable world. However, the world of the last 20 years has been anything but stable. Two great revolutions have shaken the modern economy to its foundations – information technology and globalization – and they required flexibility and adaptation. That is precisely what the institutions of the EU are bad at delivering, hence the EU's relative decline. It is surely because the US adapted better to these forces that partly explains why it has recently outperformed the EU.

There is something else as well. As the EU has continued in sharp relative decline, the concentrated effort of the European elites should have been directed towards the requirements to raise productivity, employment and investment. Instead, European leaders have been obsessed by further harmonization and integration, by treaty change and, of course, by that ultimate form of integration – the euro.

4

The Trouble with the Euro

When you come to a fork in the road, take it.
—Yogi Berra, US baseball player and philosopher

The European single currency, the euro, has become the focus of European integration – and it could yet prove to be the cause of the EU's disintegration. If this happens, it would be deeply ironic, for it was not imperative to have a single European currency and the enterprise was embarked on too early and with insufficient preparation. It was an integration too far and too soon.

It is, therefore, the best example yet of bad decision-making in the EU. But, as with so much else, the bad decision did not emerge accidentally. Rather, it derived directly from the EU's history and its essential nature. Much of what went wrong with the euro is now so well known that it is pointless to dwell on it. It is on why it went wrong, and what this tells us about the EU, that the euro saga has so much to teach us.

In what follows, I begin with the origins of the single currency and a discussion of how it ran into trouble, how it was supposed to adapt to difficulties in theory and what happened in practice. I then discuss the political lessons to emerge from the euro's travails. I conclude with an assessment of the eurozone's relative performance since 2008, including its growing trade surplus, the comparison with Japan's 'lost decade', the advent of deflation and the effects of low oil prices. Policies to save the eurozone I leave to the next chapter.

Figure 4.1 The split between EU members using the euro and not using it in 2015

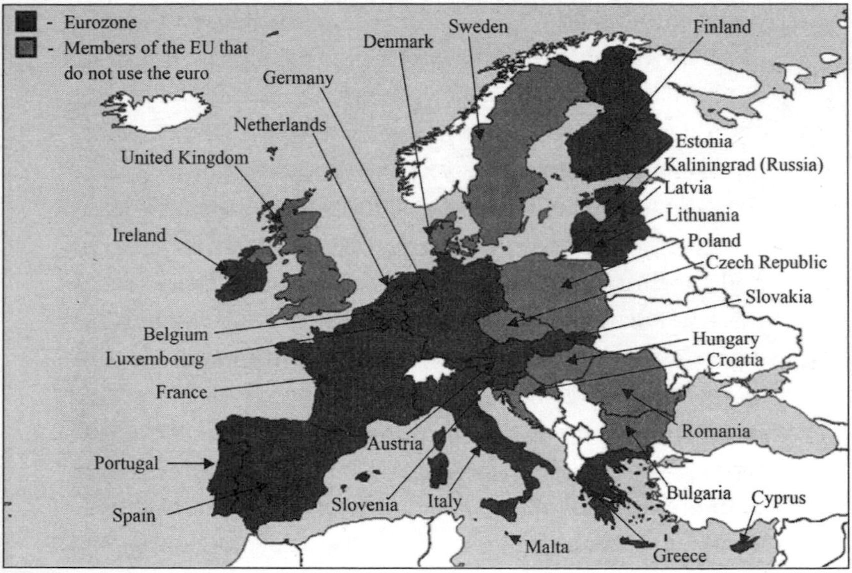

- Eurozone
- Members of the EU that do not use the euro

Sweden
Finland
Denmark
Germany
Netherlands
United Kingdom
Estonia
Kaliningrad (Russia)
Latvia
Lithuania
Poland
Czech Republic
Slovakia
Ireland
Belgium
Luxembourg
Hungary
Croatia
France
Romania
Austria
Portugal
Bulgaria
Cyprus
Slovenia
Italy
Spain
Malta
Greece

Source: www.europa.eu

The beginnings

A European single currency was debated as early as the Werner Report of 1970, which set out a three-stage process to achieve European Monetary Union (EMU) within a ten-year period. The final objective would be the irreversible convertibility of currencies, the free movement of capital and the permanent locking of exchange rates – or possibly a single currency. To achieve this, the report said there would need to be closer economic policy coordination, with interest rates and the management of reserves decided at Community level and, showing remarkable perspicacity and far-sightedness, agreed frameworks for national budgetary policies.

Subsequently, two European exchange rate schemes were implemented that built on these foundations and acted as forerunners of the euro. The Basel Agreement of 1972 introduced the 'snake in the tunnel' and, in March 1979, a new European Monetary System was formed using an Exchange Rate Mechanism (ERM) to reduce fluctuations between the currencies of member states. Neither of these currency systems was the real McCoy, though, and the ERM, already a shrunken creature compared to the early days, was replaced in January 1999 when the euro came into being in 11 member states. After 7 more countries joined it, the eurozone comprised 18 countries, leaving 10 EU members outside the zone. With the accession of Lithuania in 2015, the eurozone has expanded to 19 members, leaving 9 EU members not using the euro (see Figure 4.1).

The lure of monetary union

It is easy to see why the formation of a single currency would be a key objective for those who wanted to unite Europe. A common currency would lead to a common state. There are examples of different states using the same currency, but they are all cases of small countries sharing a currency, such as some of the Caribbean islands, or of a small country using a larger one's currency without having any say in the issue or management of that currency; Panama's use of the US dollar is an obvious example. However, I cannot think of any example of major states of roughly equal status sharing a common currency – apart from the members of the eurozone.

The nineteenth-century Gold Standard is sometimes quoted as a counter-example, since it united umpteen different countries at fixed exchange rates. But it does not really count, since the Gold Standard was not itself a currency, or even a system for managing currencies, but rather a regime that left countries in charge of their own economic and financial management, albeit with little room for manoeuvre if they wanted to stay in the system. Most importantly, the Gold Standard did not remove national sovereignty, not least because it was possible to suspend it or leave it, as the UK did twice, in 1914 and again, having returned to it in 1925, in 1931.

Currencies and states are closely linked. The taxing power of the state is one of the sources of assurance that money will be worth something. Equally, when things go wrong, it is the state that can and often does pick up the tab for failing assets and banks, as recent experience in Europe and America can attest.

The danger in sharing your currency with a neighbour over which you have no control is that it will operate policies that will undermine the currency. These may cause either a spike in bond yields, a currency collapse, an upsurge of inflation or a banking crisis – or any combination of the four – with obvious costs for your economy. That surely means that, if you are going to share your currency with other countries, you will reasonably demand some sort of control over their fiscal (i.e. budgetary) and financial policies. And if one country is going to have oversight over another's fiscal policy, how can that be done without also having some form of political union that will enable joint, or at least shared, control of fiscal policy?

So when the architects of monetary union put in place the single currency without arrangements for fiscal or political union, they were in fact constructing a halfway house. It was European integration lite.

Yet this was not entirely a case of blindly stumbling towards an unsatisfactory half-answer. Many of the euro's progenitors fully understood what they were doing. When the euro was still no more than a glint in the eye, a debate raged between the so-called German and French schools. The 'German' school argued that economic integration and full convergence should come first and then monetary union would be the coping stone that finished off the whole structure. The 'French' view was that, since political union was going to be so momentous and difficult to reach agreement on, insisting on it first would delay the whole process and perhaps even make it impossible. It would be better to start with monetary union. Admittedly, this would inevitably lead to crises, but out of these crises would come the political will to forge fiscal and political union.

As matters stand, it is too early to say which of these views was correct. While the depth of the crisis in which the single currency has been embroiled suggests that the German view was spot on, we do not yet know the final act. The euro crisis has indeed, as the French view upheld, spawned an effort to forge fiscal and political union. It may yet be successful. We shall have to wait and see.

How it happened

In economics textbooks, countries decide whether or not to form monetary unions with other countries on the basis of their economic suitability to each other. Are they subject to similar economic shocks? Where they are not, are their structures flexible enough to be able to absorb different shocks without massive dislocation and unemployment? Are countries able to live together and produce full employment without needing recourse to exchange rate changes, different interest rates or exchange controls?

A whole literature, enough to keep you busy for the best part of a lifetime, was developed by economists to answer questions such as these, culminating in the crowning glory, the Theory of Optimum Currency Areas; that is, a theory about the best (i.e. most efficient) grouping of countries to form single currency blocs. And this theoretical edifice is a pretty impressive structure, well worthy of a Nobel Prize or two.

As you may have guessed, however, this vast literature had next to no bearing on how the euro came into being or how it was structured. As things turned out, the pace of currency union was forced by events – and not even economic events at that. In November 1989 the Berlin Wall came down and just over two years later the Soviet Union disintegrated. These events made possible the reunification of Germany after nearly 50 years of separation. But not everyone saw this as an unalloyed blessing. What would Russia think? It still had nearly 400,000 troops stationed on German soil. What would France think? And what would be the UK's view?

At first, UK Prime Minister Margaret Thatcher was dead against reunification and was in close communication not only with the Soviet leader, Mikhail Gorbachev, but also with America's President, Ronald Reagan.

If reunification was going to happen, West Germany had to have the support of France, but that was not a foregone conclusion. French fears of German dominance were very real. Why make things worse, France might reasonably think, by letting Germany get bigger and stronger? After all, the French writer François Charles Mauriac had said in the 1960s that he was so fond of Germany that he was glad there were two of her. He surely spoke for many Frenchmen – and people of other nationalities.

In the event, French President François Mitterrand did agree to reunification, but he exacted a price. Germany would have to agree to submerge the deutschmark into a new European currency, subsequently to be called the euro, and in the process emasculate the Bundesbank, which had ruled the roost over the European economy for the last few decades. West Germany's Chancellor Kohl agreed to this price and so the euro was born. The greatest monetary experiment in the history of human-kind happened when it did, and how it did, because it appeared to make political sense at the time.

Trouble right from the beginning

As might be expected from the difficult circumstances of its birth, right from the start the new currency was plagued by serious design failures. In order to ensure that the countries admitted to the union were capable of coexisting in a monetary union without recourse to cur-rency changes, different levels of interest rates or the use of capital controls, certain conditions were laid down in the Maastricht Treaty of February 1992 to govern eligi-bility to join. These included a 'reference value' for the ratio of government debt to GDP of 60%. Countries were expected to be at or below this reference value.

A country could still be admitted even if its ratio was above this level, provided that the ratio was falling and was approaching 60% 'at a satisfactory pace'. In the event, Italy and Belgium, and later Greece, were admitted to the currency even though their debt ratios were well above the 60% level and even though they did not convincingly pass the qualifying test. The reason, of course, was political. Europe's leaders simply regarded it as unacceptable to keep them out.

No arrangements were put in place for a fiscal union, but instead there was a no-bailout clause in the Maastricht Treaty, which stated that there would be no external or Union-wide support for any national government that got into financial difficulties. This was supposedly to instil a sense of responsibility in individual fiscal authorities and a sense of caution in those in the financial markets who might lend to them.

Moreover, the countries of the currency area agreed to a Stability and Growth Pact, which laid down limits to their fiscal deficits. Unfortunately, this pact was very far from watertight, as both France and Germany proceeded to exceed the deficit limits without incurring any penalty. (Admittedly, one could argue that without the pact their fiscal slippage would have been greater.)

Both the no-bailout clause and the Stability and Growth Pact were paper tigers. So, in practice, there was no effective fiscal union to accompany the monetary union that was unleashed by the euro. There was no political union either. The nation states of the eurozone simply sailed on much as before.

Nor did the arrangements for the new currency involve any form of banking union. There were no agreements covering what to do in the event of a sovereign default or banks getting into trouble. In fact, the architects of the euro seemed to know very little financial history, since their restrictions and agreements regulating the criteria for entry to the euro referred solely to the fiscal realm; that is, the level of government deficits and debt.

As events turned out, when problematic conditions were encountered, although for some euro members this was because of fiscal profligacy (Greece being a prime example), in Spain and Ireland the fiscal numbers were in great shape until the recession caused by the financial crash of 2007–09 sent their fiscal deficits through the roof. Their problem was centred on a private-sector credit boom, closely associated with a property market bubble. Of this sort of disturbance the architects of monetary union seemingly had no inkling whatsoever. They certainly made no provision for it.

So when the good ship *Euro* set sail, she was equipped for moderate winds and a calm sea. When she instead encountered the violent storm unleashed by the world financial crisis of 2008, she proved to be a most unseaworthy vessel.

The anatomy of trouble

The problems of operating a single currency did not emerge at once. On the contrary, the launch of the euro in 1999 was a massive technical success and, for a time, the different economies seemed to be adjusting well to it.

Mind you, this is not surprising. The case against monetary union for ill-assorted members with substantial rigidities, poor institutional structure and a susceptibility to divergence was always that problems would build up over time – and would be exposed in a crisis. So no one should have been taken in by the fact that at first, the new currency seemed to be going swimmingly. Nevertheless, they were.

Initially, in the peripheral countries that were subsequently to be in such trouble, there was a boom. People went on a spending spree. These were countries that had traditionally tended to have relatively high interest rates and now they were able to luxuriate in a rate set by the European Central Bank (ECB) that was similar to the low rates previously enjoyed by Germany under the Bundesbank. If you like, this was a combination of British-style inflationary habits and a German cost of finance. The result was an explosion of credit and economic activity in Spain and Ireland and an associated boom in the property market with regard to both prices and levels of construction. In Greece, new-found security and the absence of an exchange rate to worry about gave the government free rein to indulge in a burst of excessive expenditure. To be alive in those days was very heaven!

Significantly, German exporters who were beneficiaries of this spending, and also German workers who, by and large, did not gain much direct benefit, did not throw their money around extravagantly.

The competitiveness gap

Then reality began to strike home, not suddenly, but stealthily. In all of these peripheral countries, costs and prices continued to rise faster than in the Germanic core of the union. They had always had this tendency, but the difference was that in the past the exchange rate had been able to depreciate to offset any lost competitiveness. Now the exchange rate safety valve had been closed off. The result was a huge loss of competitiveness in the periphery that manifested itself in large and growing current account deficits (broadly speaking, an excess of imports over exports). Meanwhile, in the Germanic core, there were large and growing current account surpluses.

At the most extreme point, the current account deficits in Ireland, Spain, Portugal and Greece were 8.5%, 12%, 14% and 20% of GDP, respectively. Correspondingly, at their highest point, the surpluses for Germany and the Netherlands were 9% and 10% of GDP, respectively.

Yet the euro elite seemed to subscribe to some equivalent of Brownian economics: there would not be a crisis because the euro had put an end to boom and bust. That was just as well. For cynics of the old persuasion, including yours truly, this was an accident waiting to happen.

Let me make one thing clear, though. Having your own currency is not a panacea for all economic problems. Moreover, umpteen countries have on occasion suffered from destabilizing exchange rate changes. In addition, the peripheral members of the eurozone had much more wrong with them than simply the fact that their costs and prices were out of line. Nevertheless, having your own currency is really important in those once-in-a-generation crises when relative prices need to adjust by 20–50%. The crisis that broke upon the world in 2007–08 was one such occasion. And just when exchange rates were needed to take some of the strain, the countries within the eurozone had to face the fact that national currencies had just been abolished.

The debt problem

When the Great Recession engulfed the world immediately after the financial crisis of 2007–08, all economies were hit badly, but the impact on the eurozone's periphery was catastrophic. As is usual in recessions, governments' budget deficits soared and this, combined with falling GDP, caused debt-to-GDP ratios to rise sharply, taking them into territory that signalled a serious risk of default. Accordingly, bond yields rose to levels that were ruinous for governments to borrow at.

Predictably, the remedy offered by the politicians was an alphabet soup of support mechanisms, typically beginning with the magical letter *E*, and more of the balm that supposedly overcomes all ills, political will. In other words: don't panic, it will be all right on the night.

But it wasn't. At the worst point in 2012, it looked as though the euro was going to break up or, at the least, some of its most vulnerable members were going to leave it. Indeed, Greece came perilously close to being expelled as the other member countries, especially Germany, were completely exasperated with it. It was only the fear that a Greek expulsion would result in a financial crisis that would bring the whole eurozone down that held Angela Merkel back.

Then came a declaration in July 2012 by the ECB President, Mario Draghi, that he would do 'whatever it takes' to save the euro. In the event, this took the form of a programme to launch so-called Outright Monetary Transactions (OMTs); that is, ECB purchases of the bonds of troubled countries, potentially without limit.

This was a stroke of genius. Bond yields fell dramatically without the ECB having to buy a single bond. Nevertheless, Draghi was sailing very close to the wind. In order to keep up the pressure on governments to improve their finances and to reform their economies, he laid down that OMTs could only be deployed to buy the bonds of countries that had entered a European bailout programme. The point was that if they were in such a programme then, as a condition of the bailout, their finances would already be subject to outside control. That was designed to placate the German Bundesbank as well as other critics.

As it happens, the two largest vulnerable countries, Spain and Italy, were not in a bailout programme and their governments were unlikely to accede to one. Their government bond yields fell all the same. Even so, the German Bundesbank President objected that the ECB programme amounted to monetary financing of governments and, as such, was illegal. In effect OMTs were a remarkable confidence trick, which has paid off – so far.

Back to the 1930s

Meanwhile, without an exchange rate to take the strain, how were the peripheral countries to regain competitiveness and thus hope to restore growth to their economies while reducing their budget deficits? The orthodox European (and especially German) answer was through austerity. Afflicted countries were to cut government spending and raise taxes in order to reduce their budget deficits, much in the way that one might do in a household.

The trouble is that economies are not households. When person A cuts their spending, this reduces the income of person B, who cuts their spending, and so on and so forth. All the while, GDP will be falling and the deficit may remain the same, or even get bigger. This Keynesian criticism of austerity economics is well known: sometimes it is justified; and sometimes it is not. There have been many times when it seemed well justified for the eurozone.

There was a second flaw to the austerity solution that was more telling. The idea was that austerity would not only improve the public finances but would also restore competitiveness, since the release of resources from the public sector as a result of spending cuts, as well as the reduction in private spending brought on by increased taxes, would reduce aggregate demand and increase unemployment. In the usual way, the resulting excess supply in the economy and increased pressure to win business and keep jobs would lower costs, prices and wages, thus improving competitiveness.

This was straightforward deflation of the sort that had been tried (and found wanting) in the 1930s. This being the EU, however, if the politicians involved could not quite alter history or blot it out, they could at least give the policy a different name. They did: they called it 'internal devaluation'. But the change of name did not make the process any the less painful, or any the more effective.

This process of 'internal devaluation' would inevitably be extremely slow. Even deflation of 1% or 2% a year would be very difficult to achieve and extremely painful. Yet some of the peripheral countries had suffered a loss of competitiveness of 30% or 40%. They would be condemned to decades of deflation. The 1930s had demonstrated that this is a recipe for misery and destruction on an epic scale. And we all know what happened subsequently, partly as a result of this economic misery.

More importantly, this strategy of deflation suffered from a huge economic weakness: deflation worsens the debt ratio. It reduces nominal tax revenues and nominal incomes and hence nominal GDP, while the outstanding value of the debt remains the same.

Now the eurozone has both a competitiveness and a debt problem. To the extent that it improves the former through domestic deflation, it worsens the latter. By the start of 2015, several of the peripheral countries had reduced their competitiveness gap against Germany

– although interestingly, Italy and France experienced continued increases in theirs – but the debt ratios of all peripheral countries continued to climb, and unemployment rates remained obstinately high. In Spain and Greece the rate fell a little, but it was still close to 25%. The eurozone's adjustment mechanism turned out to be rather like the use of a corset by someone trying to deal with obesity. The fat is still there; it just bulges out in different places.

Economic loss as the price of political gain?

While I have argued that the euro has been a failure, not everyone will agree. Some people may assert that, as with everything else to do with the EU, the essence of the project is political. To a large extent this is true – certainly as regards its origins. However, this does not mean to say that the euro had been expected to incur huge economic costs. On the contrary, the progenitors and supporters of the euro did not favour it simply as the route to political union. They believed – and asserted – that it would boost economic performance and in the process increase prosperity and create jobs.

Writing about the prospective benefits of EMU in the *Europe Quarterly* in 1999, the late Wim Duisenberg, then President of the European Central Bank, said: 'The introduction of the euro and the single monetary policy will result in higher economic growth in the euro area, while maintaining price stability.' He went on: 'It removes the risk of serious exchange rate misalignments within the euro area. This will contribute to economic growth and help to avoid any misallocation of resources.' And he concluded: 'The true benefits of the euro derive from the fact that it is a unique opportunity to shape a macroeconomic environment conducive to stability, growth and employment.'

As late as May 2008, the European Commission was still claiming that the currency union had been 'a resounding success. It has brought economic stability, promoted economic and financial integration, generated trade and growth and [provided] a framework for sound and sustainable public finances.'

It is quite clear that the euro elites did not see the euro as an economic price that had to be paid to secure the political benefits of a full union across the eurozone, but rather as the route to both political and *economic* advantage. They could not have been more wrong.

Economic performance in theory

Their key argument for the euro increasing prosperity was that currency variability reduces economic efficiency. Supposedly, it inhibits trade because firms are burdened with either increased uncertainty about effective prices and costs or the extra costs incurred by dealing with it (unsatisfactorily) through some financial hedging mechanism. Also, consumers find it difficult to compare prices across different currencies. The result is a series of nationally segmented markets that, from the standpoint of the wider group as a whole, reduces efficiency.

Meanwhile, in these conditions, capital and money markets are segmented as well. The possibility of currency changes means that interest rates and bond yields are increased by having to incorporate an uncertainty premium. Moreover, the fact that these financial markets have to be separate eliminates the advantages of large size, which again raises costs and reduces efficiency.

Equally, on the side of macro management, having umpteen national currencies rather than a single one brings problems because individual countries operating on their own risk being blown off course by events in the exchange markets. Under a single currency, therefore, governments would be able to borrow more cheaply and that too would help economic performance by allowing either lower taxes, increased public spending or lower borrowing.

It is true, the euro's proponents conceded, that giving up national currencies would remove the exchange rate safety value, but they argued that the gains from this were largely illusory. For a start, far from absorbing volatility, the exchange markets created a good deal of it themselves. Even when disturbances were generated in the domestic economy, the ability of exchange rate flexibility to offset or absorb them was limited. It is extremely difficult, they argued, to get a change in the so-called *real* exchange rate by varying the nominal rate. Any attempt to adjust to a problem in the real economy by resorting to devaluation ends in tears because inflation just moves up in tandem, leaving no real advantage.

In any case, they asserted, in a properly constructed monetary union, costs and prices would not get out of line between member countries precisely because everyone would know that there was no safety valve and macroeconomic policies would be aligned between members.

Performance in practice

If that was the idea of how the euro would pan out in theory, things have worked out very differently in practice. The gains from reduced uncertainty over exchange rates and increased market size and efficiency have proved to be very small, as some of us argued all along that they would. Trade grew no faster between eurozone members than it did between members and non-members; about which more below.

Meanwhile, again in accordance with the sceptics' fears, costs and prices did continue rising much faster in the historically high-inflation countries than in the German-led core. The result was very weak performance in the peripheral countries, thus, given only moderate performance of the core countries, making for poor performance overall.

The German economy did fairly well, but was heavily reliant on exports. Germany generated little increased domestic demand itself and its propensity to save remained high. Instead, it benefited from demand created elsewhere (which I discuss in more detail below). Meanwhile, the workings of the euro, allied to political pressure, pushed the peripheral countries into austerity programmes.

So the euro has had a strong deflationary bias, with the pressures for adjustment entirely on the deficit countries. Far from bringing a jobs bonanza, it has led to appallingly high unemployment. This is precisely the criticism of the Gold Standard made by Keynes in the 1920s and 1930s. Indeed, deflationary bias was exactly the potential problem he was so keen to avoid when designing the Bretton Woods fixed but adjustable exchange rate system for the postwar world. The euro has proved to be a modern incarnation of the Gold Standard, with all of its vices and few of its virtues.

Disappointment all round

Thus, the reasons for expecting improved macro performance from the eurozone were weak and the arguments for expecting worse performance were strong. The facts tell a clear story. (Remember that the euro was formed in 1999.) During the years 1980–98, the average annual economic growth of the area that we now call the eurozone was just over 2%. Admittedly, this was below the growth rate achieved in Australia, Norway, the US, the UK and Canada, but it was about the same as Sweden and a little higher than Switzerland. Over the years 1999–2012, however, the eurozone's average growth rate slipped to just under $1\frac{1}{2}$%.

Now, it is true that over this period, the economic environment was more difficult and many countries experienced much weaker growth. Nevertheless, it is the relative performance that is significant. Between 1999 and 2012, the eurozone's average growth rate was the lowest in the above-mentioned group of countries.

It is a similar story on the unemployment rate. Over the years 1980–98, eurozone unemployment was high, but it was below the rates in Canada and the UK. From 1999 to 2012, eurozone unemployment shot up to be the highest in this whole group, and by a decent margin.

One might think that despite disappointing macroeconomic performance overall, at least the eurozone countries would have enjoyed greatly increased trade with each other. It must surely be that, for whatever reason, this has not contributed enough advantage to outweigh whatever economic disadvantages the euro has brought. In fact, that is not what the data show. Since the creation of the euro, exports from eurozone economies to the non-eurozone have increased at a faster pace than exports to other members of the single currency bloc, for all member countries except Ireland.

The result is that there is a clear downward trend in exports to the eurozone as a percentage of total exports, for all euro members except Ireland. The majority of exports from the eurozone's two biggest economies go to non-eurozone countries while, between 2009 and 2012, Portugal, Spain and Greece all experienced sharp falls in the percentage of their exports going to other eurozone countries. In 2012, Greek exports to the eurozone represented only 30% of total exports.

Bond markets' insouciance

The eurozone's weakness continued through 2013–14. Yet, as 2014 drew to a close, if you looked at the eurozone's bond markets you could readily conclude that there was nothing to worry about. The high yields that the markets had demanded from the peripheral countries in 2012 had plunged. Pretty much across the whole continent, yields stood close to their all-time lows, as Figure 4.2 shows. And yields on peripheral countries' bonds were not that much higher than they were for the Germanic core. Indeed, if you lent to the Italian government for ten years you would receive a slightly lower return than if you lent to the US government. So the markets were saying that the crisis of the euro was well and truly over.

The trouble is, as a glance at Figure 4.2 will confirm, the markets were in a similar state of insouciance immediately before the existential crisis of 2012 blew up. The truth is that although financial markets are wonderful at assessing and valuing events or circumstances that are

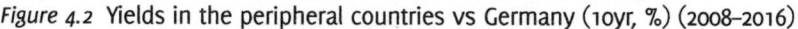

Figure 4.2 Yields in the peripheral countries vs Germany (10yr, %) (2008–2016)

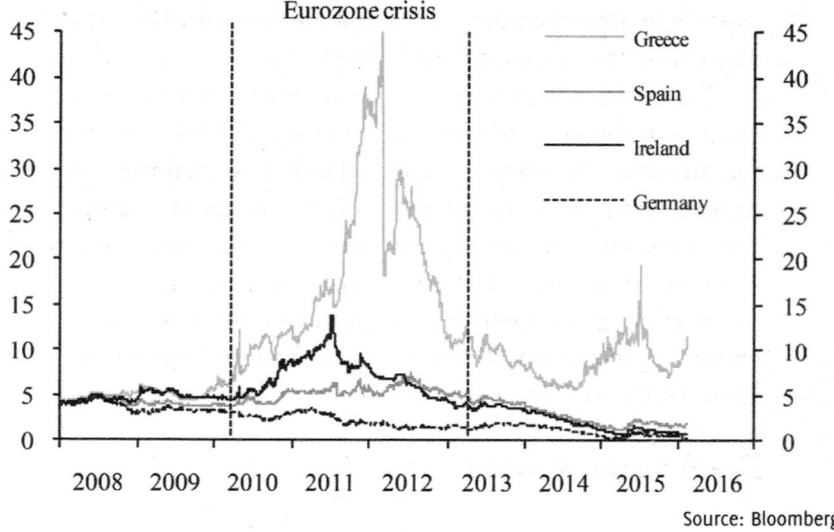

Source: Bloomberg

fairly concrete and immediate, with regard to the uncertain and possibly distant, they are very bad.

Their typical reaction to profound uncertainty is implicitly to make some blithe assumption and then to ignore the issue. In a contest for the market's attention between the uncertain and possibly distant prospect of euro break-up and the US non-farm payroll figures, due out at 1.30 pm, the payroll figures win hands down.

At the end of 2014, the markets may have been pretty sanguine about the situation, but the state of the economy was dire – and the eurozone's policy-makers were waking up to how serious it was.

Economic catastrophe

The acute problems of the eurozone first became crystal clear during the financial crisis of 2008. That crisis spawned what is now being referred to as the Great Recession, which saw output fall across just about every country in the developed world. By the end of 2014, however, some parts of the developed world were recovering nicely – but not the eurozone.

If we compare the performance of output from the beginning of 2008 to the end of 2014, thereby encompassing the crisis period, the recession and the subsequent recovery, the extent of the disaster in the eurozone becomes clear. From the beginning of 2008 to Q3 of 2014, the US economy grew by 8.4%, while the equivalent figures for the UK, Canada and the world as a whole are 3.4%, 11.2% and 17.3%. By contrast, the eurozone economy contracted by 2.2%. Within that total, Germany managed growth of 3% and France about half that. The equivalent figures for Spain, Portugal, Italy and Greece were *minus* 6.4%, 7.3%, 9.5% and 26%. This catastrophic fall of Greek GDP is roughly the equivalent of the drop that occurred in the US and Germany during the 1930s.

By the way, the figures for other continental European countries that are not in the EU are interesting. Over the same period, Norway and Switzerland grew by 6% and 8%, respectively. But the comparison that really lays bare the extent of the European crisis is with China. Over this period of just six years, the Chinese economy has grown by 70%. Putting this another way, the increase in China's GDP has been roughly equal to the level of GDP in Germany and Italy. That's right: in six years the Chinese economy has added another Germany and Italy combined.

You might readily seek comfort in the idea that this is all about Chinese exceptionalism. To some extent this is right. Comparisons with other countries are less startling – but they are still pretty shocking. Over this period, India's GDP has risen by 32%, while the equivalent figures for Hong Kong, Korea, Malaysia, Singapore and Taiwan are 20%, 22%, 36%, 29% and 20%, respectively. Something may or may not be wrong in the state of Denmark, but there is clearly something catastrophically wrong in the would-be state of Europe.

What is wrong is a continuation of the trends towards underperformance that I analysed in Chapter 3, combined with the acute problems of the euro that I analysed in this chapter, but with some new twists that have served to intensify the problem. I will first discuss Germany and France together, before going on to consider the problems of the peripheral economies, the transformation of the eurozone's international trading performance and the danger of deflation. I discuss possible policy responses in Chapter 5.

The contrast between Germany and France

For most of the euro's existence, the German economy has done reasonably well. This has not been because domestic demand has been strong, but rather because German exports have grown well. In 2014, though, this changed. German exports were hit by the slowdown in China (which is a large market for German heavy machinery and consumer durables); the crisis in relations with Russia, which saw sanctions imposed on Russia and the Russian economy coming close to recession; and the continued weak performance of the rest of the euro-zone, combined with the recovery in competitiveness of some of the peripheral countries. In 2014 the German economy grew by about 1.6% – and about the same, or slightly less, in 2015 – above the eurozone as a whole but still low by international standards.

The situation in France is intriguing. In the early years of the euro, the French economy performed more or less in tandem with Germany. Whatever variable you look at, the numbers were very similar: growth, unemployment, inflation, the public finances. Even the external accounts were similar. Germany ran a larger current account surplus, but France was in the black as well. Then from about 2006 this started to change, with French relative performance falling back on all counts.

There seem to be two fundamental reasons. The Hartz labour market reforms in Germany in 2003–05 appear to have made a big difference, enabling German unemployment to come down and to stay down. By contrast, France has made hardly any reforms at all. Second, and perhaps relatedly, German companies have done extraordinarily well in keeping costs down and hence gaining in competitiveness.

As France's performance has started to diverge from its erstwhile close partner, increasingly it is coming to resemble the peripheral countries rather than the Germanic core of the monetary union. Moreover, without deep and fundamental reforms, it is difficult to see matters changing. Since such reforms would strike at the essence of the French model, and would be seen by many in France as an abandonment of the 'French way', they seem politically impossible to implement. In short, not only has the 'Franco-German motor' stalled, but the vehicle has been shunted off the road.

Trouble disguised in the periphery

The story of the peripheral countries is more nuanced. One country stands out from all the others: Ireland. Its output has started to recover strongly. It still has its major problems, notably in the public finances and the banking sector. But as a small, open economy, it has benefited from the improvement in competitiveness brought on by a period of domestic deflation that included huge cuts in public-sector pay – and from growth in its two main markets, the UK and the US. In 2015 exports grew by 13%.

The other four peripheral countries present a rather different picture. In Spain and Portugal, on some measures there has been a quite impressive recovery in competitiveness – thanks to domestic deflation, including wage cuts.

In fact, this improvement seems more impressive than it really is. It is true that in these countries there has been a massive turnaround in the current account that has shifted it from large deficit to small surplus. What is more, this has happened partly because exports have revived. (This supports the improved competitiveness story.) However, a large part of the turnaround in trade performance is due to the deep depression of imports, which is simply a response to the collapse of domestic demand. Indeed, when, in 2014, domestic demand in Spain and Portugal started to revive, imports soared and the current account deteriorated.

Admittedly, though, in both these countries the economic situation has improved. GDP has risen and unemployment has fallen. And the reductions in the government's fiscal deficit have been astounding. Yet, for the reasons explained earlier in this chapter, this has done nothing to reduce the debt-to-GDP ratio. Indeed, in all three countries it has continued to climb. After all the painful austerity they have endured, this is a bitter blow. They have been running faster and faster in order to go backwards. In Greece this has led to a new crisis. At the end of 2014, Greek bond yields spiked up, anticipating an anti-austerity Syriza government in Athens – despite the evidence that the Greek economy had turned the corner. Syriza did win; it buckled to German pressure; and the Greek economy fell back into recession.

The country that stands out from the other peripheral nations is Italy. It has had the same experience of the debt ratio climbing; indeed, the ratio is now about 130%. But unlike the others, Italy has not undergone a painful deflation of prices and wages and there is no sign of an improvement in competitiveness. Accordingly, GDP has recovered only modestly (and thanks mainly to low oil prices) and unemployment is still over 12%. Moreover, there seems no realistic prospect of the radical reforms that would be needed to set the country on the right path. Rather like France, the political system seems incapable of delivering what the country needs. It is as though Italy is frozen in its current state. Interestingly, Italy's three main opposition parties are against the euro.

Turning Teutonic

The German tendency to save rather than spend, and accordingly to run up large current account surpluses, has been well known for some time. I wrote about it earlier in this chapter. For most of the eurozone's existence, these surpluses have been mirrored by deficits in the peripheral countries, thereby leaving the eurozone as a whole with its trade pretty much balanced. With the depression of demand in the periphery, however, and the improvements in some peripheral countries' competitiveness, this has all started to change. Now the eurozone as a whole is running a significant current account surplus of the order of about 0.5% of world GDP. In 2015, this was slightly larger than China's surplus.

This is highly significant, not just for Europe, but also for the world. In my previous book, *The Trouble with Markets*, I attributed much of the blame for the factors that led up to the financial crisis of 2008 to the world's tendency to save too much, with several countries 'oversaving' and building up large current account surpluses. In recent years, though, this situation has changed greatly. The Japanese surplus has all but disappeared, the Chinese surplus has halved, and the oil producers' surpluses are on the way to extinction. Just as this has happened, however, a new source of imbalance has emerged – the eurozone. Indeed, in 2015 as the oil-based surpluses evaporated, the eurozone had the world's largest current account surplus.

The euro has turned the whole eurozone Teutonic. Contrary to what some German opinion might hold, this is not a badge of honour. These countries are not Teutonic in their productivity performance; and their current account surpluses are created mainly by their domestic demand being bludgeoned. But the result for the eurozone – and the world – is Teutonic, just the same.

This has now become a serious problem for the world economy. It would be far healthier if the surplus disappeared thanks to higher domestic demand leading to a burst of imports than through a collapse of exports. As it is, the strong current account performance was surely one of the leading reasons behind the strength of the euro on the exchanges – and that has served to intensify one of the eurozone's looming problems, namely the threat of deflation.

Deflation and the Japanese comparison

As the eurozone has continued to disappoint, more and more commentators have come to see it as resembling, or in danger of coming to resemble, Japan. There are indeed some close comparisons. Strikingly, if we compare the path of bank lending in Japan from the beginning of its troubled period in 1991 with what has happened in the eurozone since the beginning of 2008, the eurozone has been almost as weak (see Figure 4.3). Indeed, at the end of 2014, bank lending in the eurozone was falling. This is critical. The weakness of the banking system and its limited ability to support recovery were a continuing leit-motif during Japan's difficult times. It is hard to see the eurozone recovering while bank lending is so weak.

Various commentators have foreseen the danger of what they would regard as a terrible fate; that is to say, that the eurozone, like Japan, might endure a 'lost decade'. They could not be more wrong. In relation to Japan, the expression 'lost decade' is a complete misnomer. Indeed, it is remarkable that so much error can be contained in so short an expression: two words and two major mistakes. For the period in question lasted not one decade but two. More importantly, the period was not 'lost'. Output continued to grow. Indeed, at the equivalent point to where the eurozone stands now in relation to the starting point in 2008, GDP was 7% up. In the eurozone it is about flat (see Figure 4.4). So the correct reply to those eurozone

Figure 4.3 Japan and eurozone bank lending to the private sector (Q1 1991/2008 = 100)

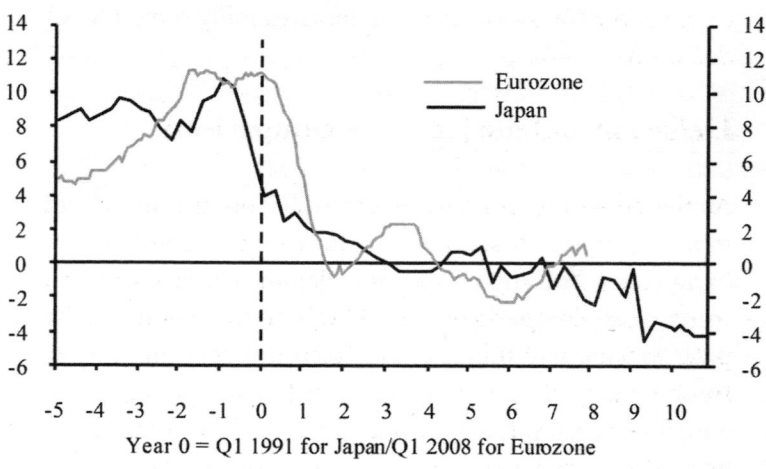

Year 0 = Q1 1991 for Japan/Q1 2008 for Eurozone

Source: Thomson Datastream

Figure 4.4 Japan and eurozone GDP (Q1 1991/2008 = 100)

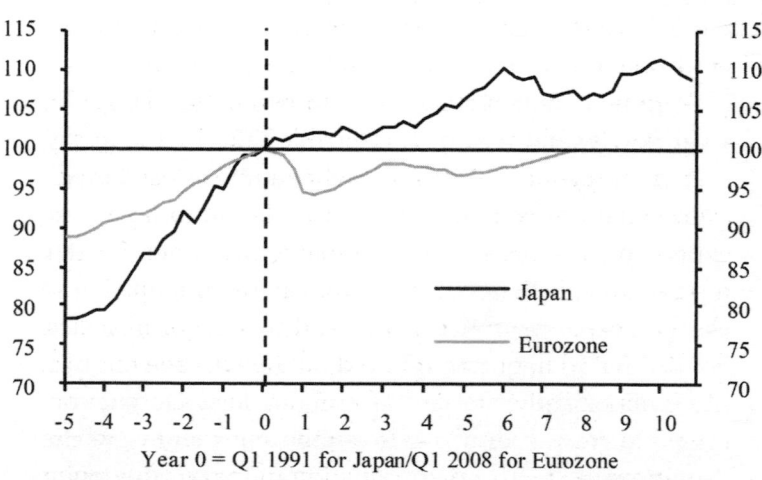

Year 0 = Q1 1991 for Japan/Q1 2008 for Eurozone

Source: Thomson Datastream

commentators who say that they fear things turning out like Japan is: 'You should be so lucky.'

One key component of Japan's difficulties during its two decades-long period of travail was deflation; that is to say, the opposite of inflation, a tendency for prices and most other nominal magnitudes to fall over time. Deflation tends to depress economic activity, as it encourages both firms and households to postpone spending. More importantly for current circumstances, other things being equal, deflation increases the real value of government debt. Just as in Japan, most countries in the eurozone already have high levels of government debt. If they enter a period of deflation, debt ratios will rise, threatening a major financial crisis.

At the end of 2014, in the peripheral countries where the debt problem is worst, deflation was already there. At the end of 2014, prices were falling in Greece, Spain and Portugal. This should hardly come as a surprise. After all, according to the orthodox policies advocated by Germany, in the absence of an exchange rate to depreciate, deflation (aka internal devaluation) is the way for the peripheral countries to regain competitiveness.

But by late 2014, the eurozone as a whole had dipped into deflation. Never mind the peripheral countries, where deflation, far from being an unfortunate accident, was actually part of the game plan; even in Germany deflation was perilously close. The German inflation rate was just 0.2%. What is more, this situation continued during 2015, and looked likely to persist during 2016. Again comparing the eurozone with Japan, as Figure 4.5 shows, at the equivalent stage to now, in Japan prices were still rising – indeed, at about the same rate as now in the eurozone. Persistent deflation only began eight years after 1991.

Figure 4.5 Eurozone and Japan CPI (%y/y)

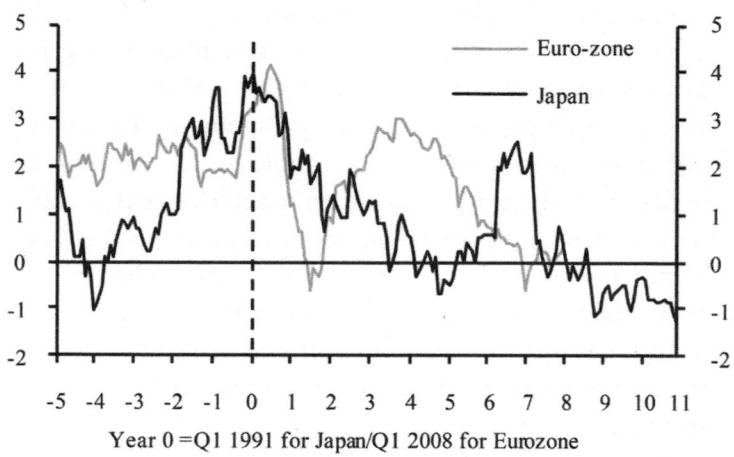

Year 0 = Q1 1991 for Japan/Q1 2008 for Eurozone

Source: Thomson Datastream

Again, as regards the negative aspects, the eurozone is in line with the Japanese experience.

Pouring oil on troubled waters

Help could be at hand for the eurozone. In early 2016, international oil prices were running at about $30 a barrel. They had recently been as high as $143. No one knows whether this recent drop is a flash in the pan, but as I write in March 2016, it does not look like it. Indeed, prices could even fall further. For most of the world (outside the oil producers) this is a jolly good thing. It will reduce the costs of production and put more purchasing power in the hands of firms and households throughout the oil-consuming countries.

Admittedly, this gain is counterbalanced by losses of purchasing power among the oil producers. But these countries tend not to spend all their incomes. Accordingly, lower oil prices transfer income from high savers to high spenders, giving a net boost to demand. (Admittedly, in 2015/16 it seemed as though the negative effects of lower oil prices on the world economy outweighed the positive effects, at least initially.) This represents the correction of one of the leading imbalances in the world economy, as discussed earlier. It should eventually cause the global economy's growth rate to pick up. Indeed, it helped to bring a bit of a revival in the eurozone in 2015.

However, for the eurozone lower oil prices also have a significant downside. They tend to reduce the consumer price index and thereby, other things being equal, lead to a lower rate of inflation, at least temporarily. Generally speaking that is not a problem, but when you are perilously close to persistent deflation it is.

The danger is that the experience of prices falling leads people to expect them to go on falling. As I said all those years ago in *The Death of Inflation*, if this happens, deflation has got into the most dangerous place of all; that is to say, it has entered people's minds. And, just as with inflation, once deflation is established there, it is devilishly difficult to shift. That is exactly what happened with Japan and it could easily happen in the eurozone, thereby worsening economic performance and intensifying the problems confronting the eurozone's policy-makers.

5

Policies to Prevent an Economic Disaster

Investment is needed but not with new borrowing ...
We want to stick to the Stability and Growth Pact.
This is also about growth and that is why we must
reject a debate about austerity against growth.
— Angela Merkel, German Chancellor,
November 2014

Given how serious the eurozone's predicament is, one would normally expect a policy response. What could it be? There are four options: muddling through and doing nothing; relying on fiscal transfers to relieve pressure on the peripheral countries; a fiscal expansion; and expansionary monetary policy innvolving lower interest rates and quantitative easing (QE). I examine all four below.

Just teething trouble?

There is a view that the difficulties of the euro and the associated poor economic performance of eurozone members are merely temporary. Accordingly, the only policy response required is to sit tight and wait. In any case, no monetary union is perfect. In the US and the UK, differences between different parts of those unions persist, but the unions themselves have carried on. (Admittedly, there is a strong separatist party in Scotland that could lead to the British monetary union being broken.) Might the euro not be the same? Moreover, the euro has begun in most inauspicious times. In a better era, whatever difficulties remain, surely the countries of the union, and the union itself, will fare better. Why cast it asunder now?

There is something in this view. If the wider benefits of European cohesion, if not a fully integrated fiscal and political union, are that great, it could be worth putting up with some temporary costs brought on by monetary union. However, even if they are of a temporary nature, the costs seem to be absolutely huge, not least in the shape of a whole generation of young people in southern Europe without work and without hope.

Moreover, these 'temporary' effects can have long-lasting consequences. In depressed economies, there is no incentive to invest heavily in plant and equipment, so the capital stock ends up lower than it would otherwise have been. In addition, the result of large-scale unemployment will be loss of skills and motivation on a massive scale. This could lead on to huge social problems – drug abuse, alcoholism and family breakdown – not to mention fostering the rise of racism and fascism. Even if the incompatibilities and inflexibilities that meant countries like Italy and Greece were ill-suited to joining a monetary union with Germany were eventually sorted out, the bad effects of the current euro depression would linger for years, if not decades.

In this regard, there is an example from history that is quite disturbing. For centuries, Italy was a patchwork of city states and kingdoms (see Figure 5.1). When it was unified in the 1860s, along with this political unification came monetary and fiscal union. Ever since, the south, which broadly corresponds to the Bourbon Kingdom of the Two Sicilies, has been depressed. After unification, the south's industry was ruined and its agriculture was sent

Figure 5.1 Italy in 1820*

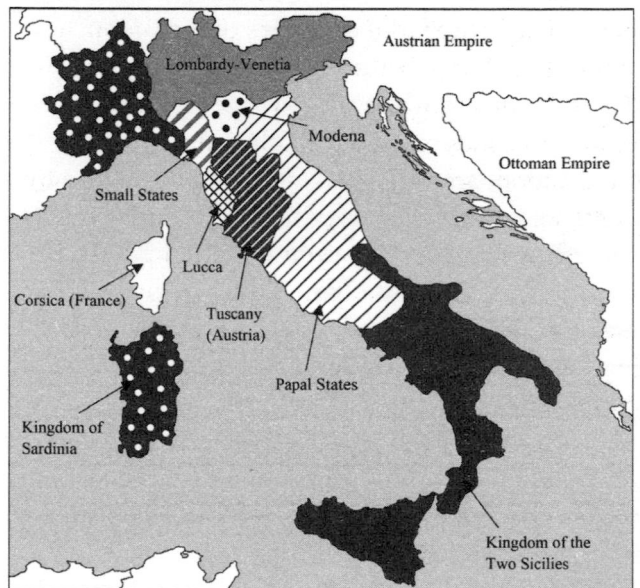

Source: www.timemaps.com

into decline. Many of its people were so poor that they were forced to leave. Over the next two decades, millions of people from Sicily and the southern mainland gave up on Italy[14] and emigrated to North and South America. Indeed, there are disturbing parallels with Greece today, where the working-age population has fallen to its lowest level since the country joined the euro.

According to historian David Gilmour,[15] many southern Italian leaders came to see unification as a serious mistake. He quotes Sicilian priest Luigi Sturzo, who became the inspiration for the future Christian Democratic Party:

Leave us in the south to govern ourselves, plan our own taxes, take responsibility for our own public works and find our own remedies for our difficulties

... we are not school children, we have no need of the North's concerned protection.

Transfers for how long?

The position of southern Italy is closely connected with the issue of 'fiscal transfers' within a fiscal and monetary union. The economic literature about such transfers is extensive. The dominant paradigm concerns so-called asymmetric shocks; that is, economic events that affect different regions, or countries, differently. The idea is that within a monetary and fiscal union, when country (or region) A goes through a bad patch, country (or region) B helps it out. And then when country (or region) B goes through a bad patch, country (or region) A helps it out in return.

This happens automatically, and on a large scale, within sovereign states, including the US, the UK, Germany and Italy. Such transfers clearly help to cushion the blow whenever a temporary setback of some sort causes regional GDP to fall.

Sometimes what happens between different countries or regions does roughly correspond to this paradigm, but often it does not. Rather than a region going through a bad patch followed by a good patch, and therefore going from being a net recipient of funds to a net donor, the region goes into a serious decline and stays in that state for decades to come. That is the story of the former industrial and coalmining districts of Belgium, northern France and northern England, and it is especially the story of the Italian Mezzogiorno. More or less continually since unification, there has been a constant flow of money from Milan in the north to Naples in the south, where it has disappeared, largely without trace. There has hardly ever been a flow in the opposite direction.

Why is this? It is far from clear that long-lasting transfers help the suffering region to adjust and recover when the problem is structural, especially since such transfers often take the form of financial relief for unemployment. Much needed though this is, if it is too generous it can inhibit full adjustment. Despite the ability to sustain consumption at a basic level, the affected region continues to be characterized by high levels of unemployment, with all of the usual associated economic and social ill-effects.

Furthermore, if the transfers take the form of some sort of assistance to companies, the danger is that this confirms and reinforces an inefficient industrial structure. Consequently, the money will effectively be wasted. The dangers are even greater if the transfer of money goes direct to governments, which have a congenital habit of spending it badly, or even counter-productively.

The Austrian, or Hayekian, solution to such problems, of course, is to let the awful current events that have caused a sharp fall in regional GDP, whatever they are, play themselves out. While I would not go that far, there is certainly much validity in the Austrian critique of attempts to ease current pain by financial palliatives.

The problems of adjustment are even worse when there is the possibility of significant corruption. Famously, this is often the case in Italy. For decades now, huge amounts of money from Rome have regularly headed south for a variety of infrastructure projects, with much of the dosh being siphoned off along the way. The result is that whatever gets built is late, badly done and over budget – if it gets built at all. The fact that so much money is available from the state increases the rewards for corruption and so there is more corruption. The strengthening of corrupt individuals, institutions and practices then makes it more likely that corruption envelops other activities in the region.

Outside Europe, we have learned so much about how international aid, especially of the intergovernmental variety, can increase corruption and strengthen the very forces that are holding a country back. That was essentially the conclusion of the great economist Peter Bauer's life's work. Yet much the same logic applies within Europe.

We also know from countless studies that high levels of corruption are a major inhibitor of economic growth. In the case of Italy, a significant part of the factors that are holding back the south is bound up with the flow of transfer money from the north.

The attraction of a region being able to adjust via a lower exchange rate is that this gives it the chance to keep unemployment down and economic activity up through net exports. Admittedly, all of us who criticize the rigidity of the euro must recognize that exchange rate changes are not the answer to a maiden's prayer. Nevertheless, if the Kingdom of the Two Sicilies had been able to run a separate monetary policy after unification, might its history have been different? A lower exchange rate for the south and the ability for it to go still lower might have kept southern industries in the game and hence boosted investment in the south. Mere fiscal transfers are no real substitute for this and they may well have made matters worse.

The German nightmare

Clearly, most German citizens are anxious about the financial burdens they are being asked to shoulder to support the periphery. Their true contribution, and their exposure to future losses, is shielded from them by the opaque way in which assistance is given – by the Bundesbank through the mysterious Target 2 balances, or through an alphabet soup of support funds, ESM, EFSF and many more. (See the Glossary for a brief explanation.) Meanwhile, they hear their leaders talk of a banking union, a fiscal union and a transfer union. They can easily be bamboozled by this variety of support mechanisms. Indeed, the politicians intend them to be confused and overwhelmed by the complication of it all so as to disguise the true cost.

In practice, German citizens can put all these niceties aside. There are only three key concepts that they need to understand and decide whether they can accept:

- Over-spending and over-borrowing by the peripheral countries in the past, to be paid for by Germany.
- Over-spending and over-borrowing by the peripheral countries in the present, to be paid for by Germany.
- Over-spending and over-borrowing by the peripheral countries in the future, to be paid for by Germany.

Even if they are prepared to sign up to the first of these – that is, to write off a good proportion of the debt that is owed to them – agreeing to fund current excess is a different kettle of fish. And surely, agreeing to arrangements that would put them on the hook to fund future profligacy in the periphery is the ultimate no-no.

Yet without really tight controls over spending and borrowing throughout the union, that is what fiscal union would imply. German citizens need to take a long and hard look at Italy and ask themselves whether they are prepared to play Milan to southern Europe's Mezzogiorno. It is surely a scene worthy of Dante's *Inferno*.

A fiscal response?

So something must be done to revive the eurozone economy. But what? One possible policy option is for the members of the eurozone to engage in fiscal expansion, or at least to go slow on the pace of further fiscal consolidation. But nearly all of them are facing a serious fiscal problem as already huge ratios of debt to GDP head even higher. Even with a free hand, there would be clear limits to what they could do. And they do not have a free hand. The Stability and Growth Pact and their agreed targets for deficit reduction limit what they can do. The German government is standing over their shoulder watching for any sign of backsliding.

By contrast, there is considerable room for manoeuvre by Germany. For the next several years Germany is due to run a structural budget surplus and its debt ratio is set to fall from just over 75% of GDP in 2014 to under 65% in 2018. Moreover, there is an urgent need for the country to spend more on public investment. As a share of GDP, public investment in Germany is running at only about 1.5%, less than in Italy and, remarkably, less than in the UK.

Even so, the chances of a major fiscal relaxation by Germany look slim. Part of the problem is that German politicians and officials seem not to accept the Keynesian approach to aggregate demand, preferring the precepts of Gladstonian finance, or even thinking of the finances of the state in the same way they would a household. Another element in German thinking is that they believe that their country has to be tough on itself, because if it is not, weaker states will open the floodgates and deficits and debt levels will soar, destabilizing the eurozone and potentially landing Germany with some heavy costs.

When it comes to understanding the Keynesian arguments about aggregate demand, it seems that the Germans just don't get it. The German response to all economic difficulties, regardless of type, seems to be that we must all make painful structural changes and cut back. This approach reminds me of those doctors who, when you visit them about an ingrowing toenail, tell you to drink less and lose weight.

On this aspect of economics, so many German officials and economists seem to have a mental block. They appear to believe that if only the rest of the world could be like Germany, all would be well. There are many respects in which this might be true, but not with regard to current account surpluses. For every surplus there must be a corresponding deficit. Accordingly, for Germany to be able to enjoy surpluses, someone, somewhere, needs to be running deficits.

Herr Schäuble, the German Finance Minister, told the *Financial Times* on 20 May 2010:

> *I hear from Tim Geithner (the US Treasury Secretary), that Germany must do more for growth. But I must ask: what should I do to grow faster? It cannot be by building up bigger deficits, contrary to the stability and growth pact. That is crazy. I must reduce my deficit.*

And that is exactly what Germany has done. In 2013, just as the peripheral countries were in dire need of extra European demand, Germany was busy tightening its budget. So although a major German fiscal relaxation may be both feasible and desirable, it also looks decidedly unlikely.

The ECB to the rescue?

Accordingly, the spotlight falls on the ECB. Faced with the conditions that exist in the eurozone today, the classic (I cannot quite say orthodox) Anglo-Saxon response would be to flood the system with money; that is to say, for the central bank to buy up assets, paid for with newly created money. The colloquial name for such a strategy is 'printing money', although in the modern world hardly any money is actually printed. Rather, it is created electronically as the central bank credits the sellers of securities with deposits at itself. In this process the balance sheet of the central bank increases.

This policy is an extension of trying to stimulate the economy by lowering interest rates (the price of money). That too has been pursued, even to the point of taking interest rates into negative territory. QE is typically pursued when rates cannot be lowered any further. (The eurozone is close to this limit.) Accordingly, the central bank switches from trying to influence the price of money to influencing its quantity. That is why the policy is now known as quantitative easing, or QE. (When Keynes advocated this in the 1930s, it was called 'open-market operations'.)

This is the strategy pursued by the Federal Reserve in the US and by the Bank of England in the UK. It is also the strategy pursued hesitantly by the Bank of Japan over the last 20 years and now embraced more wholeheartedly as part of 'Abenomics'. But it has been largely eschewed by the ECB – until it announced in January 2015 that it would, finally, go ahead with QE. The reason for its reluctance speaks volumes about the nature of the euro project – and the fate of the EU.

How QE works

Quantitative easing works through a number of different channels. First, it floods the banks with liquidity on which they earn next to no interest. In normal conditions they will seek to reduce their holdings of central bank money by lending it out and, in normal conditions, this will tend to stoke increased aggregate demand. Unfortunately, when QE is used it is precisely because conditions are not normal. Indeed, they may be so abnormal that the banks would rather sit there holding the idle money for fear of making a loss if they lent it out. (That has broadly been the experience in the US, UK and Japan.)

Second, QE tends to raise the price of the assets bought and thereby depresses their yield. This both increases wealth levels and reduces the cost of finance.

Third, QE alters the balance of portfolios as economic agents finds themselves with more central bank money or its equivalent, and fewer, risky, higher-yielding assets. This should encourage them to buy other assets and thereby to push the expansionary impulse elsewhere through the economy.

Fourth, with more of one country's money in issue in comparison with others', wealth holders will typically respond by trying to adjust their portfolios through selling some of their domestic money for foreign currency, thereby depressing the exchange rate, with all the usual consequences for competitiveness and the price level.

In practice, in an economy whose financial system has been shattered by a major crisis, channels 1–3 are likely to prove pretty ineffective. In that case, QE must rely on the fourth channel, a weaker exchange rate, to have its effect. And this effect can be powerful, provided that the exchange rate is allowed/encouraged to fall a long way.

However, in the eurozone there are two problems. First, will Germany be happy with a scenario in which the euro, which is after all its currency, is deliberately made to be weak on the exchanges?

Second, will other countries outside the single currency, such as the US, China, Japan and the UK, permit the eurozone to climb out of its problems via a weak exchange rate? After all, this represents the export of its deflationary tendencies to other countries. If all countries are operating QE to the same extent, then there is no prospect of any one being able to depreciate against the others. And all countries in the world cannot depreciate. So QE can be extremely powerful or totally useless, depending on the circumstances at the time and how it is implemented. So far, the ECB has overcome German objections and other countries have accepted a much weaker euro.

German financial orthodoxy

Let us be clear: QE is not a magic wand. What's more, it can lead to severe distortions in both financial markets and the real economy. Even so, it just might get the eurozone economy moving. So why was the ECB initially reluctant to pursue QE?

Here again, we come up against German financial orthodoxy: such activity is inflationary; and inflation is public enemy number one. The concern is that if governments are able to get finance through the central bank, that will remove any market discipline on their spending. Once that discipline has gone, then society is on the road to Harare (in Zimbabwe); that is, hyper-inflation. Even if the central bank buys debt in the secondary market rather than supplying governments with the money directly, that effectively comes to the same thing. Monetary financing (of government) is the road to perdition.

Jens Weidmann, President of the Bundesbank, said in October 2014:

Monetary financing is prohibited for good reason, and this prohibition should not be allowed to be circumvented through secondary market purchases.

And again:

Asset purchases may act like a sweet poison for governments. The rude awakening may come when the purchases are reduced or stopped altogether.

Accordingly, in the teeth of stern German opposition, the ECB had its hands tied. As a matter of fact, it engaged in activities that are very much like QE. They should have had the effect of boosting the size of the ECB's balance sheet. But in order to spare the Bundesbank's blushes they are called something else, and the amounts were kept comparatively minor. Indeed, for a time after 2012, the ECB's balance sheet was contracting, which is exactly the opposite of what should happen under QE.

In January 2015, the ECB finally bit the bullet when it announced that it would embark on a programme involving extra asset purchases of €50 billion per month, i.e. €60 billion in all. It subsequently extended this programme to March 2017, making a grand total of €1.3 trillion. And it may well do more.

There were two concessions to the Germans. First, the ECB will not allow its holdings of any one country's debt to exceed 33% of the total. This cleverly prevented it from buying Greek debt – at least for now. Second, for 80% of its purchases, the credit risk will reside with individual national central banks, rather than being pooled.

The worst way to do QE

So is the eurozone about to be saved by a massive splurge of QE? One trillion euros sounds like a lot of money. As it happens, after all these bond buy-ins, in early 2016 all that has been achieved is to return the ECB's balance sheet to where it was in 2012. (See Figure 5.2.) This means that since the beginning of 2008, the ECB's balance sheet has expanded by about 150%. By contrast, the Bank of England's balance sheet has expanded by about 300% and the Fed's by about 400%. So the ECB's monetary expansion is a minnow by comparison – and yet the eurozone's plight is much greater and the danger of deflation more pressing.

More than that, the manner of the ECB's adoption of QE is almost guaranteed to have minimal impact. Even in the US and the UK, it is far from clear that QE has had a massive effect, although a number of academic studies have credited it with turning the economy round and boosting it quite considerably. The problem is that in the extreme conditions under which QE is enacted, normal

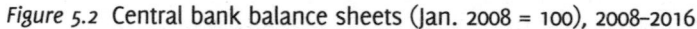

Figure 5.2 Central bank balance sheets (Jan. 2008 = 100), 2008–2016

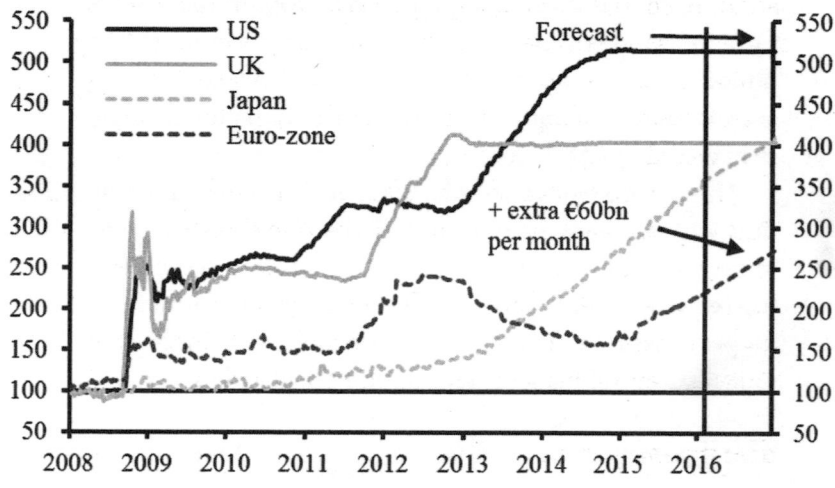

monetary relationships break down. The so-called velocity of circulation of money (the ratio of money GDP to the quantity of money) falls. The result is that no one can be sure of the extent of QE that will be needed to achieve a given increase in money GDP.

Nevertheless, according to the textbooks, QE is potentially highly effective because, in theory, there should be no limit to the amount of its own money that a central bank can and should be prepared to create. So, although it will not know how much QE it needs to do the job, it can relax in the knowledge that if a certain dose does not do the trick, it can proceed with a higher dose, and so on ad infinitum. Moreover, it can tell the markets this – and they can readily believe the message.

Accordingly, the private sector can be brought to behave in a way that the authorities want – that is, to spend – by the sheer and overwhelming power of money creation. What is more, if the central bank plays its cards right and easily convinces the markets of its will and power, then it may not actually need to do that much QE to achieve what it wants. What the central bank needs to do is to demonstrate its will, determination and confidence.

This is precisely how the Bank of Japan did *not* conduct its QE programme in the 1990s. It injected modest amounts of money hesitantly, saying it was not sure that this would work and assuring people that it would not necessarily do more! It was no surprise, therefore, that Japanese QE seems to have had only limited impact.

Moreover, this is precisely how QE is likely to proceed in the eurozone – in inadequate amounts, hesitantly, in the teeth of German opposition, and with the constant threat that the programme will be halted or even reversed. You cannot imagine circumstances more likely to make a programme of QE fail.

Calling the Germans' bluff

Since the German view is evidently so important in shaping ECB policy, it is worth assessing how powerful the German opposition to QE is, and whether Mario Draghi could simply continue to override it. After all, Germany does not have a formal veto. It is only one voice in the Governing Council, albeit supported by allies. And in January 2015, Draghi managed to announce QE in the teeth of German opposition – and later extended it.

Nevertheless, if much bolder QE were pushed through against German opposition, the consequences could be severe. Jens Weidmann would probably resign, just as his predecessor did. This might well destabilize the markets and get them wondering again about the robustness of the euro. Moreover, the ECB needs heavy German involvement in whatever financial programmes are in place to support vulnerable countries. As it is, the Bundesbank's participation in such programmes is under scrutiny by the German Constitutional Court. Another Bundesbank President resigning could just push it over the edge.

Bear in mind also that, unlike in previous years, there is now a eurosceptic political party in Germany, AFD. Under the circumstances discussed here, its support would be bound to rise, making things more difficult for the German government.

The ultimate danger that Draghi has to guard against is that Germany, out of sheer frustration and exasperation, and fearing a monetary and financial catastrophe, exits from the euro. That would leave him up the proverbial creek without a paddle. So he has to move towards his objective gradually and craftily, in the hope that Germany can be kept, if not happy, then at least complaisant.

Monetary theology and political reality

Given that QE has been embraced with open arms by both the Fed and the Bank of England, and given also that it appears to have been pretty successful in stimulating a recovery with no sign of an inflationary upsurge, why is the Bundesbank so dead set against it in the eurozone? Are the Bundesbank's leaders simply mad? The answer is no. The reasons why the Bundesbank takes a different view from the two leading Anglo-Saxon central banks go right to the heart of the European integrationist project. In my view, they also explain why it is unlikely to succeed.

When you listen to senior Bundesbankers opining about the great evils to be unleashed by some sort of arcane monetary action rather than another, what seems to be in dispute is a form of monetary theology. The Bundesbankers sound like a group of mediaeval schoolmen disputing how many angels can stand on the head of a pin.

But in fact their stance is both readily understandable and highly relevant to the practical situation at hand. The reason that the Bundesbank gives for its reluctance to support QE is essentially the danger of effectively letting spendthrift governments off the hook by allowing them to finance themselves with 'printed' money.

Yet this is also a legitimate concern in other countries, including the US, the UK and Japan, which all, nevertheless, have enacted QE. The reason they felt able to proceed with it while the Bundesbank does not is that, in the case of these three countries, the debt in question was issued by *their* governments. What the Bundesbank fears is letting other governments off the hook, principally the governments of Italy, Spain, Portugal, Greece and, increasingly, France. Its worry is that ultimately it would be German taxpayers that picked up the tab for these other governments' profligacy.

In other words, German reluctance to enact the ultimate monetary stimulus is closely related to the lack of a fiscal and political union to run side by side with monetary union. It derives from the fact, stressed in this book, that, as currently constituted, the euro is a halfway house.

Inflation worries

This is also the key factor behind a second reason for the Bundesbank's reluctance: the fear of stimulating inflation.

This has particular resonance for German people because of the experience of hyper-inflation in 1923, and again at the end of the Second World War. Interestingly, even in the US and the UK, QE ran into a great deal of opposition from those who argued that it would eventually be massively inflationary. Indeed, some argued that this result was simply inevitable when the huge increase in central bank money eventually came to be activated.

In fact, this viewpoint was never entirely fair or properly justified. The point is that just as central bank money can be created, so it can be destroyed. The operation that created the money in the first place simply needs to be put into reverse; that is to say, the bonds that the central bank purchased need to be sold back or, at the least, allowed to run off when they mature (with appropriate management of the liquidity consequences for the money markets). Alternatively, the central banks can freeze the deposits of commercial banks and thereby prevent them from using the excess cash to increase lending.

Nevertheless, there are two quibbles with this, one technical and the other essentially political. The technical one is whether, when it comes to it, the central banks will be able to spot the inflationary pressures building and will be able to take adequate action in good time to stop them from being realized.

This is indeed tricky, but it is not notably different from other decisions that routinely face central banks. Moreover, there is no reason to believe that the ECB would be any less perspicacious than the US Fed or the Bank of England in seeing the pressures building, nor less technically competent in conducting an effective operation to head them off.

However, things are different on the second issue I mentioned, namely the political aspect. There is a serious question mark over whether, when push comes to shove, the central bank and, standing behind it, the government will be willing to take the action necessary to stop the money injected by the central bank from causing inflation. The easy option might be simply to let the opening of the monetary floodgates cause higher inflation. Indeed, if there is a problem of heavy public indebtedness this might be a convenient solution.

This point would not have been lost on the central bankers in the Fed and the Bank of England. Yet they are sufficiently confident in the integrity of their institutions, and in the attitudes of their own governments, that this concern has not proved to be a major constraint on their actions. It might even be that, if they have explicitly considered the matter, they have concluded that if, when it comes to it, the democratically elected government of the day chooses to allow or even encourage a burst of inflation, perhaps to reduce the burden of the public debt, then that is beyond the remit of mere central bankers to anticipate, still less to resist.

Now consider how different this is from the position of the Bundesbank and its senior leaders. Suppose that it allows a massive expansion of the ECB's balance sheet to relieve the current situation. Just as in the US and the UK, at first this brings not much effect, and when it does start to be effective the results are wholly beneficial: demand increases and the economy recovers – and without bringing higher inflation.

But suppose that, when inflation subsequently looks like becoming a problem and the time comes to reabsorb or freeze the money, the members of the ECB Council take a different line. They may well dress it up some other way, but in essence some members may have concluded that a burst of inflation is the best way to escape from the eurozone's horrific problem with public debt. Far from being feared or resisted, higher inflation could actually be welcomed as part of the solution. Yet, *ex hypothesi*, Germany would not have a huge problem with public debt, and even if it did, it might well not endorse the inflation solution to it.

For German policy-makers this is perhaps an even worse nightmare than the one described earlier. After all that Germany has been through, it has to endure another destructive burst of inflation, perhaps hyper-inflation, in order to liquidate the debts of profligate southern countries that many Germans thought should not be allowed into the eurozone in the first place. Grasp this prospect and suddenly the Bundesbank's position does not seem so theological or mediaeval after all. On the contrary, it seems perfectly sensible.

The euro is at the root of the trouble

It is critical to understand what reconciles the Bundesbank's anxieties with the apparent success of QE in the Anglo-Saxon countries. The need for the Bundesbank to take this stance arises precisely from the partial union of different sovereign states with different problems and different values; in other words, it arises from the absence of fiscal and political union. It is a direct consequence of the dog's breakfast that is the euro.

Indeed, although the Bundesbank has always had a penchant for sounding theological when it comes to monetary matters, in the days of its pomp, before the formation of the euro, when it managed the deutschmark and was the de facto central bank for much of Europe, it was often much more flexible than its rhetoric would have led you to expect. It talked monetary orthodoxy, but its actions were pure pragmatism. The point is that with credibility in the bank (so to speak) and confident in itself as an institution and in its secure place in the German state and in national life, when it was necessary, it could afford to depart from the orthodoxy.

I would go further. Imagine that the euro had not been formed; I suspect that if Germany had been afflicted by the conditions existing in the eurozone now, with the deflation danger looming, the Bundesbank would have been prepared to embrace QE, just as the Fed and the Bank of England have done. What is more, with the Bundesbank embracing QE, given its de facto leadership of pretty much all European central banks, effectively all of Europe would have adopted QE.

So, after contributing so much to the weak performance of the European economy, the euro, this creature of the European elites that was supposed to boost European prosperity, has stood in the way of effective action to prevent a deflationary disaster. It is really beyond parody. We can only hope that a revival of the world economy succeeds in lifting the eurozone as well, and that somehow, by muddling through, the current dire situation improves such that the awful dangers of a financial crisis are avoided. If this does not happen, then those politicians who shoehorned the countries of Europe into the euro will have a very heavy responsibility to bear.

What needs to be done to make the euro work

The countries of the eurozone are at a crossroads – and they know it. To make the currency work, they now have to press ahead with arrangements for fiscal and political union. However, that is not an easy assignment. Imagine what is involved: umpteen sovereign countries with different fiscal, political and parliamentary traditions have to agree on how each other's fiscal policy should be run and coordinated, and on political institutions for the whole eurozone that will exercise this power, while being democratically accountable.

This is all the more difficult because different member countries have different ideas about the role of the nation state. While Germany seems to be prepared to submerge its identity in some common Europeanness, this does not appear to be how France views its future. There are doubtless umpteen positions in between taken by the other countries.

Moreover, quite apart from the manifest political difficulties everywhere, in Germany in particular there are acute legal difficulties. The German Constitutional Court has asserted the supremacy of German law over EU law. Although it backed the Lisbon Treaty, it stated that Europe's states are 'Masters of the Treaties' and has ruled that it would not be lawful for the Bundestag to alienate its tax and spending powers to EU bodies. If Germany were to create a political union, that would require a new constitution, which could only be implemented after a referendum.

Political lessons from the euro's failure

We are where we are because of the astounding arrogance and incompetence of the European political elite. The saying is that democratic electorates get the leaders they deserve; heaven knows what the peoples of Europe have done to deserve their current leaders.

Nevertheless, they cannot say they were not warned. Largely, but not exclusively, from the UK, eurosceptic economists have waxed lyrical about the dangers of uniting so many disparate countries in a monetary union without real convergence and without robust, common fiscal and political institutions; interestingly, in private, senior officials of the German Bundesbank argued much the same. Although the eurosceptics were vilified by the establishment, both in the UK and on the continent, they have been vindicated.

Faced with the evidence of the failure on a huge scale of a project that was both unnecessary and badly structured, the response of the euro elites should by now have been fully predictable; namely, to push on with it, regardless of the economic costs, believing that sheer political will is going to see them through. But no amount of political will can enable you to reach the moon with a peashooter.

The conclusion is that the euro has been a disaster from the beginning. It shows the quality of EU decision-making at its worst, driven by national politics, horse-trading, considerations of national prestige and childlike visions of future European unity – with scant regard for economic reality.

One of the most important issues to emerge from the analysis of this disaster, though, is what the euro's survival or break-up would imply for the future growth of the EU. Could the end of the euro be part of the EU's salvation? And if not, what could?

6

Europe's Economic Future

Prediction is very difficult, especially if it's about the future.
>   —Niels Bohr, Nobel Laureate in Physics

It is impossible to know the future, whether about the EU or indeed anything else. The EU may have a very bright economic future or it may not. It is for statements like this that economists are justly notorious, yet they and other forecasters make a living by peering into the future. At the very least, we have the past, and current trends, to guide us. There can be no certainty, but there are things that can be said about the likely shape of the future.

When analysing the likely future growth of the EU economy, first of all I discuss the prospects of economic performance improving, assuming that the euro remains in situ, before going on to discuss how a break-up of the euro could improve matters, including the effects on the two key countries, France and Germany. I then turn to a non-economic subject with huge economic implications: Europe's demographic outlook. This enables me to come up with some plausible scenarios for Europe's long-term GDP prospects in comparison with the rest of the world.

Prospects for higher economic growth

The key point is that, as I showed in Chapter 3, the EU has been a comparative economic failure, with persistently low growth rates compared not only to the emerging markets, but even to other developed economies. Could this change?

It could. My analysis in this book is that weak growth is fundamentally due to bad policies at national and Union level. But these policies could change. The key issues concern labour market regulation, as discussed in Chapter 3: the EU needs to raise its rate of productivity growth and the employment rate. Although the latter in itself would not raise labour productivity – in fact, initially it would do the opposite – it would raise the level of output per head of the population and that would stimulate investment. Moreover, greater labour market flexibility would also encourage companies to expand.

Equally, it is possible to imagine a programme of tax reform to stimulate investment and employment. Furthermore, it is possible to imagine that when the state of the public finances allows this, taxes could be cut. It is even possible to imagine a shift in austerity programmes in France and Italy towards more emphasis on expenditure reduction and less emphasis on tax rises. Or, to be less prosaic, it is possible to imagine the EU actually implementing the so-called Lisbon Agenda.

It is possible to imagine all these things, but do they seem likely? For the EU to move in this direction would require fundamental reform of the EU itself, almost to the point of changing its very nature. In Chapter 7, I address the question of whether the EU could successfully reform itself. The answer is that of course it could, but it is unlikely to do so. As I have shown, there are systematic reasons why the EU tends to make bad decisions that suppress economic growth. The euro episode, which I related in Chapter 4, tells the story. Bad decisions are the natural outcome of both the structures of the EU and its dominant ideas.

Accordingly, many of the sources of weak economic performance are likely to continue, or even to get worse. Later in this chapter I will show what 'no change' would imply for the EU's relative importance in the world economy. First, I discuss something that could improve the EU's performance – the break-up, or partial break-up, of the euro.

How an end to the euro could improve economic performance

While this is not the place to debate the likelihood of the euro surviving or breaking up, it is important to recognize that it could break up, either partially or wholly. After the Greek crisis of 2012, it is impossible to pretend that the euro is necessarily for ever – all for one and one for all. We now know that it is possible for a country to leave the euro. What is more, during the Greek crisis the then French President, Nicolas Sarkozy, said as much, as did the German Chancellor, Angela Merkel. In addition, not least thanks to the essays submitted in pursuit of the 2012 Wolfson Prize, which my firm, Capital Economics, won, we know *how* it can be done. The 19 musketeers may not stick together after all.

That said, my interest here is solely about the economic consequences of the two possible scenarios: euro survival and euro break-up. Most people, both among the public at large and in the financial markets, now believe that the euro is going to survive. They may prove to be right. Despite its obvious difficulties, it is still perfectly possible that the euro will be saved by a deal involving lots of zeros, accompanied by handshakes and smiles all round.

If this does happen, all the ways in which the euro is holding back economic growth in the EU, which I analysed in Chapter 4, would remain in place. The peripheral countries would be stuck with extremely high unemployment and locked into austerity while Germany continued to 'set an example'. That would provide no basis to hope for stronger economic growth in Europe.

What if my own view – namely, that the euro is likely to break up – proves correct? It is widely believed, even accepted as beyond contention, that, in the spirit of *1066 and All That*, euro break-up would be a bad thing; indeed, that it could be disastrous, not only for Europe but for the world as a whole. There is no doubt that it could cause a financial crisis greater than anything yet experienced – Lehmans on steroids. Yet, for reasons I will spell out in a moment, there are good reasons why a euro break-up would bring improved economic performance in the medium term. So here, I am arguing, is something that could plausibly sustain a hope for better European economic growth in the future: the break-up of the euro.

Overturning the conventional wisdom

This idea will appear shocking to many readers. Nevertheless, the long-term results of a major economic crisis are often the complete opposite of the immediate impression registered at the time, by both people at large and the intellectual and policy establishments.

In 1931, just about all members of the UK's National (i.e. Coalition) government subscribed to a programme of extreme austerity – or at least, they thought that there was no alternative. When Britain was forced off the Gold Standard in September 1931, this was widely believed to

be a disaster. Yet the economy was able to benefit immediately from low interest rates and was to benefit over the
next several years from a more competitive exchange rate,
which ushered in the fastest economic growth in Britain's
history. As Sidney Webb, a former Labour Minister, said,
'Nobody told us we could do that.' In fact, this was, to
put it charitably, a misunderstanding. Keynes had been
saying it for years.

It was the same story in 1992 when the UK was trapped
inside one of the euro's forerunners, the Exchange Rate
Mechanism (ERM). Trying to keep the pound above the
specified minimum against the deutschmark required the
UK to set interest rates at a level much too high for the
domestic economy. It was obvious to all but those blinded
by an intellectual obsession, that something had to give.
Unemployment was soaring, businesses were going bust
by the thousand, the economy was in recession and inflation and the rate of wage increase were low. Nevertheless,
the Treasury and most of the commentariat said that if the
UK came out of the ERM, the results would be disastrous.
Bizarrely, they claimed that interest rates would have to rise
and the recession would intensify.

Meanwhile, a few independent-minded economists,
including, I am proud to say, yours truly, argued the exact
opposite. We claimed that outside the ERM interest rates
would fall, inflation would hardly rise at all and might
even drop, and the economy would benefit from a vig-
orous recovery, just as it had after the financial crisis of
1931.

When the UK was forced out of the ERM on 16
September 1992, even though this was widely regarded
as a catastrophe, the minority counter-view proved to be
correct. Interest rates fell and, before too long, a decent

economic recovery was underway. A date originally known as Black Wednesday became White Wednesday and finally Golden Wednesday.

It could be just the same with the break-up of the euro.

How could the euro break up?

There are several ways in which the euro as currently constructed could break up. It is important briefly to consider these, because they may have different economic consequences.

Leaving from weakness

The most frequently discussed form of partial break-up is through the chosen departure of a weak country. The most often considered candidate has been Greece or, more recently, Cyprus. If one country leaves, of course, it may be that more countries follow later. I have always thought that much would depend on whether the first leaver succeeded outside the single currency. In that event, forces pushing the other weak peripheral countries out would be irresistible.

I know it must seem incredible that a country like Greece, which has been so badly governed for so long, could successfully manage an exit and an accompanying large devaluation. Nevertheless, Argentina achieved something similar when it broke the peso's peg to the dollar in 2001. Greece might be able to pull off such a feat – or Italy, or Spain.

If any of these countries left the euro, doubtless the initial impact would be to create chaos. For a time at least, the leaders of other peripheral countries could say to their people: 'Look, we must go on taking Mrs Merkel's ghastly medicine, or we will end up like Greece (or whoever).' But if Greece (or whoever) was doing well outside the euro, the people would be likely to reply: 'Please, let us end up like Greece (or whoever).'

Of course, a weak country could be *asked* to leave. This possibility has been admitted over the last few years by Wolfgang Schäuble, the German Finance Minister, who wrote in an article in the *Financial Times*:

> *Should a Euro-zone member ultimately find itself unable to consolidate its budgets or restore its competitiveness, this country should, as a last resort, exit the monetary union while being able to remain a member of the EU.*

And because by definition, in some sense or another, each vulnerable country is dependent on outside funds, being asked to leave would effectively kick it out. Once it was denied financial support, the only way to prevent complete economic and financial collapse would be to leave. There were times over the last few years when the French and German governments came to the point of complete exasperation with Greece and might have decided that they would be better off without it. Although they recovered from these feelings, they could easily return at some future stage.

Leaving from strength

Alternatively, a strong country could choose to leave. The most obvious candidate is Germany, although the Netherlands and Finland are other possibilities. For the time being, it seems unlikely that Germany could choose to leave, but the longer the crisis of the euro continues and the more Germany is asked to pay to keep it together, the greater becomes the chance that Germany could leave. The euro is far from being wildly popular among the German public, many of whom would like to see a return to the deutschmark. However, many have bought the line that the euro has been good for Germany because it has helped German exports, an argument I disputed in Chapter 4.

Moreover, quite a few people believe that the euro in particular, but also the EU in general, is the key to German security. For peace and stability they are prepared to pay a heavy price. This is why the revelation that Germany is paying an awful lot to keep the euro show on the road has not already provoked such outrage as to force it out of the system. Because of this, the size of the bill that would persuade Germany that it must leave is that much greater than it would be for a normal country. Still, 70 years after the end of the war, Germany is not quite a normal country.

Mind you, the size of the bill is rising all the time and the German psyche is gradually changing. It is interesting that finally, after many years during which the eurosceptic cause hardly found any voice in Germany, a new party, Alternative für Deutschland (Alternative for Germany), has been founded on an anti-euro ticket. It may not win many votes yet, but the journey of a thousand miles begins with a single step.

North–south splits

Perhaps the most appealing form of euro break-up is a split of the eurozone into two, euro-north and euro-south. What is particularly intriguing about this idea is the scope it gives for different outcomes for the euro as a currency, and what it implies about the problems of managing a new currency, depending on which countries leave the existing euro.

Suppose that the southern countries, Italy, Spain, Portugal and Greece, leave the euro and set up their own new currency. That currency would certainly be weak and these countries would still be saddled with enormous debts denominated in euros. They would have to default on a very large scale, thereby probably triggering a banking crisis across Europe, if not worldwide.

By contrast, if Germany and the other northern core countries departed, leaving the southern members to continue with the euro, the position would be much more comfortable. In this case, the euro would be a weak currency and the new northern one would be a strong currency. The group of strong countries would have to grapple with the problems of establishing a new currency. Meanwhile, in the south default would not be automatic, because their currency would continue to be the one in which their debt was denominated, the euro.

While this is an appealing solution to the problem of the euro, as things stand it is not very likely, not least because of the difficulty of effective coordination between the northern countries. Perhaps a more probable scenario is one in which Germany leaves and then the other northern countries leave later to join it. Even that, though, looks to be a long way off.

The French connection

Since Germany has been so closely twinned with France for the last 60 years, thinking about the German situation (which I will discuss in more detail in a moment) leads naturally to wondering about the future of France.

I have always thought that the really interesting question about France is not why it is doing so badly, but rather why it is doing so well. By that I do not mean to suggest that France is a spectacular success – which it isn't – but rather, that it seems to operate some extremely destructive policies and yet somehow the results do not seem to be too bad. Indeed, if the UK ran its economy the way the French run theirs, it would have gone bust long ago.

I have been troubled by this question for some time, without coming up with a wholly satisfactory answer. I find myself juggling with four (not necessarily contradictory) possible answers. First, France is a large, inherently strong country. Second, even the daft things it does (such as the 35-hour week), it manages to do well. This links to my third possible reason: both the French managerial class and its cadre of senior civil servants are extremely well trained and hugely effective in promoting French interests.

So far it sounds like cause for a quick chorus of 'Vive la France!' However, my last reason is much less comfortable: it takes a long time for things to go badly wrong. Moreover, when the deterioration does come, it is not necessarily obvious. This sounds somewhat like Adam Smith's pronouncement: 'There is an awful lot of ruin in a nation.' But once the rot does set in, it is difficult to stop. The decline of the British Empire is one distant example, with Japan's fall from grace in the 1990s and the collapse of the Soviet Union being more recent cases. If France continues on the current path, it is difficult to see anything except persistent relative decline, not only against the rising powers of Asia but also against Germany and even the US and the UK. And it could be a good deal worse. Finally, finally, *les poulets* are coming home to roost.

One of my favourite factoids is that there are roughly as many British people living in France as there are French people living in the UK. The crucial difference is that the British living in France are mostly old and retired, whereas the French living in the UK are mostly young and employed. That speaks volumes. France may have (at least in the south) a better climate and an attractive, even beguiling, way of life. But for the young and enterprising and for anyone wanting to start a business, the country is a nightmare.

France has made a very large bet on its relationship with Germany and their joint construction of monetary union. While the euro may have been a French diplomatic triumph, in economic terms it has worked in favour of Germany. Furthermore, it has created a Frankenstein's monster of a currency that could yet pull down the whole of Europe, France included.

So if the euro were to split, which way would France go? Would it stick with Germany and be part of the strong northern core? Its current economic performance does not compare well with Germany's. Its fiscal deficit, at almost 4% of GDP, is much higher than Germany's, although lower than the UK's. However, the government debt ratio is only marginally behind the UK's and France is going to struggle to get this ratio lower as economic growth remains sluggish. Meanwhile, the unemployment rate runs at roughly double the German equivalent.

If France stayed tied to Germany in a northern euro, then I suspect that French economic performance would be really dire. A German-led northern euro – or new deutschmark, call it what you will – would soar on the exchanges, thereby making France even more uncompetitive, causing its GDP to slump and unemployment to rocket. Now that would make French politics really interesting.

If, by contrast, France broke with Germany, it could either operate its own currency or be part of a southern euro. Either way, it could lead the southern countries in what, encompassing Italy and Spain, would be an economic bloc as large as, or even larger than, the German-led north. And either way, if France broke the link with Germany, its economy would enjoy an immediate improvement in competitiveness, just like Italy and the other peripheral countries.

This choice mirrors the one France faced in the 1930s with regard to the disastrous currency regime of the day, the Gold Standard. While Britain left it in 1931 and enjoyed a rapid economic recovery, France stayed on and languished.

I have no doubt that if the French establishment were confronted with the choice now, it would choose to stay with Germany. Moreover, it would do so pretty much unthinkingly. Therein lies much of the problem. Whether the German establishment would want France in, however, is a different question.

Effects on third parties

Suppose the euro did split into north and south, or in some other way disintegrated, what would be the effect on European countries not in the euro, such as the UK, Sweden and Switzerland?

First of all, their exchange rates would go in opposite directions against the two groups. Let us take the UK as an example. The pound would go up against the southern euro and down against the northern euro. There is no way of knowing, a priori, how the balance of these two opposing movements would pan out for overall competitiveness.

However, the opportunity to expand aggregate demand in the south, and the possibility of a more relaxed fiscal and monetary policy in the north (more on this in a moment), holds out the likelihood of net benefits to the UK. At its simplest, the interests of the UK, and of other European countries, are best served by having a prosperous economy in the countries that currently constitute the eurozone. As I have argued here, the most plausible way to achieve those conditions is for the euro to break up.

Just to emphasize the point, when I say that the euro is one of the causes of Europe's weak economic performance, I am not using 'Europe' loosely as a stand-in for 'the countries of the eurozone'. The weak performance of the countries locked in the euro straitjacket is an important factor restraining the economic growth of other European countries, like the UK, that have close and extensive trade relationships with the eurozone.

The economic benefits of euro break-up

Whatever form the break-up took, if the euro were to split there would be a boost to economic performance from two related sources. First, the peripheral economies (perhaps joined by France) would regain competitiveness immediately as their currencies fell. They would enjoy a boost from exports. Moreover, improved economic activity would increase tax revenues and thus lower fiscal deficits. Accordingly, it might be possible to ease up on the austerity drive. Where appropriate, it might even be possible for some of these countries to launch their own programmes of quantitative easing, which would enable indirect central bank funding of government borrowing.

These possible gains are clear enough. However, suppose that, for a variety of reasons, a let-up in the austerity drive and/or the adoption of QE is not possible. Then we would be left with exchange rate changes as the only source of benefit. Yet gains in competitiveness from exchange rate changes are a zero-sum game; that is, for the system as a whole, what is gained on the swings is lost on the roundabouts. If the countries of the periphery enjoyed improved competitiveness as their currencies fell, the flipside would be that the countries of the core would suffer reduced competitiveness as their currencies rose. So how would this bring an improvement overall?

This is where we come on to the second factor. As I pointed out above, we must presume that after any departure of the weaker countries or a full break-up, the exchange rate of Germany (and the other northern core members) would rise sharply. This would tend to reduce German exports and increase German imports, thus reducing German GDP and increasing German unemployment. As a by-product, the German inflation rate would fall. These changes would alter the balance of the German economy. As prices in the shops fell, German workers' real incomes would rise. As a result, they would increase their spending.

It is important to realize that since the euro's formation, the German economy has been seriously unbalanced. It has performed quite well, although not spectacularly well by its own past standards, nor in comparison to other developed economies around the world. However, its success has been heavily dependent on exports, to both the rest of the eurozone and countries outside it. The combination of restraint on wages and the German exchange rate being kept down by the existence of the euro has transferred real income from wages to profits, from workers to companies. Companies have tended not to spend much of their extra income, while workers have restrained their spending.

If Germany somehow left the euro or the euro disintegrated, these factors would go into reverse. It is possible that the mere transfer of income from companies (which are, in current circumstances, reluctant to spend) to consumers (who would tend to spend a good proportion of their increased income) would boost aggregate demand sufficiently to more than offset the blow to GDP from reduced German exports. If so, German overall GDP would be higher. And that would mean, of course, that it would be higher for the current eurozone as a whole, since the boost to competitiveness for the peripheral countries would increase their GDP.

However, if this effect were not strong enough – as it might well not be – then there would be scope for economic policy to give it a push. German fiscal policy could be relaxed and there would be a case for Germany to adopt QE (which the Bundesbank might now agree to). At the very least, monetary policy could be kept looser for longer.

In this regard, the effect of a strong exchange rate in reducing inflation is critical. It would give Germany the ability and the encouragement to try to expand domestic demand. What such a development would do is return Germany to the sort of position it was in with the deutschmark, before the advent of the euro. That was hardly a period of economic failure.

Indeed, the deutschmark was central to the success of the German economy and the participation of ordinary German workers in that success. Just as it is now, under the deutschmark Germany was brilliant at manufacturing and exporting, and its businesses were successful at keeping the rate of increase in costs down. Meanwhile, German consumers were prudent. This meant that Germany had a persistent tendency towards running a large trade surplus. But the deutschmark tended to rise and this largely offset the effects of low increases in costs. While this attenuated the growth of exports, it ensured that consumers' real incomes, and hence consumers' expenditure, rose.

The facts speak for themselves. From 1970–98 – that is, until the last year before the euro's formation – the average annual growth rate of German consumer spending was 2.5%. Under the euro, from 1999–2014, the annual average growth rate was 0.9%. From 1970–98, the average current account surplus was 0.8% of GDP. From 1999–2014, the average surplus was 4% of GDP. From 1999 to Q3 2014, the total increase in real GDP in the US was 36%, against 34% in the UK and 21% in Germany. The equivalent figures for consumers' expenditure are even more striking: for the US, growth of 44%; for the UK, 38%; and for Germany, only 13%.

There should be no puzzlement about why German consumption growth has recently been so weak. The simple truth is that German workers have not been paid very much. The fruits of German export success have gone largely to their employers, who have then sat on the money. From the formation of the euro in 1999 to the end of 2014, real compensation per employee has increased by about 12% in France and 17% in Finland, but in Germany it has actually fallen by about 3%.

Has Germany benefited from the euro?

Nevertheless, there is a widespread belief that although the eurozone may not have been a success, at least Germany has done well out of it. It seems to follow from this that Germany would do badly from a euro break-up.

As the above discussion makes clear, I think this argument is basically right – as far as it goes, which is not very far. There are two serious flaws in it. First, it is true that German exports have been strong, but because Germany has not bought corresponding amounts from its trade partners, including its fellow members of the eurozone, it has amassed substantial net claims on other countries. Putting it crudely, Germany has sold umpteen BMWs and Mercedes to Greece and has lent it the money to pay for them (partly through the inter-mediation of the ECB). Greece is in no position to pay the money back, so Germany has effectively *given* the BMWs and Mercedes to Greece. That does not sound like good business to me.

Countries can get hung up on export success. Nevertheless, man cannot live by exports alone – not even German man. The ultimate end of economic activity is consumption. Producing things for others to consume does you no (direct) good at all. Exports are merely the price you pay for imports.

There is another country that suffers from export fetishism – China. It is even more absurd for a country as poor as China to run a huge current account surplus. The problem is not so much the exports themselves as the lack of corresponding spending on imports. The result is lower living standards for the Chinese people than would be possible under a different policy. The similarities between the policy approaches of Germany and China are so great that British economist Martin Wolf has coined the term 'Chermany'.

The second flaw is that although German exports have been strong, as I pointed out above, German consumption has not been. Accordingly, although the German economy has bounced back well from the crisis of 2008–09, over the whole period since the formation of the euro German GDP growth has not been that wonderful. So, as argued above, it is by no means clear that the German economy overall is better off under the euro than it would have been under the deutschmark. Meanwhile, the countries of the periphery are unambiguously worse off.

Furthermore, as a result of the euro, German monetary and financial management is mired in the most ghastly mess: monetary transactions by the ECB, which according to German monetary orthodoxy threaten an inflationary disaster at some point, and continued fiscal transfers to the south, which, in some form or other, imply a continuing burden on the German taxpayer.

The end of the euro as the answer?

Therefore, the end of the euro could, in my view, improve Europe's relative economic performance. Whether the EU could survive the collapse of the euro is a subject I take up in Chapter 8.

Let us put this into perspective. The EU was doing badly before the introduction of the euro, as I made clear in Chapter 3. Excessive regulation, the drive towards harmonization and the tendency towards ever-increasing interference in more and more aspects of economic life were tendencies of the EU before the advent of the euro. Accordingly, unless something else changed radically, even without the euro the EU would be likely to go on being a relatively poor performer.

So, although the end of the euro would help the EU's performance, in the absence of other changes it would not be a game changer. Yet there is something else that has got nothing whatever to do with the euro that is liable to make a big difference to the EU's performance: they just aren't making enough Europeans any more.

The demographic timebomb

Of all the problems besetting the European continent that cannot be laid at the door of the EU, surely Europe's dire demographic outlook is one of the most obvious. Indeed, European countries that are outside the EU, such as Switzerland and Norway, also have low birth rates.

Low birth rates mean that populations are ageing and, before long, the workforce will be falling. Soon after that, the absolute level of the population will be falling. I am not arguing that having a larger population is necessarily better than having a small population, nor am I suggesting that there is an automatic link between the level of population and the level of GDP per head. The point is simply that the smaller the population is, other things being equal, the smaller will be the total size of GDP.

Of course, other things are not always equal. For a time it is possible for an economy to offset the effects of a falling population by increasing the so-called participation rate, the proportion of the population of working age that works, or by putting back the age of retirement. Nevertheless, in the end the scope for doing this will run out and a lower population will imply lower GDP; that is, a smaller economy.

In 2011, according to the World Bank, the number of births per woman was running at 1.6 for the EU as a whole and as low as 1.4 for Austria, Germany, Greece, Italy, Spain and Portugal. According to the Population Division of the United Nations Secretariat, by about 2031 the EU's population should be starting to fall and it will carry on falling to 2050. Within the total, though, there should be some marked shifts. The UK's population is forecast to continue rising, but Germany's is projected to fall quite sharply. By 2049, Germany's population is forecast to be about the same as the UK's.

In the outside world, China's population is projected to fall from 2031 onwards, but in India and the US numbers are projected to carry on rising. For the world as a whole, there are projected to be about 2½ billion more people in 2050 than there were in 2010. Accordingly, the EU's share of the world's population is projected to fall from 7.3% to 5.4%.

One way of avoiding the consequences of low European birth rates for the size of the population, and hence ultimately the size of the economy, is to allow this development to be offset by large-scale immigration. This might well happen and if it does it might be the way, or at least part of the way, in which the EU could avoid a sharp fall in its share of global GDP. However, since electorates have turned against this option just about everywhere in Europe, it seems unlikely to be taken. (I examine the issues raised by recent migration into the EU in Chapter 11.)

Medium-term GDP forecasts

So what does all of this imply for the prospects for the EU's GDP over the next few decades, compared to other countries? This is an area where angels should fear to tread. Forecasting long-term trends in population growth and the growth of output per head may well be worse than forecasting the weather or the macroeconomy. Still, here goes.

First, let me clarify a conceptual issue. The growth of output per head is influenced by more factors than simply the growth of productivity, including workforce participation rates and the level of unemployment. Nevertheless, over the long time periods considered here, the scope for these to vary is limited. So the growth of output per head comes down to the growth of productivity. Accordingly, hereafter I use the term 'productivity growth' to stand for the growth of output per head.

Despite the huge uncertainties, there are some useful things that can be said. On the basis of plausible assumptions about productivity growth in Europe and elsewhere in the world, given the population prospects that I discussed above, a possible future path for the share of the EU in the world's GDP can be suggested.

Rather than rely on a single-point forecast, though, I think the best way forward is to look at three scenarios. Under all three, the EU's share of world GDP is projected to decline quite sharply. This is due to a combination of slower population and productivity growth in the EU than in China, India and other emerging markets. However, the pace of these changes varies depending on the assumptions made about productivity and population growth. (In this instance, though, the assumptions about population growth are the same in all three scenarios.) For simplicity, the GDP projections for Japan, Brazil and Russia are also unchanged in all three scenarios.

Under the first scenario, productivity is assumed to grow by 1.7% in the EU, compared to a world average rate of 2.4% and a rate for China and India of 4.5%. Although the uncertainties about the future are so huge that it seems rash to say that any proposition appears reasonable, given recent experience this scenario can be described as a plausible central case. It is significant, then, that in this 'plausible central case' the EU's share of world GDP is projected to decline from 19.4% at present to 9.8% in 2060. Meanwhile, in 2060 India and China would together account for almost 40% of world GDP, compared to about 25% for the US and the EU combined.

The second scenario assumes marginally faster productivity growth in China and India, with both averaging 4.75% per annum. By contrast, productivity growth at 1% per annum in the EU and at 1.5% in the US is slower than in the base scenario. In this case, in 2060 India and China would represent 46% of world GDP, compared to less than 20% for the US and the EU combined.

While the third scenario is more favourable to the EU, it is also, for the reasons given in this book, the one that I judge to be the least likely. Here, the growth of productivity in the EU picks up to an average of 2.3% per annum; the same figure is assumed for the US. Both China and India experience slightly slower growth in productivity than in the other scenarios, at only 4% per annum. In this case, in 2060 India and China would represent 32.5% of world GDP, compared to about 30% for the US and the EU combined.

Let me make clear that no one should take these figures seriously as a forecast of what is actually going to happen. They represent an exercise in imaginative thinking that draws out the implications of current trends and the way in which they may develop in future.

What is striking is that even in the most unlikely, optimistic scenario, which includes markedly higher European productivity growth, perhaps linked to fundamental reform of the EU, in 2060 the EU's share of world GDP would be well below that of the US and China and only just a little bigger than India's.

In relation to the world that existed in the mid-1950s when what we now call the EU was conceived, the picture revealed by these projections is startling. The idea behind what was to become the EU was to strengthen Europe's economy through integration and to increase its influence in the world. It would have been incredible then to suggest that by 2060 the EU could end up as a smaller economy than India.

It is noticeable also from the scenarios discussed above that in the coming decades no country will enjoy the commanding preponderance that America once did. This also marks out the future as being significantly different from the early postwar world, dominated by America and the Soviet Union – the world in which the EU was conceived.

I am not trying to suggest that the EU's prospective fall in relative importance is all its own fault. Even if the EU were a paragon of virtue in relation to economic management and even if national governments were to act in ways most favourable to economic growth, with the result that European growth rates were higher, they would still, almost certainly, be lower than those enjoyed in the emerging markets, led by China and India.

Moreover, as the EU as a whole falls in relative size and importance compared to other parts of the global economy, the same will tend to happen to its member states. Indeed, they may be so small that they cease to matter to the Indias and Chinas of this world and accordingly lose the ability to negotiate satisfactory trade relationships with them. However, as I argue in Chapters 9 and 10, this seems unlikely. It may well be that most European countries would enjoy higher economic growth, and therefore slower relative decline, if they were outside the EU, and it should be possible for them to trade successfully across the world.

The importance of decline

There are three major factors operating against the EU's economic prospects:

♦ The workings of the euro, which impose a deflationary bias across the monetary union.
♦ The persistent tendency towards low productivity growth, allied to weak investment and excessive anti-business interference in markets.
♦ Severely adverse demographic trends, which will see the EU's population shrinking sharply as a share of the world total.

Of course, the biggest factor in the EU's prospective relative decline is something about which the Europeans can do nothing, namely the continuing rise of the emerging markets. Nevertheless, being a relatively slow growth area and losing share of world GDP is not necessarily a disaster. But while membership of the EU might still confer net benefits, each member state's relations with the rest of the world would grow in relative importance. If the EU were to set up barriers against interaction with the rest of the world as the rest of the world got bigger, the balance of advantages from being inside the union would shift towards the negative.

Moreover, a lower European share of world GDP would imply a weakening of Europe's influence in the world. It would also call into question the rationale for being a member of this bloc of countries and even whether the bloc of countries should exist at all. Putting it more provocatively, belonging to the EU would become less and less relevant. What would be most important for each and every European country would be to ensure that it derived maximum benefit from the opportunities afforded by the rapid growth of the emerging markets.

In fact, this development has already begun. The EU's economic growth rates have been low compared even to most other developed countries, but especially compared to the emerging markets, and European businesses have started to wake up to the implications.

Although the prospective relative decline of Europe seems inexorable, if Europeans want to slow this decline, short of creating more Europeans, the EU's economic performance needs to be radically improved. This means that the EU needs to be fundamentally reformed – or dissolved.

Part III

Reform, Dissolution or Departure

7

Could the EU Willingly Embrace Reform?

If you open that Pandora's box, you never know what Trojan 'orses will jump out.
—Ernest Bevin, UK Foreign Secretary, referring to the Council of Europe in 1949

I have argued that the EU is far from being an economic success and that its relative performance is likely to deteriorate further. Its governing elites are committed to pressing on towards 'ever closer union', even though this is economically irrelevant at best and, at worst, extremely dangerous politically, not least when the European public is becoming increasingly eurosceptic.

So, what to do? In Chapter 5, I outlined economic policies that might save the euro. In this chapter I consider the possible political reforms that might save the EU. I start by discussing whether, just like the economic difficulties of the euro, the EU's current political problems can be regarded as teething troubles. I then go on to consider how small changes to the EU's operations could be made without major disruption, before analysing the issues concerning more radical reform. Here I discuss both what would be required, including by eurosceptics in the UK and elsewhere, and what would be possible.

The troubles of youth?

One could argue that the defects of both policies and institutional arrangements that I discussed in Chapter 2 are a direct result of the fact that the EU is in an in-between position. It has assumed many of the roles usually taken by sovereign states, but it is not fully sovereign over its own territory. Accordingly, for most issues decisions are made as the result of a process of horse-trading between the EU's member countries, particularly its 'big two', France and Germany. So once the process of integration were complete and nation states had sunk back in importance, if not actually disappeared, perhaps the quality of decision-making in the EU would improve.

After all, the United States of America did not emerge as the finished article in 1776. Indeed, it had to pass through a bloody and deeply traumatic civil war less than a century after its foundation. Its subsequent stellar success was far from obvious either before or immediately after that conflict. Why should we expect the United States of Europe to emerge perfectly formed?

In any case, why does the EU need to be perfectly formed? Even if the US, the UK, Germany, France or any of today's sovereign states are broadly well functioning, they are not paragons of good government, and each has its fair share of mistakes, problems and horror stories. Perfection is too high a standard. The more appropriate question to ask is whether it is reasonable to assume that, after its teething troubles had been overcome, the EU, or whatever it called itself then, would be likely to work tolerably well as a political entity.

Problems with a European democracy

Even if the United States of Europe were fully established as the sovereign body for the territory of the EU (or the United States of the eurozone established as the sovereign body for that grouping of countries), there are good grounds to believe that it would not function well as a political entity. Accordingly, the quality of its governance would probably be low.

First, the population of the EU is about 500 million people, with an electorate of just over 400 million, compared to a population of 312 million and an electorate of 240 million for the United States. This would make the United States of Europe the world's second largest democracy, behind India, which has a population of about 1.2 billion people and an electorate of about 740 million. The larger the polity, the more difficult it is to get genuine engagement from the electorate and the greater the danger of politics being enmeshed in webs of corruption and special-interest pleading.

Putting India aside as a case *sui generis* and a country at a completely different level of development, for purposes of comparison we should concentrate on the United States. It is noteworthy that the US is experiencing severe political problems. The participation rate at elections has fallen to extremely low levels and there is widespread disillusion with politics and politicians. This could have damaging consequences. Notably, the American political system has been unable to produce a clear decision on the level of public spending and borrowing, to the point where, in 2013, the US government was forced to shut down and the country came close to default.

Second, the countries of the EU do not share a common language. Without this, people in different European countries cannot watch the same television shows, listen to the same radio programmes, read the same newspapers or blogs – or listen to the same party political broadcasts.

Accordingly, it is extremely difficult to see how there could be Europe-wide political parties. As the late Enoch Powell once put it, there cannot be a European democracy because there isn't a European *demos*.

Third, EU members have very different institutions, political cultures and histories, encompassing everything from deeply ingrained democracy (as in the Netherlands and Sweden) to dictatorship (Germany and the former eastern bloc, as well as Greece, Portugal, Spain and Italy) and dysfunctional government (Italy again). This is in marked contrast to the US, which forged its institutions and its political culture as it went along, without there being much existing beforehand to get in the way.

Democracy and freedom

If the EU formed a full political union and reshaped its institutions, it would presumably have all the trappings of a normal western democracy. But you don't have to be Einstein to realize that this is not the answer to everything. Today, the signs of disenchantment with democracy are everywhere to be seen, especially among the disaffected voters of Europe.

If the EU achieved full integration, it is possible that it would have a very strong president with powers well above those enjoyed at present by western presidents and prime ministers. Or perhaps it would end up with a system of non-government, rather like the one 'enjoyed' by Italy over the last seven decades. Either way, the odds are that an EU democracy would not work well. That could only lead to bad decision-making – and perhaps worse.

There is an important issue beyond the mechanics of the electoral process. In the West we have become obsessed with the idea of voting as the key to freedom. It is not. In Britain, universal suffrage was not granted until 1928, yet from the eighteenth century onwards it was widely recognized that the independence of the judiciary and the freedom of the press meant that it was a free country. Institutions really matter. The EU is being cavalier in the way that its elites create institutions and shoehorn states with different histories and characteristics into an artificial common identity.

It is ironic that the integrationist impulse is dominated by the noble objective of avoiding war, something that has been such a scarring part of Europe's history. For the proponents of full integration seem to have given little thought to something else that has scarred Europe's history, deriving from the malfunctioning of the political system. The latest, and most terrible, of the wars that we all so keenly want to avoid happened as a direct result of the institutional weakness of Weimar Germany and, through the democratic process, of the collapse of democracy. The recent rise of the Golden Dawn party in Greece has eerie parallels with the rise of the Nazis in Germany in the early 1930s.

Moreover, Communism, whose icy embrace once stretched across half the European continent, arose out of the mixture of an enfeebled autocratic regime in Russia and its defeat in war. Going back further, could something like the Napoleonic wars have happened without the collapse of the *ancien régime* in France?

Without a clear vision of a united Europe's future political institutions, with several arguments as to why, whatever they are, they might not function well, and in view of Europe's history, to pursue the objective of full integration willy-nilly is surely an unprecedented gamble. The stakes could not be higher.

Ending petty annoyances

Insofar as the institutions of the EU are found wanting, how reasonable is it to expect radical reform to change them into a condition where they are both effective and acceptable to the voters? Is it in the EU's nature to be reformable? If the EU were serious about reforming itself, many of the petty things that annoy eurosceptics could easily be fixed without requiring fundamental reform. For instance, the EU could finally abolish the absurd duplication of the European Parliament's buildings and resources in Brussels and Strasbourg and the expensive shuttling between the two, simply by restricting itself to one site (presumably Brussels). It could also end the practice of employing umpteen translators by declaring that its institutions would work in only three languages, English, French and German. As an example of the absurdity of current arrangements, at present, although just about everybody in Malta speaks English, the EU provides translations between Maltese and the EU's other languages. With an establishment of around 1,750 linguists and 600 support staff, the European Commission has one of the largest translation services in the world.

Furthermore, the EU could begin to address the issue of excessive regulation by declaring that for every new regulation that is brought in, an existing one (or even two) has to be dropped; an approach that has been adopted by the UK's Coalition government. As if to show that such a development is possible, in October 2013 the European Commission announced its intention to withdraw a series of proposed regulations covering everything from soil quality to occupational standards for hairdressers, which would have, among other things, prevented hairdressers from wearing high heels at work. Moreover, the Commission President, José Manuel Barroso, had a plan entitled 'Refit', for reviewing EU laws and then simplifying, reducing or repealing them and dropping proposals for new measures that are thought to be impractical or unnecessary. He said that these developments reflected 'a cultural change in the way the EU works'[16] – although the plans quickly ran into opposition from France, which feared that this could weaken the EU's 'social protection'.

Barroso's recommendations just predated the report of a panel of leading British businesspeople, set up by UK Prime Minister David Cameron, to look into how to cut European red tape. The report came up with 30 proposals, including the exemption of companies with fewer than 10 employees from all new employment laws and scrapping the need for small businesses in low-risk sectors to keep written health and safety records. Adoption of such an agenda could both improve economic performance and make the EU more popular.

Equally, some of the EU's obvious failings that so annoy eurosceptics could simply fade away. As it is, spending on the Common Agricultural Policy (CAP) as a percentage of all EU spending has fallen from 75% in 1985 to 44% in the latest figures, published in 2013. (Mind you, this is because the overall budget has risen, rather than because the money spent on the CAP has fallen.)

Requirements for fundamental reform

Yet none of this gets to the fundamental issues, which relate to the competences of the EU and the relationship between it and its member states. Of course, what fundamental reforms of the EU are regarded as desirable, or even necessary, to make belonging to the EU worthwhile will differ from individual to individual and country to country. (I give my own views on this in Chapter 10.) A good place to start a discussion of the possibilities of reform, though, is the speech by David Cameron at Bloomberg on 23 January 2013. In that speech he laid out five principles for a new European Union, fit for the twenty-first century:

1. Competitiveness:
- At the heart of the EU must be the single market, but it must now be completed by encompassing services, energy and digital.
- Trade deals should be completed with the US, Japan and India as part of the drive towards global free trade.
- Europe's smallest entrepreneurial companies should be exempt from more EU Directives.
- The Commission should shrink its budget and be made less bureaucratic.
- There should be a new Single Market Council.
2. Flexibility:
- The Union should encompass countries with different levels of integration.
- In particular, while some countries may wish to pursue the goal of ever closer union, Britain does not and some other EU members may share its view.
3. A transfer of powers back to member states:
- We need to recognize that not everything has to be harmonized.
4. A bigger role for national parliaments:
- It is to their national parliaments that European leaders are, and should remain, accountable.

5. Fairness:
- ♦ Whatever new arrangements are enacted for the eurozone, they must work fairly for those both inside and outside it.
- ♦ There is no reason why the single market and the single currency should have the same boundaries.

Cameron said that he preferred to enshrine these changes in a new treaty, not only for Britain but for the whole EU. However, if there is not the appetite for a new treaty, then these five principles would form the core of what the UK would try to negotiate with its European partners. Much to (almost) everyone's surprise (including Cameron's), he duly won the 2015 general election and, having promised a referendum if he won, became committed to holding one by the end of 2017. In the event, what the prime minister asked for in his negotiations with the EU in the lead-up to the vote fell far short of the Bloomberg speech agenda. (I discuss the outcome of Cameron's negotiations in the new final chapter.)

Nevertheless, it is revealing to analyse the Bloomberg agenda. To help assess the fundamental issues, the UK government launched a major initiative: the Review of Competences between the EU and the UK, announced by the Foreign Secretary in July 2012. This consists of 32 separate reports on a variety of subjects ranging from the Single Market to animal health and welfare, with the full array of publications due to be available by the end of 2014. These reports threw up some serious issues for discussion between Britain and the rest of the EU; although none revealed anything radical or shifted the debate.

Nevertheless, we had a clear idea of the sort of changes a Cameron-led government would want. At the seemingly prosaic end of the spectrum, the Prime Minister was concerned to close loopholes in EU free movement legislation that critics say lead to so-called benefit tourism, whereby citizens of other EU countries come to the UK to avail themselves of various benefits, including free health treatment, which leads to huge costs to the NHS. Interestingly, when asked by the European Commission for evidence of 'benefit tourism', the British Home Office was unable to provide any. In October 2013, it stated that it does not have data on the number of non-British EU nationals compared to British nationals claiming benefits over a given period, nor on the number of EU migrants making fraudulent claims.[17]

In fact, shortly afterwards the European Commission published a report claiming to show that in 2011, out of 1.4 million jobless benefit claims in the UK, fewer than 38,000 were made by non-UK EU citizens, less than 3% of the total. Moreover, in 2013 EU Justice Commissioner Viviane Reding pointed out that some of what Britain was complaining about was its own fault. She said: 'It seems that some national systems are too generous. Don't blame the Commission or EU rules for national choices and national regulatory systems.'

This issue is less prosaic than it appears, for if EU member countries are able to impose different conditions and regulations on the citizens of other EU members, this strikes right at the heart of the Single Market; that is, the free movement of people within the Union and access to all facilities and opportunities, as though it were one country. However, since there is such concern, not only in the UK but in many other countries as well, about the level of net migration, it may be necessary for the EU to make concessions on the issue of benefit entitlements to non-nationals in order to preserve the wider and more important issue of freedom of movement. In this respect, Cameron has found some support on the continent. (I take up the issue of the free movement of labour in the next chapter, and the Cameron 'deal' in Chapter 11.)

Still, there is enormous scope for dangerous rows. In January 2014, Cameron suggested that Britain should not be paying child benefit for children living in Poland whose parents are working in Britain. This elicited a furious response from the Polish Foreign Secretary, Radoslaw Sikorski, who pointed out that such Polish workers in Britain were paying taxes to the UK Treasury and helping the British economy. He even suggested that Britain was stigmatizing Polish immigrants and said that they should return home.

In addition to a limit on benefit tourism, Cameron originally wanted the repatriation of social and employment law, the protection of the City and greater powers for national parliaments. More fundamentally, whatever he is prepared to say to his European counterparts, the starting point for the UK to be satisfied with its position in the EU would be either the end of the ambition for ever closer union, or the ability of the UK, perhaps joined by some other countries, to 'unsubscribe' to this objective, while others were at liberty to continue to pursue it.

If ever closer union were abandoned as an objective, the consequences would be serious. Gone would be all pretensions to the United States of Europe. The idea would have to be to return Europe to a continent of competing nation states, albeit under a close association of friendship and cooperation. Essentially, Europe would be *renationalized.*

The possibility of reform

If it approached matters in the right way, the UK might seem to be in a strong position to negotiate radical reforms of the EU. On the face of it, it had a strong hand because the necessary measures needed to make the euro work would require a change to the EU treaties, and here the UK has the power of veto. Theoretically, this would enable the UK to demand radical changes to the EU, including the repatriation of certain powers, as the price of its agreement.

In practice, though, this approach was not likely to be fruitful and risked stirring up anti-British sentiment. If the British were seen to be stopping measures needed to make the eurozone work, this might prompt eurozone members to go ahead under a different framework, outside the EU treaties, thereby leading to a fragmentation of the EU and risking the future of the Single Market.

The UK was more likely to make progress if it were less confrontational. It would be important for the tone not to be petulant and strident, but rather to convey a reasoned and closely argued case for a reformed EU that would work, not only for the UK but for other EU members as well. The UK would be aided in this endeavour by the well-acknowledged capabilities of its diplomats and by the continuing continental respect for its experience and pragmatism. In the event, in its attempts to negotiate reform of the EU, the UK did not ask for much, and did not get much, as I discuss in Chapter 11.

As it happens, it is not only the British who want the end of 'ever closer union'. In June 2013, the Dutch government said: 'The Netherlands is convinced that the time of an "ever closer union" in every possible policy area is behind us.'[18] The ruling party in the Netherlands said in the autumn of 2013 that it would like to see 'whole policy areas' returned to national governments, and it has called for ways to overturn or challenge rulings by the European Court of Justice. Moreover, a recent poll by the think tank Open Europe found that, by a majority of 2 to 1, German voters favour a decentralization of powers from Brussels. Furthermore, the Italian Prime Minister said that a return of powers 'could be possible and it could be useful for us too'.

In fact, in late 2013 a conference was held in Messina, Sicily, hosted by the former Italian Foreign Minister and eurosceptic Antonio Martino. The meeting, organized under the banner of the Alliance of European Conservatives and Reformists (AECR), included representatives of parties from across Europe, gathered to discuss how a European Common Market might be formed. What made this meeting particularly poignant was that it was held at the same hotel as the 1955 Messina Conference of the European Steel and Coal Community, the forerunner of the EEC. What is more, at the earlier conference one of those present was Gaetano Martino, then Italian Foreign Minister, father of Antonio Martino.

The very shift of popular opinion in Europe against the EU, which I analysed in Chapter 2, argues that across Europe political pressure for fundamental reform will be strong. In that case, the UK could be pushing on an open door. One could reasonably argue that, whereas a decade ago the integration fundamentalists were pressing for an EU army and justice department to build on the base of a successful monetary union, this is now widely regarded as *passé*. The watershed moment was reached in 2005 when the French and Dutch rejected the EU constitution in referendums. After that, the dream of the European super-state was dead. Nation states are on the way back.

It is even possible to imagine a drive to reform the EU involving a close degree of cooperation between Germany and the UK. After all, Germany has never been fully signed up to the 'statist' tradition that so dominates French thinking and it is well aware of the way in which so many EU laws and practices hold back EU economic performance. Now that Germany is stronger as a country and with Angela Merkel indubitably the strongest politician in the EU, it is possible that Germany could throw its economic weight behind a programme of radical reform.

Germany would be keener to keep the UK in the EU than it is prepared to admit. Relations with France have become strained, not only over the euro crisis but also over foreign policy. When Germany sided with China and Russia over Libya in 2011, this caused consternation in Paris; this happened again when Germany refused its support for the French intervention in Mali. Meanwhile, German policy-makers are well aware that without the UK in the EU, Germany would become both more dominant and more resented, while France might seek to establish an informal grouping of Latin states against it. In addition, other countries would support Germany in wanting EU reform and the UK's continued membership of the Union: the Netherlands, Ireland, Italy, Finland, Sweden, Denmark and Poland.

Putting French and German mutual suspicion aside, something that might strengthen the urge to reform is the need to unite against a common enemy. The most obvious candidate here is Russia, which has recently taken a more belligerent tone in its dealings with the outside world and which sees itself as a rival to the EU with regard to association with former Soviet republics and satellites.

As I mentioned in Chapter 2, in late 2013, well before the seizure of Crimea, Russia managed to persuade Ukraine to back out of a planned trade deal with the EU, through a combination of financial inducements and veiled threats. Just before Latvia became the 18th member of the eurozone on 1 January 2014, its finance minister mentioned this fact and implicitly referred to Latvia's vulnerable position vis-à-vis Russia, when noting that Latvia would now be firmly tied into the institutions of the West: NATO, the EU and the euro. If Russia continues in its current vein, then surely the countries of the EU will want to make sure that they stick together. If reform is necessary to make them stick together and to make them stronger, then they will surely have a clear motive to support it.

With regard to the *possibility* of reform, it must be remembered that the EU has changed dramatically in the last 50 years. When the Delors Commission came out in 1985 with a blueprint for the Single Market, cynics were dismissive. Although it is not perfect, the Single Market now exists. Even the Common Agricultural Policy has been radically reformed, with the result that subsidies are no longer linked to production (which resulted in 'butter mountains' and 'wine lakes'), but are instead related to the area cultivated. So if the EU managed to make these radical changes in the past, why can't it reform itself now?

Barriers to reform

The chance for radical reform to emerge from Cameron's renegotiation has passed, but could the EU still choose to follow a path of radical reform? The fact that the Netherlands might join the UK in opposing ever closer union sounds encouraging, but in practice, getting an agreement on the future shape of the EU would be fraught with difficulty. Different countries have different requirements for fundamental EU reform, which is one of the major factors arguing against the reforms necessary to satisfy the EU's critics being possible.

The German Chancellor in particular fears that if countries are able to 'cherry pick' which bits of the EU they would like and which they would not, the whole edifice could unravel. Meanwhile, a German–British pro-reform alliance, although possible, does not seem at all likely. It would mean a fracturing of the close relationship with France that, despite current tensions, remains the cornerstone of German foreign policy. Quite apart from anything else, a Franco–German split would have serious consequences for the ability to hold the euro together.

Indeed, in November 2013 Gerhard Schröder, Germany's Chancellor before Merkel, blamed Britain for the eurozone financial crisis and for blocking EU measures designed to sort matters out. He said:

> *The problem has a name and that's Britain. As long as the British block these moves, nothing will happen ... We can be sure that Britain is no longer willing to join the euro area. Countries that are not in the euro area cannot prevent greater integration ... It's tough but you cannot say: 'I will not be there but I want a say.'*

The EU has more chance of achieving reforms that do not need treaty change, not least because such changes have to be ratified by national parliaments and in some cases by referendums. Several countries, most notably France, are fearful that the EU is now so unpopular that they would not get a new treaty approved in a referendum. The trouble is that a reform package that did not require treaty changes would be unable to satisfy the demands of leading British eurosceptics.

For instance, the Fresh Start group of British MPs is reasonable and moderate and would like the UK to remain in the EU. They have come up with some proposals that do not involve treaty change. However, they recently put forward a proposal for EU reform[19] consisting of the following:

- An emergency brake for any member state regarding future EU legislation that affects financial services.
- A repatriation of EU competence in the area of social and employment law to member states.
- An opt-out for the UK from all existing EU policing and criminal justice measures not covered by the Lisbon Treaty block opt-out.
- A new safeguard for the Single Market to ensure that there is no discrimination against non-eurozone member interests.
- The abolition of the Strasbourg seat of the European Parliament, the Economic and Social Committee and the Committee of the Regions.

At least the first two points in the above package would require treaty change.

More strikingly, in January 2014 almost 100 Conservative MPs sent a letter to David Cameron asking for the UK parliament to be able to overrule European regulations. This is tantamount to calling for the UK to leave the EU, unless the latter is so fundamentally reformed as to be unrecognizable. After all, as the Union is currently constituted, EU membership is all about accepting the primacy of European law. So in trying to negotiate a new deal for Britain within the EU, Cameron is caught between Scylla and Charybdis.

Just to underline how difficult it would be for the UK and other countries to achieve fundamental reform of the EU, in October 2013 the President of the European Commission, José Manuel Barroso, said that Cameron's aim of bringing EU competences back to Britain was 'theological, unreasonable' and 'doomed to failure'. He added that reform of the European Union could only be accomplished through review of the 'acquis'; that is, the body of legislation, thought to comprise more than 150,000 pages, on a case-by-case basis. You can imagine what a tortuous process that would be, with different countries arguing the toss over each point.

Moreover, whatever support for reform might come from the Netherlands and the Nordics, there would be bound to be strong opposition from France. There, the tradition of an interventionist, protectionist state, going back to Colbert in the seventeenth century, is deeply embedded. Indeed, on the idea that the UK would encounter considerable support from other countries for a review of EU treaties, Barroso said that other European leaders (perhaps thinking of the French President?) would veto such British proposals.[20]

Furthermore, although public opinion may be turning against greater integration, this is unlikely to cut much ice with the policy-making elites in Europe. They have always been in the driving seat of this project and in the past they have never shown much deference to public opinion.

As to the notion that fear of a common enemy, Russia, might unite Europe, if it does, this is likely to push it in the direction of further integration rather than reform. That would ensure that at least one key member of the Union, namely the UK, departed.

It is interesting that some of the EU's greatest failings and weaknesses have been in the foreign policy/defence arena. Perhaps this is because NATO provides an effective defence umbrella for Europe (see the discussion of NATO in Chapter 9). It is also worth noting that in the past, Russia has been adept at forging bilateral deals and relationships with individual EU members. It would be tempted to pursue this course again. It is not obvious that, faced with a combination of Russian bribes and threats (e.g. over energy supply), the members of the EU would be able to put up a united front. They barely managed it after Russia's seizure of Crimea in 2014.

The Soviet example

The tension over the Crimean issue is relevant to the question of possible reform of the EU in another way, because it invites comparison with the issue of Russian, or more particularly Soviet, reform. We all know that the Soviet Union collapsed. Could this result have been avoided if the Soviet Union had been radically reformed?

Clearly, General Secretary Gorbachev tried, with his policies of *glasnost* (openness) and *perestroika* (restructuring). But he failed, and for good reason.

First of all, there was a territorial problem. The Soviet Union was territorially the continuation of the old Tsarist empire. If some form of freedom and self-determination were conceded, nationalist sentiment, which had so long been suppressed, would well up and ensure that the territory of the Soviet Union shrank back to Russia proper, shorn of its colonies, which is pretty much what happened. (There could be an element of this in the current debates about the EU. Perhaps, though, the UK and one or two other recalcitrants could depart, leaving the essential core of the EU unchanged.)

As regards the elements of political culture and political life rather than territory, could they have survived in a 'Soviet' way as opposed to Russia becoming a western, liberal democracy? In many ways these Soviet elements have survived, in particular in the continued role and influence of the former KGB, the extra-legal behaviour of much of the state and the near dictatorial powers and conduct of the Russian President, Vladimir Putin. However, this hardly provides an attractive role model for the EU. Indeed, in some ways the 'reformed' Russia is worse than the old Communist Russia. In place of the tired and rotten value system of Communism, the prime value and objective of the modern Russian state is quite simply *pro bono Putino*.

In short, the Soviet Union was not, and could not be, reformed into a liberal, democratic state. I suspect that the EU is similarly incapable of the radical reform that would make it a force for good across Europe and accepted by its citizens as a vital part of their identity, rather than a burden and an imposition to be borne.

Radical reform requires irresistible pressure

Thus, although it is possible to imagine that the EU could willingly subject itself to fundamental reform, this would encounter major difficulties. History suggests that the problem is deep-seated. Essentially, the EU would need to reinvent itself and change into something that it essentially is not, never has been and has never intended itself to be. In particular, a renationalization of Europe would be such a major climbdown by the European elites that they would be unlikely to choose it willingly. It would be more likely to come about through pressure, perhaps as a result of tension over mass migration across the EU, or from the eurozone moving on to full fiscal and political union, or a break-up of the euro, or one country deciding to leave the EU. These are the possibilities to which I turn in the next chapter.

8

What Could Force Radical Change?

> *You cannot create a federation to save a currency.*
> *Money has to be at the service of the political struc-*
> *ture, not the other way round.*
> —Professor François Heisbourg, 2013

In the last chapter I established that there are wide-spread pressures for reform of the EU, but there are also some major barriers that stand in the way of a solution. However, there are some key issues that are pushing their way up the agenda and are so substantial that, one way or another, they will change the EU fundamentally – either because they force the EU to embrace radical change or because they act as a catalyst for it to break up.

I begin with one of the most contentious issues of all, namely the free movement of labour across the union, before going on to consider the drive towards fiscal and monetary union in the eurozone, the possibility of a break-up of the euro, and the implications for the EU of the Scottish referendum. I then consider the impact on the rest of the EU of a UK withdrawal.

The free movement of labour

Although the UK has had a difficult relationship with the EU for just about the whole span of UK membership, the issues that have been at the forefront of public concern have waxed and waned. There is no doubt that over the last few years the issue that has shot up the agenda most is the scale of immigration from the rest of the EU to the UK. What is more, it seems that increasing concern about this is the leading issue behind the increase in support for the UK Independence Party (UKIP), which has placed enormous political pressure on the Conservative Party under David Cameron.

What most UKIP supporters want is a limit on the number of EU citizens allowed into the UK. After his general election victory in May 2015, David Cameron was under enormous pressure to demand this. However, as I discuss in Chapter 11, he did not quite ask for it and he got nothing like it.

The free movement of labour is taken as a right within any normal democratic state. Accordingly, it is not surprising that it was included in the Treaty of Rome as one of the 'four freedoms', the others being the free movement of goods, services and capital. Furthermore, it has a clear economic justification.

The economic principles

The economic justification for the free movement of labour comes from the basic theory of resource allocation. Output and welfare are maximized if people are able to find jobs that they want to do anywhere inside the Union. After all, that is exactly what happens in any single country. Accordingly, someone from the UK might want to live and work in Berlin, while someone from Germany wants to live and work in Paris, and someone from France wants to live and work in London.

When such movements are allowed to happen, employers can select from a deeper labour pool and employees can choose between a wider variety of jobs and conditions. The result is better businesses and happier people.

But this is not quite how things have turned out. Rather, there is a tendency for large numbers of citizens from one group of countries to settle in one or more other countries. For instance, over the last ten years the UK has accepted up to a million immigrants from the former Eastern Europe, especially Poland, but hardly any British citizens have chosen to move to Poland. Accordingly, individual countries such as the UK have lost control of their borders and the size of their populations is at the mercy of these migrations of people.

Nevertheless, you could argue that the mass immigration of people to a country like the UK is advantageous. There have been several studies that have suggested this. Certainly, the higher numbers of workers in the country will tend to boost the size of the UK's GDP. Indeed, increased labour supply is one of the leading reasons behind the UK's recently good relative economic performance.

But why does the absolute size of a country's GDP matter if GDP per capita is unaffected? In fact, there is one sense in which it can be thought to matter, and this has a major bearing on the position of a country like the UK whether it stays in the EU or leaves it; namely, the extent of its power and influence. Other things being equal, the more workers the UK has, the bigger its GDP will be and the weightier it will be in international negotiations. (I take up the relevance of this point to the UK's position if it were to leave the EU in Chapter 10.)

There is no doubt, though, that the effect of immigration on per capita GDP is of more importance – certainly in the mind of indigenous workers. And here the evidence is not at all persuasive in favour of allowing unlimited immigration.

Admittedly, even this is not an open-and-shut case, since the issue is not solely about the impact on the real incomes of indigenous people now. Depending on the type of people coming into the country, their skills, work ethic and culture, they may energize the receiving country and strengthen its gene pool. There is a good deal of evidence that immigrants tend to be more highly motivated and driven than the average in the societies that they have left.

A long history of immigration

Moreover, not only in the US, which is obviously a country of immigrants, but also in the UK, immigration has been a leading factor that has shaped its development over hundreds, if not thousands, of years. Well before the modern era, the British were a mixture of Celts, Romans, Anglo-Saxons, Vikings and Normans (who were themselves an immigrant people twice over, since they were descended from the Norsemen who invaded Northern France).

In the seventeenth century, substantial numbers of Huguenots came to England, fleeing religious persecution on the continent. And after Cromwell readmitted the Jews to England (following their expulsion by King Edward I in 1290) there was a flow of Jewish immigrants. This became a flood in the late nineteenth and early twentieth centuries as thousands fled the pogroms in Russia and Poland. And, of course, there was another influx from central Europe in the 1930s with Jews fleeing Hitler's murderous tyranny.

Meanwhile, hundreds of thousands of Irish people came to Britain following Irish independence in 1922 and this immigration continued in the decades immediately following the Second World War. In the 1960s, substantial immigration began from the Caribbean, soon followed by large numbers of other people from the New Commonwealth, especially India and Pakistan, but also from Africa and the Middle East. The UK has also received substantial numbers of people from Hong Kong, Australia, South Africa and Latin America. More recently, there has been a wave of immigration from the former Soviet bloc. Interestingly, this has not been restricted to people from EU countries; substantial numbers of Russians have also settled in the UK.

You could argue that recent immigration should be seen as of a piece with this long line of immigrants who have made Britain what it is. You could argue it, but you would not find much sympathy from the men and women on the Clapham omnibus – even though many of these men and women would themselves be recent immigrants. And whatever *bien pensant* opinion thinks about this issue, the state of popular opinion will be the deciding factor in the debate about the UK's membership of the EU.

Ironically, across Europe most of the upsurge of popular resentment against immigration has centred on opposition to more Islamic immigration from states that are not members of the EU, and never likely to become so, rather than to immigration from other parts of the Union. Admittedly, some migrants from other parts of the EU might be followers of Islam. But the bulk of intra-EU migrants would be Christians or, more accurately, those who are nominally Christian but are in effect completely secular. No matter, in the public mind these two issues may be readily fused together into opposition to immigration in general.

Interestingly, here is an issue that really does seem to unite people across Europe. Anxiety about immigration is far from being a uniquely, or even especially, British phenomenon. There have recently been strong anti-Islamic protests in France, Sweden, the Netherlands and Germany.

The roots of public concern

Public concern over immigration has four elements. First, there is the sheer matter of numbers. In Britain many people think that the country is simply 'full up'. Whether or not they are right, there is no doubt that the UK population has expanded substantially over recent years and that there are 'congestion' problems with regard to traffic, housing and access to public services.

The reference to traffic is instructive. There is a well-known problem in transport economics that the costs that an extra road user inflicts on existing road users – through extra congestion – are not felt by that marginal road user. There is here what economists call an externality, which justifies attempts to limit road usage or to charge for it.

A similar point applies here to immigration – and not only with regard to traffic. The UK is congested in a more general sense, and it is quite possible that the losses to existing residents outweigh the gains to immigrants who are allowed to settle in the UK.

This touches on a wider issue. Suppose that the gains to the immigrants exceeded the losses to the original inhabitants. Does this mean that the said immigration should be allowed? Not under conventional concepts of what government should be about, which is, while adhering to international law and behaving with decency and humanity towards others outside the country, promoting the welfare of existing citizens. That is not the same as maximizing the welfare of all humanity – or even of that subgroup of it that either does live in the UK or wishes to do so. That is not the constituency to which national politicians are supposed to be responsible.

The second concern is about identity. In many European nations, the indigenous people feel that their culture and traditions are under threat from people coming from different countries. Ironically, as mentioned above, this concern is most acute with regard to immigration from outside the EU. But, in theory at least, countries like the UK are able to control this, whereas they have no such powers with regard to immigration from the EU.

The third concern is about the cost to the public purse; that is to say, the access of immigrants, or even temporary arrivals, to the benefits of the welfare state, including free healthcare, in- and out-of-work benefits and child benefit, even though they do not have a history of living in their new country and paying taxes there. This causes many British citizens to feel that they are a 'soft touch' and they are having to fork out more of their hard-earned money to those who do not deserve it.

Stolen jobs?

The fourth, and probably most important, concern is about jobs. It is widely believed that immigrants take employment opportunities from indigenous workers. In the short term this might be true, but for any length of time over which the economy can adjust it is not true. This belief corresponds to the 'lump of labour' fallacy;

that is to say, the idea that there is only a fixed number of jobs to go round. But there is not. The number of jobs is completely flexible, and can expand to match all the would-be workers who are available and willing to work.

The flipside of this point is that the argument that mass immigration has been necessary because the immigrants do jobs that indigenous people do not want to do is fallacious. If this immigration had not happened, then the real wages to be earned in those activities would have risen and that would have brought adjustment: some indigenous workers would have been incentivized to do these jobs, even though they did not 'like them', and some of the activities that give rise to this employment would have been reduced in extent because it would now have become 'too expensive' (for instance 'designer' coffees and sandwiches).

Indeed, as with most of economics, on this issue prices hold the key. An increase in labour supply brought about by immigration, without any corresponding increase in the supply of capital, can be expected to reduce the real wage at which people will be employed. Hence there is a legitimate concern of indigenous workers, who feel that their pay has been significantly eroded as a result of immigration. It has been.

And it is worth stressing that there is a decided class issue at stake here. If it is true that mass immigration into the UK has lowered the real wages of unskilled and lowly skilled people – and there is considerable evidence that it has – this has brought real benefit to many middle-class families who employ such people as builders, drivers, housekeepers, cooks and nannies. Accordingly, a cynic might say that the 'generosity and openness' of so many people on the well-heeled, liberal left is merely thinly disguised self-interest.

From free movement to mass migration

The issue of migration is another example of what has gone wrong with the EU since its foundation. The issue hardly arose after the EEC was formed in 1957, not least because, as I pointed out in Chapter 2, the member states were at roughly the same level of GDP per head, and hence roughly the same incomes and living standards.

However, recent EU expansions have brought in countries with a much lower GDP per capita than the previous EU average. This has given a clear economic incentive for substantial numbers of people to move from these new EU members to the older ones.

Meanwhile, the depressed state of the economies of most of the older EU member countries has increased the resentment of the indigenous population. Indeed, in the eurozone, since the normal means of adjusting to an excess supply of labour – that is, through the exercise of monetary or fiscal policy – are not available, immigration into these countries actually does increase the rate of unemployment. (But this point does not apply to the UK, since macroeconomic policy is free to encourage the full take-up of all available labour. Indeed, over the last couple of years at least it has been successful in achieving this.)

Possible solutions

Whatever the benefits of immigration to the host country (and there is a substantial literature on this subject, on both sides of the debate), there is no doubt that in the UK this is an explosive political issue. Concerns about the effects of uncontrolled immigration have made it more likely that the UK will opt to leave the EU in its coming referendum.

How could this issue be addressed? As discussed in the previous chapter, it might be possible for the EU to agree for there to be restrictions on the ability of immigrants to claim benefits in their new country before the expiry of a certain amount of time, or until certain other conditions are fulfilled. If successful, this might help to assuage public concern.

Moreover, a unilateral tightening of the rules governing entitlement to certain benefits applying to all residents of a country, both indigenous people and recent immigrants, might deter some immigrants from coming. The current UK government has already begun a squeeze on welfare entitlements and the squeeze is due to be intensified in future years.

But, of course, none of this goes to the heart of the matter. It does not address the three other issues that I said were at the root of concern: numbers, culture and competition in the labour market.

Perhaps it will be possible to reduce concern about these issues by applying temporary limits to the number of migrants from new EU member countries that can enter old EU member countries – or at least some of them. After all, that was done when Bulgaria and Romania joined the Union. Yet even if this were agreed, it would only be a sticking plaster. There is acute concern about immigration from states already in the EU, so placing temporary restrictions on entry from new EU entrants would not do much to relieve public anxiety.

Meanwhile, the scope to deal with these concerns radically, by placing a limit on the overall numbers of migrants from the EU allowed into a country such as the UK, is just about nil. For the freedom of movement of labour is included in the Treaty of Rome because it was intended that the Community, subsequently to be called the EU, should behave as a country. Yet in Britain, and also in other EU members, many people, perhaps a majority, want to have control of their borders – that is for the EU not to be constituted, or to be regarded, as a country. This principle could only be considered if the whole concept and vision of the EU were transformed.

Fiscal and political union

One factor that could force such a transformation is the plight of the euro.

I argued in Chapter 4 that the survival of the euro will require its members to proceed towards full fiscal and political union. That would have huge implications for the shape of the EU. As matters currently stand, given the split between those countries that use the euro and those that do not, of the 28 members of the EU, 19 would be inside a full monetary, fiscal and political union and 9 would be outside it, including the UK, Sweden and Denmark. Of course, it is possible that these outsiders would subsequently, one by one or in tandem, join the eurozone. In that case, the problems of running the EU with these two different sorts of membership would be merely a transitional phase.

This outcome does not look very likely, however. At the very least, the UK would surely stay outside the single currency for the foreseeable future and perhaps for ever. Other 'outs' may stay out. In that case, the EU would have evolved into a two-tier membership.

To some extent, of course, this has already happened, with various countries outside the euro and some outside various other arrangements. Nevertheless, while the euro is restricted to a currency union alone, the significance of this split is limited. Once the euro members press on to full fiscal and political union, the split would become more and more significant. On the question of status, it looks as though the non-euro members would be second-class or at best 'country members' of the club. More importantly, unless some special arrangements were put in place, it might be possible for the eurozone members to make laws and regulations applying to the whole EU without the fringe members being able to prevent, or even influence, them.

It might just be possible for these arrangements to evolve in a way that satisfies eurosceptics in the UK and elsewhere. Suppose that those countries that lie outside the integration that is occurring within the eurozone receive cast-iron protection against the core EU imposing its will on the fringe. Suppose, also, that they negotiate the repatriation of powers and competences from the EU that I discussed above. In that case, their links to the eurozone would be much closer to a free trade association, without any political baggage. (Even so, unless exemption from the Single Market was negotiated, the 'outs' would still be subject to EU regulations, which I discuss further in the next chapter.)

Effectively, the eurozone would then have become an even more integrated EU, fulfilling the dreams of the founding fathers, and the outsiders would effectively, although not literally, have left it, but they would have retained the trade links that they wanted in the first place. From a sceptic's point of view, such a settlement seems quite attractive. It also does not seem so far-fetched.

There are, however, three difficulties with it as a scenario to solve the problem of bad governance and poor economic performance in the EU. First, although countries in the outer ring would get what they wanted, the majority of EU members would continue to be trapped in the existing EU, only with all the extra downsides of being within a full fiscal and political union. The factors I analysed in Chapters 2 and 3 making for poor governance would remain in place, but now magnified by the even closer union. Poor European economic performance would continue and the 'democratic deficit' would widen.

Second, it is highly doubtful that the leaders of the EU would countenance such an eventuality, not least because they would fear that other countries might favour the semi-detached status of the outer ring, thereby causing the whole structure to unravel. Moreover, they would surely fear that the 'outs', led by the UK, would launch just the sort of economic and tax competition that I referred to in Chapter 3 and would start to outperform.

Third, prosaically, but probably more importantly, such a development would effectively tear up the legal basis of the current EU and would require a new set of treaties, which would be a nightmare, if not downright impossible, to negotiate.

The political consequences of euro break-up

Let us now consider the implications for the EU of the opposite scenario; that is, a euro break-up. European leaders have been saying recently that if the euro fails, Europe fails. As a matter of economic logic, this is hogwash. The euro project was never necessary for the growth of European trade and prosperity. After all, several EU members, including the UK, have not been in the euro. Meanwhile, many countries in eastern Europe have continued to grow fast without being in the euro.

What has been the secret of the success of the Asian Tigers? It has certainly not been the adoption of a single currency or the pursuit of harmonization. As I consider in Chapter 10, while there has been some discussion of an Asian monetary union, the idea has never got off the ground. Meanwhile, these countries have concentrated on the real sources of economic growth, not some bureaucratic pipedream. And, as we all know, they have continued to do extremely well – unlike their European equivalents, imprisoned by the supposed benefits of the single currency.

Logically, the break-up of the euro should have no consequences for the EU. It should merely return it to the status quo ante, which should be perfectly viable. After all, a common currency is not needed to operate a free trade area, or even a single market.

However, that is just the logic. Clearly, politics is about something more than that – and sometimes everything but that. If the euro fails, this would deal such a blow to the integrationist cause in Europe that the EU probably would not be able to survive. The sceptics would have been vindicated and popular anger against the European elites would pour forth.

Moreover, in the process of euro disintegration, surely national animosities would have been fanned: the peripheral countries against the core for imposing such austere polices and not sharing in the burden of adjustment; the core against the peripheral countries for borrowing too much and perhaps not paying their debts to the core; Germany against France for slipping towards the peripherals and failing to endorse austerity; France against Germany for being so German.

Something like this seems to be the view of the European establishment. Addressing the Bundestag on 19 May 2010, Angela Merkel said: 'It is a question of survival. The euro is in danger. If the euro fails, then Europe fails. If we succeed, Europe will be stronger.'

In 2013, the significance of the euro for the survival of the EU received support from a highly respected member of the French establishment, Professor François Heisbourg, chairman of the International Institute for Strategic Studies (IISS). But he comes to completely the opposite conclusion to Angela Merkel. In his book, *La fin du rêve européen* (The end of the European dream), he says: 'The dream has given way to nightmare. We must face the reality that the EU itself is now threatened by the euro. The current efforts to save it are endangering the Union yet further.' He argues that European leaders have their priorities back to front and says that France and Germany should together plan a break-up of the euro in secret and implement it, with a return to national currencies, over a weekend, thereby saving the EU. Of course, merely ending the euro would not necessarily lead to fundamental reform and, as I argued in Chapter 6, would not be sufficient to end European economic under-performance. Moreover, for the reasons given above, it may not be possible to overcome the bad feeling created by a euro break-up.

Jacques Attali, former head of the European Bank for Reconstruction and Development, claimed in late 2013 that contractionary policies imposed in Europe by Germany were pushing France into a situation comparable with the position in Germany in 1933, when the

National Socialists took over. While this may or may not be an exaggeration, Jean-Pierre Chevenement, who once stood for the French presidency, has compared the present mood in France to 1934 and 1935 before the Gold Standard blew up. He says that unless Germany changes course, the southern European countries will have to withdraw from the euro to prevent their industries from being irreversibly hollowed out.

On a different note, although it is impossible to be sure what would come out of the chaos that would follow a break-up of the euro, as I have suggested in Chapter 4, I suspect that a complete return to national currencies would be unlikely (and undesirable). Germany could surely operate a successful monetary union with the Netherlands, Austria and Finland and it might find this congenial. It is not impossible that Denmark and Sweden might join such a union and even, depending on its conditions and its ambitions for statehood, Norway and Switzerland.

It would be possible for France to lead a Latin monetary union consisting of itself, Spain, Italy and Portugal. Perhaps Greece would join such a group, although it might go its own way (more on this in Chapter 10).

How ironic it would be if this unnecessary and dangerous integration, namely the euro, designed to unite Europe, ends up by casting it asunder. But then, as the thrust of this book should have made clear, bad decisions are baked into the nature of the EU.

If the failure of the euro does end up breaking the EU, perhaps we should regard this as happening, as Karl Marx would have said, as the inevitable result of the EU's own internal contradictions.

Lessons from the Scottish Referendum

With or without a break-up of the euro, the aftermath of the referendum on Scottish independence in September 2014 could also prompt radical change. The debate, both before and after the referendum, stimulated interest in the question of whether, if the UK voted to leave the EU, Scotland would remain part of the UK. In addition, there is a debate about whether the new constitutional settlement for the UK that seems to be evolving after the referendum offers a template for a new EU.

It has been well known for some time that on average Scottish voters are more favourably inclined towards the EU than are their equivalents in the rest of the UK. This may well be because they see the EU as a valuable counterweight to Westminster, but for some the feeling is more radical. If the UK voted to leave the EU, it is quite possible that the pressure for another referendum in Scotland would become irresistible and, as things stand, it is quite possible that if they had to choose, a majority of Scots would prefer the EU to the UK.

But such a strict choice is unlikely to be available. During the Referendum campaign in 2014, it became clear that the EU was not minded to give the Scots the assurance of EU membership. If it left the UK, and therefore the EU, Scotland would have to wait in the queue with other prospective new members – and with no guarantee of admittance. At the very least, Scotland would face an uncomfortable time as it found itself on its own, and by no means sure that it would be able to find a home and a protective umbrella any time soon.

What is more, the EU is unlikely to be bluffing, because it faces two other leading candidates for secession from

EU member states: Catalonia from Spain and the Veneto from Italy. At the very least, those two countries are likely to insist that the EU makes it difficult for Scotland so as to deter their own secessionists. If it comes to another referendum, this alone might be sufficient to deter Scots from voting to leave the UK.

Federalism unleashed

Something more radical – and potentially more positive – came out of the referendum. In the debates running up to the vote, all the Westminster parties promised Scotland a substantial degree of autonomy if it voted to stay in the UK. Steps are now being taken to put this pledge into effect. However, this has unleashed a hornets' nest of constitutional implications for the UK. In England, there is considerable resentment that, as things stand, while Scots will have the ability to decide their own affairs, their MPs will also be able to vote on matters that affect England.

This looks as though it is going to end up with one of two possible solutions: Scottish MPs are barred from voting in the House of Commons on purely English issues; or the formation of a separate English Parliament, or even several regional Parliaments, with the Westminster Parliament responsible only for such matters that affect the UK as a whole, such as defence, foreign affairs and the environment.

It is far too early to tell how this issue is going to pan out, but the second possibility could be seen as offering a template for how the EU should evolve; that is to say, allowing considerable autonomy to its constituent parts, with institutions at federal level concentrating on the matters that genuinely apply at that level.

This is what the principle of subsidiarity is supposed to secure. But, as I pointed out in Chapter 3, this runs completely counter to the EU's current ethos, which is all about the drive towards central control and harmonization. Accordingly, whatever EU leaders might say about subsidiarity, in practice the EU is run on principles directly counter to it.

Suppose, though, that the EU did turn itself into a federal state, along the lines of the possible solution for the UK outlined above. In this case, would the existing member states of the Union retain any useful role at all?

The end of nation states?

Take the UK case as an example. Scotland, Wales and Northern Ireland already have their own devolved administrations. Now suppose that England is divided into a series of regions with their own administrations, of which London would surely be one. And suppose, also, that defence, foreign affairs and the environment had been transferred to the EU level. What, precisely, would be left as the area of competence of the UK parliament and the UK government? Indeed, what exactly would be the point of the UK itself? It is not difficult to imagine it dissolving altogether.

Similar things could happen in other countries: with the regions of Italy separating and the country again coming to resemble the patchwork of small states shown in Figure 5.1; with the regions of Germany separating, perhaps along lines similar to the separate states that existed prior to German unification in 1870; the Spanish regions of Catalonia, Andalucía, Galicia and the Basque Country separating from Castile; and Belgium splitting between the Flemish-speaking north and the French-speaking south, as mentioned earlier.

At first sight, France might seem likely to resist break-up, as it has been a unified state for hundreds of years and, superficially at least, it seems united. But there are separatist movements in Corsica, Brittany and the French Basque Country. It might not be too fanciful to see Normandy as a separate mini-state under the European umbrella. Meanwhile, the Alpine country of the south-east might unite with north-west Italy, renewing ancient associations that existed under the Duchy of Savoy.

Other countries might undergo similar separations. And perhaps there could even be the re-emergence of European city states. I have already mentioned London as a possible candidate, but there are others: Berlin, Munich, Paris, Madrid, Rome, Milan, Venice and many more.

Whether this sounds like a nightmare or a dream come true depends, I suppose, on where you stand on the great questions of identity that underlie the issues discussed in this book. For those who feel thoroughly European, it may sound like an appealing prospect. And for many people who feel primary allegiance to a region rather than a country, as is true in much of Italy, it could also seem tempting. It will be anathema, of course, to all those who believe in the nation state, or at least in their nation state, or, in the case of the UK, in their four-nation state.

Like it or not, though, this is not a ridiculous vision. The prospect of regions and cities flourishing as autonomous entities within an overarching, common European umbrella corresponds to the vision of so many of Europe's leaders, as discussed in Chapter 1. What it amounts to is a reversal of the last few hundred years of European history – or much less in the case of the new 'nation' states of

Germany and Italy that were only formed in the second half of the nineteenth century.

An idea whose time has passed?

Indeed, many of the countries of eastern Europe, including several states that are already in the EU and a few that are in the queue to join, have had even shorter histories as independent nation states. For some, their heritage is as part of the Russian empire. For others, it is as part of the polyglot Austro-Hungarian Empire. And the same goes, of course, for Austria and Hungary themselves.

So a federal Europe without nation states is not completely out of the question. Yet I sense that the moment has passed, as political support for any form of federalism has faded. And this radical form would, of course, involve a complete recasting of all EU arrangements and all EU treaties, which, after all, are between member states. As things stand, this seems impossible.

Moreover, at the more prosaic level of their everyday lives, European people have to confront the reality of the EU's economic failure. This hardly seems to be the time to go for broke on 'more Europe', to the point of dissolving nation states, both ancient and modern. Indeed, while the EU's greatest creation, the euro, is in danger of breaking up, the EU itself is in a fight for survival.

The effect of a British departure on the EU

In the previous chapter and earlier in this one, I touched on the subject of possible British withdrawal from the EU. In the next chapter I will examine the pros and cons of such a departure for the UK. But there is another, related issue that needs to be discussed here, namely how the EU would be affected if a single large member withdrew. Would this further or retard the forces making for reform? Could it precipitate the break-up of the EU? Any country could decide to leave the Union, but why beat about the bush? The UK is the most likely to do so. So, in what follows, the UK is the example I take. Nevertheless, most of the analysis would apply to other countries that might consider leaving. In the next chapter, although I concentrate on the prospect of a UK withdrawal, I also briefly consider the case of the Netherlands.

The implications of a withdrawal from the EU would be considerable. The UK's withdrawal would represent the loss to the EU of about 15% of its economy, nearly 12.5% of its population and almost 20% of its exports (excluding intra-EU trade). Moreover, at the very least, there would have to be extensive negotiations within the remaining EU about changing its institutions, quotas, budgets and voting procedures.

Admittedly, in 2014 the UK's net contribution to the EU budget amounted to less than 0.1% of the Union's combined GDP. It should be possible for the EU to cope with the loss of such a comparatively small amount. Nevertheless, the enforced reallocation of several billion euros between other member states would cause acrimonious discussions between them about their relative contributions. Indeed, this could precipitate a wholesale review of the EU's expenditure and funding arrangements.

There would also need to be an adjustment within the European Council to reflect the disappearance of the UK's 29 votes; and within the European Parliament as Britain's 73 seats disappeared, or were reallocated. Similar issues would arise in relation to the loss of Britain's European

Commissioner, the departure of British judges from the European Court of Justice and quotas regarding the employment of Britons or British representatives on various EU bodies. All of these changes could perhaps be accomplished easily, but would be more likely to result in wrangling, which could easily lead on to calls for fundamental reform of the institutions.

A British departure would also affect the political balance and predispositions of the remaining Union. Some fear that the withdrawal of one of the EU's most liberal members, and one of its strongest supporters of markets, could push the EU in the direction of greater regulation and protectionism. This is a fear most frequently expressed by businesspeople and politicians in countries that tend to agree with Britain on such issues; that is, Denmark, Sweden and the Netherlands.

Sweden's *Aftonbladet* newspaper made it clear that a British exit would be 'to Britain, Europe and Sweden's disadvantage'. It explained:

> *For the Swedish part, we would lose an important partner in the EU, we are close to the UK on many issues and it would be unfortunate for the Swedish political interests. The EU as a whole is losing a strong and important State. As the UK is one of the three heavy-weight countries in the EU, the whole Union would be hit hard by an exit. With Britain outside the EU would be a weaker Europe. It brings economic strength, military reach and credibility in international politics.*

On the other side of the account, some observers argue that since the UK is the EU's most awkward member, its departure would make the Union easier to manage and easier to drive towards closer integration. Mind you, Britain's decision not to join the euro did not obviously allow the management of the currency to be a major success.

There is also the risk that a UK departure could make it more difficult to keep the rest of the EU together – particularly if the UK appeared to have obtained a good deal and seemed to be doing well outside, while the remaining EU, now without British influence, moved in the direction of more regulation, integration and/or protectionism. The chances of this happening would be all the greater if the financial and political issues unleashed by Britain's departure, as discussed above, led to acrimonious disputes between remaining members.

This is clearly on the mind of leading European politicians. Swedish Foreign Minister Carl Bildt has said: 'Flexibility sounds fine, but if you open up to a 28-speed Europe, at the end of the day there is no Europe at all. Just a mess.' This also seems to be the view of another Foreign Minister, Germany's Guido Westerwelle: 'Germany wants the United Kingdom to remain an active and constructive part of the European Union ... But cherry picking is not an option. Europe isn't the sum of national interests but a community with a common fate in difficult times.'

It would be deeply ironic if, having been a semidetached member of the EU for some time, the UK managed to prompt its dissolution by leaving it.

Splitting hairs?

So I have argued that although public concern about immigration and/or any one of three plausible events

– fiscal and political union for the eurozone, a break-up of the euro and the UK leaving the EU – could precipitate fundamental reforms that enabled the EU to continue, in practice any of these would be more likely to precipitate the break-up of the EU.

Yet on paper anyway, there may be only a thin line between what a suitably reformed EU would be like – cut down to size, renationalized, limited and properly controlled democratically – and the arrangements for European cooperation that might emerge if the current members of the EU started from a blank sheet of paper without the Union. In the first case, there would still be an entity called the EU, but it would look and behave as a radically different institution. In the second, there would not be an institution called the EU, but there would be some form of cooperation and integration to which the EU already subscribes – or aspires.

Provided that we ended up in the same place, analytically, which of these two ways it happened would make no difference. In this sense, the innocent observer could say that, in principle, he was indifferent between the objectives of reform and dissolution.

In practice, though, there are some real differences. On the negative side, dissolution carries some serious risks: that full cooperation on trade issues would not be forthcoming, for instance, or that it would be impossible to construct the suitable institutions for European cooperation on subjects like the environment or security.

Equally, given what I have written here about the inherent nature of the European Union and both the self-interest and the ideology of EU elites, gaining agreement on radical reform is going to be extremely difficult. A clean sheet of paper has a stronger appeal.

This argues, it seems to me, that those countries, like the UK, that want a radically reformed EU should start off by trying to secure this reform, but then not be surprised if they fail. In that case, the exit would beckon. The same goes for any widespread attempt across the EU to press for reform.

Of course, any country contemplating leaving the EU would need to assess a whole raft of possible costs and benefits. How these stack up is the subject of the next chapter.

9

The Costs and Benefits of Leaving the EU

For the EU, Britain's exit would be a heavy blow, but for the British it would be a real disaster...
　　　　　—Joschka Fischer, former German Foreign Minister

There is no definitive study of the economic impact of the UK's EU membership, or equivalently, the costs and benefits of withdrawal. Framing the aggregate impact in terms of a single number, or even irrefutably demonstrating that the net effects are positive or negative, is a formidably difficult exercise.
—Daniel Harari and Gavin Thompson, *The Economic Impact of EU Membership on the UK*, 2013

My analysis so far has centred on three broad scenarios: the EU sails on, much as at present; it continues but on a much reformed basis; or it disintegrates. Yet there is a fourth scenario, referred to in the last chapter, which needs to be considered now in detail: the EU continues but an individual country decides to leave. How should such a country weigh up the pros and cons of exiting?

I start by considering how a country might leave, since this affects the possible outcomes. For the sake of simplicity, as well as verisimilitude, I assume that this country is the UK, although similar considerations would be relevant for other countries. I then discuss several key issues bearing on whether the UK would be a net gainer by leaving: the EU membership fee; the Common Agricultural Policy; trade relationships and the various options that the UK would face; the Single Market; the position of car manufacturers; the possible reaction of foreign-owned firms with operations in the UK; the interests of the City of London; and the implications for jobs. I conclude with an overall assessment.

How a country could leave the EU

It is often suggested that the withdrawal of a member state from the EU would be both unprecedented and unthinkable. In fact, Algeria withdrew in 1962 and Greenland in 1985. This prompted concerns that they set precedents for other withdrawals, but since both countries were overseas territories, they provided no real guide to how a full member might withdraw.

Indeed, no EU treaty mentioned the idea of a member state voluntarily withdrawing from the EU, or its predecessor organizations, before this appeared in the draft European Constitution. Yet under international law it has always been possible for a country to withdraw, if it wished. This had, after all, been the subject of the referendum Britain held in 1975, which no other member state contested; and there is nothing to stop the UK from unilaterally withdrawing now. It would involve parliament repealing the 1972 European Communities Act and under Article 20 of the Lisbon Treaty the EU is bound to accept a country's withdrawal.

While withdrawal would be legal and would represent the assertion that London's parliament was sovereign, in practice this would not be the end of the matter. If it withdrew from the EU, the UK would still have to abide by many of the obligations it has entered into with the Union. More importantly, the complexity of economic, political and legal relationships means that the UK would have to work with the EU to negotiate, and subsequently manage, the implications of a withdrawal.

How the UK could successfully withdraw and what would have to be done to achieve this is a large subject in itself. However, I do not think these matters need detain the reader of this book very long. Suffice it to say that a fully legal withdrawal could be accomplished. It is now time to look at the various costs and benefits to see whether such a withdrawal would make good sense.

The EU membership fee

The most basic cost of EU membership is, of course, the contribution to the EU budget. One might readily imagine that this is a non-controversial matter, but in fact it is not quite so straightforward.

In 2014, the UK government's payments to EU institutions amounted to just over £19 billion.[21] However, the government received a rebate on its contributions to the EU budget of just under £5 billion, making its net payment just over £14 billion. The UK public sector also received from the EU about £4.5 billion in various sorts of disbursements, making the overall figure just short of £10 billion, amounting to about 0.6% of nominal GDP.

Over and above these amounts flowing to and from the public sector, there are also various payments to and from the UK's private sector.

For some purposes it is appropriate to look at the gross cost to the government; in some cases the net cost to the government; in others, the gross or net cost to the UK as a whole. The key point is that although, whichever definitions you take, the sums are not tiny (and they are tending to rise), neither are they gargantuan. Moreover, the UK might discover that, rather like Norway and Switzerland (see below), even outside the EU, depending on the exact nature of its arrangements, it might be obliged to make some contribution to EU funds.

The UK's contribution to the EU budget is a subject of great interest in the UK media, who typically refer to the gross, rather than the net, figure. I do not wish to downplay the importance of the budget contribution: due account must be taken of it in any assessment of costs and benefits. Nevertheless, these are not the sort of sums on which the fate of great nations depends – nor on which momentous decisions about EU membership should be made.

The Common Agricultural Policy

A related topic that figures large in the UK media is the cost of the Common Agricultural Policy (CAP). The CAP provides subsidies to European farmers and keeps the prices of agricultural products artificially high. As a net importer of such goods, the UK ends up as a net loser and its consumers pay more for food than they would if the UK were able to buy food freely on world markets.

Care is needed here to avoid double counting. To the extent that CAP spending is paid for out of the EU budget, it is already included in the estimates made above. It is only any further economic losses caused by the distortions to behaviour brought about by the CAP that should be added to the cost of EU budgetary contributions.

Estimates of the cost of the CAP have varied widely over the years, with the figures generally falling over time, at least when expressed as a share of GDP. Estimates by the OECD in 1993 seemed to imply a total cost to the UK from the CAP of 4% of GDP, including government transfers. A more up-to-date study by Open Europe, published in 2012, put the cost at about 1.1% of GDP, again including the fiscal costs.

The non-fiscal costs incurred as a result of resource misallocation, resulting from the EU's subsidies to domestic producers and its tariffs on agricultural imports, total about 0.5% of GDP, slightly less than the cost of the UK's net budgetary contribution to the EU. This would mean that the CAP costs were substantial, but far from overwhelming. Compared to the years immediately before and after the UK's entry to the EU in 1973, when food prices figured large in the debate, the CAP has faded in relative importance.

Media attention is drawn to issues like the budget contributions and the cost of the CAP partly because to the ordinary person they can seem so large (in return for so little), but partly also because they are – or at least appear to be – readily quantifiable. Yet, as so often in economics, the easily quantifiable bit is likely to be the minor part of the equation. It is the elements over which there is much uncertainty, and on which judgement must be exercised, that are likely to prove the most important.

Trade relationships

The most significant of these uncertain elements is the UK's trade relationship with the EU and, linked to this, the outlook for employment and prosperity. This has a general aspect and some specific issues that need to be considered separately. First of all, I discuss general trade issues, including the UK's various options for trading relationships with the EU.

Even when it comes to the bare facts about the extent of trade with the EU, there is considerable scope for misunderstanding. Just over 50% of the UK's exports of goods go to other EU members and over 57% to the whole of Europe. Sometimes these figures are given undue prominence. However, as well as goods, the UK is also a large exporter of *services* and the appropriate numbers to consider are the ones involving goods *and* services. Looking at goods and services combined, the UK exports over 30% of its GDP. Of that, about 45% is exported to the EU, or roughly 14% of GDP. The UK also earns considerable amounts of money from overseas investments. If these are included along with exports of goods and services, then the proportion of total receipts from abroad coming from the EU is just over 40%.

In fact, there is controversy about how far even these figures give an accurate picture. There is a good deal of economic activity that is dependent on these exports to the EU, and a very large number of jobs, an issue to which I will turn in a moment. So it is possible to argue that a larger proportion of GDP is directly or indirectly dependent on trade with the EU. Mind you, once you start to deal in indirect linkages, you are really standing on very slippery ground. After all, the more than 50% of exports that is not accounted for by exports to the EU will also have indirect connections with other parts of the UK's GDP.

Moreover, there is an adjustment to be made in the other direction. A large proportion of the UK's exports that pass through the ports of Antwerp and Rotterdam, and are therefore counted as exports to the EU, are in fact bound for re-export to countries outside the EU. In addition, there is the so-called Netherlands Distortion, arising from the practice of UK companies, for tax reasons, channelling the income on investment abroad through 'brassplate' holding companies domiciled in other countries, including the Netherlands Antilles, income that is recorded in the UK national accounts as originating in the Netherlands. There is a similar distortion involving Luxembourg. Some estimates of these distortions put their combined extent at as large as 5% of GDP.[22]

Even taking account of these effects, though, there is no doubt that the UK's trade with the rest of the EU is enormous. How this would fare if the UK were to withdraw is a supremely important issue. Accordingly, in what follows, I operate with the figures as officially recorded. Nevertheless, the reader should bear in mind the likelihood that they exaggerate the true importance of the EU in British trade.

Is there life after departure?

It is wrong to presume that all British exports to the EU would cease as soon as the UK left the Union. A good proportion would continue, pretty much come what may. Exactly what would happen depends on what sort of trade relations were agreed. We cannot be sure of the answer, but we can get quite some way by focusing on considerations of self-interest and the structure of existing international arrangements. One thing is clear, though: there would be enormous advantages for both sides in continuing a very close commercial relationship. And that is the most likely outcome.

The UK is in a strong position to negotiate. It is a huge market for many continental firms. Indeed, it is not widely realized that the UK is the rest of the EU's largest single export market, larger even than the US. For many continental firms that will mean their largest market full stop. The Italian firm Ferrari, for instance, recently announced that the UK had become its biggest market.

Moreover, the rest of the EU's trade balance with the UK is decidedly positive; that is, it exports more to the UK than the UK exports to the rest of the EU. (Note, though, that this does not mean than the UK 'makes a loss' on its trade with the EU. The extent of the gain from trading relationships is complex, but it includes being able to import from abroad more cheaply than you can make things yourself. In addition, there is no need or even benefit in having balanced trade with each and every trading partner.)

So, after a UK departure from the EU, umpteen European firms, including German car manufacturers BMW and Mercedes, would be desperate to maintain free and open trading links with the UK. (I will discuss car manufacturing and the special factors affecting foreign-owned businesses in the UK in a moment.) They would lobby their governments and the EU accordingly. Indeed, because the UK's trade relations with the EU are so close and extensive, it might be possible for Britain to negotiate an especially favourable trading relationship.

There are umpteen conceivable sets of arrangements that could qualify, with sometimes only minor differences between them. However, if we take remaining in the EU as currently constituted as Option 1, there are six other major options, depicted in Table 9.1. I have tried to put the options in descending order of closeness to full EU membership, although the distinctions between the different options are not always neat. (Note that this table refers only to the sorts of arrangements governing trade between a departing country and the remaining EU. What options might exist concerning wider global trade, and what arrangements might be possible for the countries of Europe if the EU were to break up, are discussed in Chapter 10.)

Option 2 is to try to negotiate something similar to Norway's arrangements. Norway is not a member of the EU, but it is a member of the European Economic Area (EEA) and thereby is a member of the Single Market, the importance of which I discuss in a moment. Mind you, Norway's access to the EU market is subject to the implementation of the EU's Rules of Origin. For example, if a car is imported from China to Norway and then exported to an EU country, it would be subject to duty. However, the advantage of the EEA for Norway is that it is outside the CAP, the EU fishing rules and the EU-wide regional policy.

Option 4 – I will come to Option 3 in a moment – is to try to replicate the arrangements that Switzerland enjoys with the EU. Switzerland also misses out on those three EU 'benefits'. In fact, it belongs to neither the EU nor the EEA, but maintains close relationships with the EU through a series of bilateral agreements, which give it tariff-free – and hassle-free – access to the Single Market for its goods exports. These agreements do not cover services, including financial services.

Appearance and reality

These arrangements for Norway and Switzerland should not be taken simply at face value. In practice, although both countries are outside the EU, they are closely

Table 9.1   The UK's options for trading relationships with the EU

	ACCESS TO SINGLE MARKET	NON-EU TRADE
1 **EU** Full EU membership	Full access via the customs union. Additional 'four freedoms': labour, capital, goods and services	Conducted under the EU's Common Commercial Policy (CCP) and EU FTAs
2 **EEA** Nearly but not quite an EU member; the 'Norwegian option'	Full access via EEA agreement subject to rules of origin (ROO). Four freedoms	Conducted under EFTAs, FTAs or separate bilateral agreements
3 **EEA Lite** Midway between the Norwegian and Swiss options	Full access for goods exported to the EU but Single Market rules not applied to rest of economy	Same as EEA
4 **Switzerland** A free trade agreement – a tailored bilateral deal	Access in most areas subject to ROO. Limited access in services. Free movement of labour, capital and goods	Conducted under EFTAs, FTAs or separate bilateral agreements
5 **Turkey** A stripped-back customs with the EU; the 'Turkish option'	Full access for goods. Agricultural products and services are not covered by the customs union, as customs unions only cover physical goods	Subject to the EU's CCP for industrial goods but not agricultural produce. Required to start FTA negotiations with any country that signs an EU FTA
6 **Free Trade Agreement** (FTA); the 'Bootle' option	No tariffs applied but not part of the Single Market. Free movement of goods but not labour	No restraints on EU trade
7 **The 'American' option** Sometimes referred to as the 'WTO-only option'; no special arrangements	EU members treated the same as any other country, but EU tariffs applied to exports to the EU	No restraints on EU trade

Source: Adapted from S. Booth & C. Howarth (2012) *Trading Places: Is EU Membership Still the Best Option for UK Trade?* London: Open Europe. Permission is gratefully acknowledged.

SOCIAL AND EMPLOYMENT LEGISLATION	PRODUCT REGULATIONS	EU BUDGET CONTRIBUTIONS	CAP, CFP AND REGULATORY POLICY	SOVEREIGNTY
All	All	Yes	Yes	Ability to influence and vote (or be outvoted)
All	All	Contribution for areas of participation on a % of GDP basis + voluntary contribution to EEA fund	No	Limited influence and no votes. Regulations legally enforceable
None	Only affecting exports to the EU	Voluntary contribution	No	Limited influence and no votes
None	All voluntary	'Voluntary' contribution to Swiss development fund and EU infrastructure	No	Bilateral adoption of regulations
None	All	No	No	Product regulations apply. Limited scope to influence CCP in goods
None	EU regulations only for exports to the EU	No	No	Full sovereignty but no influence on the EU
None	EU regulations only for exports to the EU	No	No	Full sovereignty but no influence on the EU

intertwined with it and both make some budgetary contribution to the EU.

Moreover, there is considerable dissatisfaction with their arrangements. In the case of Norway, the dissatisfaction is mainly on the Norwegian side, as it is obliged to accept EU legislation and regulation but has no say in them, an arrangement that has been described as 'government by fax from Brussels'. Actually, this widely quoted phrase is rather misleading. Quite apart from the extraordinarily old-fashioned reference to fax machines, the fact is that Norway does not have to adopt all EU legislation. In 2004, the Norwegian government said that of the pieces of EU legislation enacted between 1997 and 2003, it had adopted 18.5% of them.

Switzerland is not bound to accept EU rules, but in practice it does accept a good deal. One notable advantage of the Swiss arrangements, though, is that Switzerland is free to conduct its own trade policy with countries outside the EU. Indeed, Switzerland has recently negotiated a free trade agreement with China. The EU is trying to negotiate an agreement and if it secures one, then the UK, as a member of the EU, would benefit (more on this in Chapter 10). But, crucially, while it is a member of the EU, the UK is not able to negotiate its own free trade agreement with China, or any other country.

However, the Swiss arrangements have caused increasing irritation in Brussels. Effectively the EU would like the Swiss to accept something like the Norwegian arrangements, which would be accomplished by Switzerland joining the EEA, although this was rejected by the Swiss people in a referendum 20 years ago.

Option 3 corresponds to the suggestion put forward by Conservative MEP David Campbell Bannerman in his book *Time to Jump*. He names this option EEA Lite. It stands midway between the Swiss and Norwegian arrangements. Under this set-up, the UK would belong to the EEA but would leave the Single Market. It would have to apply Single Market rules in the production of goods exported to the EU, but not in the overwhelmingly larger part of the economy not consisting of exports to the EU. The UK would be able to repeal existing EU legislation and would no longer be required to enact new EU legislation. It would also operate Swiss-style immigration controls, which differentiate between citizens of different EU member countries and put a cap on the number of citizens from specific countries allowed in during a specified period.

This EEA Lite proposal would undoubtedly appeal to many British eurosceptics, but is it feasible? Bearing in mind the EU's dissatisfaction with the Swiss position, it is far from clear that the EU would ever agree to EEA Lite for the UK.

Option 5 is to replicate Turkey's set-up with the EU. The Turkish option is effectively a form of stripped-back customs union with the EU, which gives full access for goods, but not agricultural products or services. The disadvantage of these arrangements is that Turkey is still subject to EU regulations over non-EU trade and it has limited scope to influence the EU in these or any other matters. The advantages are that Turkey has no budget contributions to make and it is not subject to EU social and employment legislation.

Other options

Option 6 for the UK is to negotiate a free trade agreement (FTA) with the EU without all the bells and whistles of the Swiss arrangements. In particular, although goods would be traded freely between the UK and the EU, there would be no freedom of movement of labour. This would put the UK on the same footing as other countries that have FTAs with the EU. There is a huge number of these, including South Africa, Columbia, Peru, Morocco, Israel and South Korea. Indeed, the EU is negotiating a whole lot more, including agreements with the US, India and Japan.

These arrangements would be attractive from a UK perspective and the chances of securing an FTA would be very high. After all, pretty soon the whole world will have some sort of FTA with the EU. The chances of the UK, the EU's largest export market, not being able to secure one are small. Even so, it would not be wise for the UK to assume that it would be bound to obtain an attractive deal. Indeed, partly *pour décourager les autres*, the EU might be uncooperative.

So, even though the chances of this being realized may be remote, it would be well to consider the ultimate downside; namely, that the UK has no special arrangements with the EU (presumably because these cannot be negotiated on acceptable terms). This is Option 7 in Table 9.1. While it may sound disastrous, it would not be. It would place the UK in the same position that the US is currently in, along with India, China and Japan, all of which manage to export to the EU relatively easily.

This option is sometimes referred to as the 'WTO only' option, indicating that the only protection against discriminatory trade practices would be the World Trade Organization. But I have called this the 'American' option, indicating that it would place the UK in the same position as the US is currently. Mind you, if the US manages to negotiate an FTA with the EU, then it would move up from Option 7 to Option 6.

The 'American' option would mean, however, that British exports to the EU would face the common external tariff. In fact, this should hold no terrors for us. The EU's average tariff is about 5%. If they were obliged to pay this, it would cost British businesses about £7bn per annum – a substantial sum, but not overwhelming. Indeed this potential loss has already been more than offset by the effects of the fall of the pound caused by Brexit fears.

Some UK businesses worry that, quite apart from the tariff wall, EU members might seek to discriminate against imports from the UK. In fact, such discrimination would be illegal under the provisions of the WTO – although that would not necessarily stop it. After all, relying on the WTO presumes that it survives and continues to be effective. (I take up this subject in Chapter 10.)

In fact, the important differentiator between these various options is not really the danger of facing the common external tariff, nor even the possibility of trade discrimination, but rather membership of the Single Market. For the EU is not simply a free trade area or a customs union. The Single Market combines tariff-free access with a series of common regulations imposed equally across its membership. How attractive the various trade options are depends to a considerable degree on how important membership of the Single Market is.

The Single Market

Access to the Single Market dominates debate about trade relations. Ironically, it was two British Commissioners who developed and pushed through the Single Market idea and made it a reality. The driving force was the desire to reduce regulatory obstructions to trade. In some ways it has been a great success. The Single Market now unites 28 countries into the world's largest integrated trading bloc, with a combined GDP of some €12 trillion.

The point is that by being within the Single Market and meeting all its regulatory requirements and standards, British exports enter continental markets on an equal footing with goods produced there. If Britain were outside the Single Market and thereby able to apply different regulations and standards, the danger is that manufacturers would have to use two sets of labelling and packaging – or, in the worst case, two manufacturing processes. The downside of belonging, though, is that since the original vision of a Single Market with a common, minimal level of regulation, in practice regulation has grown like Topsy – and it is applied across the whole economy.

Wise heads and craggy diplomats, lofty businessmen and grizzled politicians all nod sagely in agreement when someone suggests that it is vital that the UK remains part of the Single Market. Yet this is not the open-and-shut case that it is often made out to be.

A misleading comparison

When supporters of the EU speak of the possibility that the UK will leave the EU, they often talk about it 'turning its back on', or even 'being shut out' of, the Single Market. This sounds, and is meant to sound, pretty apocalyptic. With such a large share (probably between 40 and 45%) of our exports going to the EU, it holds out the threat of some sort of economic disaster.

The image seems to be of some internal space where the Single Market is located and within which it does its business. Perhaps we can imagine a hall that is the centre for the trading of financial securities, just like Stock Exchanges past and present – or perhaps one of those grand buildings in old market towns that served as the Corn Exchange. Entry to this trading space is secured by a door. Leaving the EU amounts to closing the door – or having it slammed shut – behind you, and thereby losing access to the market.

Admittedly, some commentators seem to envisage the possibility of a halfway house because they talk of departure as removing or closing 'full access' to the Single Market. The image seems to be one in which non-members are allowed into part of the space, but not all of it, or perhaps allowed into all of it but only for some of the time, maybe Mondays and Tuesdays only, or every day but only between the hours of 11 am and 3 pm.

This image is completely misleading. Every country in the world has access to this room. It is merely that non-members may have to pay some sort of entrance fee at the door (the common external tariff) and in order to offer goods for sale inside this trading hall, they have to comply with all the conditions and standards laid down under the rules of the Exchange. But that is all: no locked doors, no limited hours of access. As to having to obey all the rules and standards of the Single Market, this is exactly what exporters have to do when they sell into any other market around the world. When Britain exports to America, it has to obey American rules and meet American standards, and similarly if it exports to China or Australia. The difference is that the UK does not have to apply American, Chinese or Australian rules and standards to the whole economy.

And it is perfectly feasible to export into the Single Market without being a member of it. After all, the United States, China, Japan, India and a host of other countries manage to export successfully to the EU without being part of the Single Market. As I mentioned above, they are all trying to get an FTA with the EU (i.e. Option 6), but this does not involve belonging to the Single Market. So why is it so essential for the UK to be part of it?

Confronting the evidence

Although it might be perfectly possible to sell into the Single Market from outside it, there must be a presumption that this would put a country at a disadvantage compared with being inside it. This might be a reasonable presumption, but the evidence does not offer much support for it. From the UK's entry into the EU in 1973 until 2012, the proportion of its goods exports going to the EU14 (that is, all the other EU members, apart from the UK, except those who joined in the expansions of 2004, 2007 and 2013) *fell*, from 64% to 62%. About a quarter of this drop occurred during the period of the Single Market, which commenced in 1993.[23] Interestingly, in the period from 1960 to 1972, when the UK was outside what we now call the EU, the proportion of British goods exports going to the EU14 rose by 12%.

Moreover, the evidence suggests that many countries outside the Single Market have done better at exporting to it than the UK has, even though the UK is on the inside. Over the first 19 years of the Single Market, from 1993 to 2011, in a league table of the 35 fastest-growing exporters to the 11 (other) founder members of the Single Market, the UK comes in at number 28, just below Egypt.

As regards the growth of goods exports between members, over the first 19 years of the Single Market's existence, the weighted mean is an increase of 92%. Over this period the equivalent figure for Norway and Switzerland was 114%, while for the US, Canada, New Zealand and Australia the figures were 126%, 142%, 147% and 243%.

Now, of course, the EU is the single biggest market for the UK's exports, but it has to be recognized that, for all the supposed advantages of being inside the Single Market, the growth of the UK's exports to it has been pitifully low compared to exports to other parts of the world. Over the period 1993 to 2011, the percentage growth of UK exports to the EU11 (the other original Single Market member countries) was only 81%, putting the EU 26th in a list of the top 33 fastest-growing markets for UK exports. The growth rates for exports to Australia, India, the United Arab Emirates and Russia were 159%, 269%, 413% and 508%. The top of this table was Qatar at 16,141% (from a very low starting level).[24]

None of the above numerical comparisons makes a conclusive case. In particular, any analysis suffers from the bane of the economist's life, namely the absence of a 'counter-factual'. That is to say, we do not know what these figures for the UK would have been like if it had been outside the Single Market. It is possible that UK exports to the Single Market countries would have been even weaker than they turned out to be in practice. But at the very least, these figures cast serious doubt on the thesis that for the UK, membership of the Single Market is absolutely vital. Indeed, they suggest that the benefits of Single Market membership are probably rather small. The really important factor appears to be the overall health of an economy and its growth rate.

Taking account of the costs

Moreover, whatever advantages a country gains from being part of the Single Market have to be compared with the losses. The UK, or any other country that considered leaving the EU, would have to weigh up what it loses by being a member through having to apply the common external tariff to imports from outside the Union and, most importantly, what it loses from having to apply the rules of the Single Market, and other forms of EU regulation, to those parts of the economy that are not involved in trade with Europe. Even for an open economy like the UK, these parts of the economy overwhelm the parts involved in all trade, never mind trade with Europe.

As I pointed out above, roughly 14% of the UK's GDP is directly accounted for by exports to the EU. That means, of course, that some 86% is not accounted for by exports to the EU. (If one makes a reasonable allowance for the Rotterdam/Antwerp effect, the proportion of GDP not involved in exports to the EU might be as high as 90%.) In almost all western countries, the bulk of GDP and employment concerns the satisfaction of basic consumer wants and these are supplied within the domestic economy: the retail trade, utilities, entertainment, bars and restaurants, services such as dry cleaning and home repairs and maintenance. The list goes on and on.

Under current arrangements, such purely domestic activities are severely affected by various sorts of EU regulation. For instance, the number of hours doctors can work in the British National Health Service (along with all other workers in the economy) is proscribed by the European Working Time Directive, which came into force in the UK in 2009. It limits working hours to an average of 48 per week, measured over a reference period of 26 weeks, as well as imposing other obligations and limitations concerning rest and breaks.

The results for the NHS have been disastrous, since it has been customary for junior doctors to work very long hours and in the process to build up substantial experience quite quickly. The restrictions now imposed by the EU mean that there is a shortage of experienced doctors and accordingly a shortage of would-be consultants.

Moreover, when thinking about losses from being outside the Single Market, due recognition must be made of the fact that across much of the service sector, the Single Market does not work at all. This is particularly pertinent to the UK, as it is in this sector that much of its comparative advantage lies.

The free movement of people

There is another extremely important question that receives much attention in itself, but is seldom seen in the popular debate as part of the Single Market issue – the free movement of people, which I appraised in the last chapter. To the architects of the Single Market it was an article of faith that the free movement of people within the Union would be a clear gain. Of course, the Union was then much smaller and more homogeneous. To the people of western Europe, now experiencing uncontrolled, and uncontrollable, numbers of immigrants coming in from other member states, it has proved to be a burden on public services, housing provision, welfare provision – and the tolerance of the indigenous population.

To be acceptable to the electorates of western Europe, a reformed EU would have to include limits on the free movement of people within the Union. If it fails to impose limits on the movement of people, the simplest way for a single country to do this is to stand outside the Single Market and thereby retake control of national borders.

This issue acquired more immediate importance beginning in 2014 as temporary restrictions that the EU had imposed on the movement of people from Romania and Bulgaria expired. In the UK, this gave rise to fears that there would be a huge influx of migrants from these countries, thereby placing intolerable burdens on public services. These fears were heightened when it was suspected that Romania and Bulgaria were liberally issuing passports to migrants from Moldova and other non-EU member states, which would then give these people the right to free movement across the whole of the EU.

The car industry

Having reviewed these general considerations affecting trade relationships, it could be helpful to consider the position of two particular industries that are at the heart of deliberations about UK membership, the automotive industry and the financial services industry, starting with the former.

The automotive industry employs over 700,000 people in the UK and accounts for about 10% of total export volumes. The UK's car exports to the EU are heavily outweighed by its imports, whereas the reverse is true for trade with countries outside the EU. There are no British-owned volume car manufacturers. The bulk of UK production is accounted for by German, French, American and Japanese firms, so the possible effects of an EU withdrawal are closely connected with the attitude of foreign business owners, to which I will turn in a moment.

The UK's car industry is a success story, but the overall industry trends are dominated by global over-capacity in car production and its shift to the emerging markets, where costs are lower. Germany is the world's third largest car manufacturer, after China and Japan, followed by Korea, India, the US, Brazil, France, Spain, Russia, Mexico, Iran – and the UK, in 13th place.[25]

If the UK withdrew from the EU, there would clearly be massive industry pressure to forge an FTA with the EU. If that were not forthcoming, exports from the UK to the EU would face the EU's external tariff, which is currently 10% on cars and 5% on imported components. That is a significant barrier, although not insurmountable. It would have the same effect as a 10% rise in the exchange rate and could be counteracted by a 10% fall in the exchange rate. Currency movements of this magnitude are pretty common, certainly from one year to the next and sometimes over much shorter periods.

If the EU imposed the tariff, it would then be open to the UK to impose a similar tariff on car imports into the UK from the EU. Such tit-for-tat games are not to be recommended, but it should be emphasized that if the UK did respond in this way, the net effect on aggregate demand in the UK would probably be positive, since the UK imports more cars from the EU than it exports to the EU. Of course, the immediate effect on aggregate demand is not the be-all and end-all of the matter, not least because of the effect on foreign-owned firms' decisions about whether to continue operations in the UK.

Yet this effect on aggregate demand needs to be borne in mind when the leaders of the car industry wax lyrical about the huge dangers to their industry, and hence to the UK, from a UK withdrawal from the EU.

Foreign reaction

Given the predominance of foreign owners in UK car manufacturing, as well as in some other industries, their concerns deserve special consideration. In July 2013, the Japanese government sent a note to the UK Foreign Office warning that Japanese companies invest in the UK because they see it as a gateway to European markets and hinting that 130,000 British jobs could be at risk if the UK pulled out of the Union. The document said that there were about 1,300 Japanese firms with operations in Britain that could review their position if Britain did not continue to play a 'major role' in the EU.

As if to back up this view, in October 2013 Toshiyuki Shiya, Chief Operating Officer for Nissan, which employs 6,400 people at its plant in Sunderland in northeast England, said that it was 'very important' that the UK was a member of the EU. He also said that the threat of import tariffs imposed by the EU on British-made cars if the UK left the EU was an 'obstacle' for Nissan.

It is possible, indeed, that if the UK withdrew from the EU it could lose some FDI, including Japanese FDI already in place. Nevertheless, this remains unlikely. The idea behind the fear is that such investment in the UK is made because the UK is a member of the EU. It is true that Japanese firms have invested in the UK not primarily to supply the UK market, which is comparatively small, but rather to use the UK to supply the whole EU market.

Yet the UK's attractiveness for FDI is not solely about membership of the EU. There are several reasons why Japanese and other foreign-owned firms choose to locate operations in the UK. Tariff-free, and interference-free, access to the rest of the EU is only one of them. The UK's advantages include the English language, a legal system that can be relied on and trusted, a flexible workforce, a favourable cost structure, a welcoming social and political culture and global links.

Interestingly, the Japanese government and Japanese firms are not well known for making acute judgements on major European matters. In fact, they made much the same noises in the late 1990s and early 2000s about the UK not being in the euro. They turned out to be completely wrong.

As if to prove that concerns about EU withdrawal are not a uniquely Japanese phenomenon, in January 2014 Steve Odell, Chief Executive of Ford's manufacturing operations in Europe, the Middle East and Africa, said that if the UK left it would be 'cutting off its nose to spite its face' and that it would be calamitous for British jobs and businesses. (Ford employs nearly 15,000 people in the UK.)

To some extent, for Japanese, American and other exporters from the UK, matters depend on how much of a tariff barrier those exports would face. On current form the answer appears to be not a lot. The tariff regime described above is hardly onerous. Moreover, it is likely, as I argued above, that after it had left the Union the UK would enjoy some pretty favourable trade access deals with the rest of the EU that would mean that tariffs were not imposed.

In any case, even if the UK did not secure favourable access, this need not present an insuperable barrier.

After all, as I pointed out above, countries all round the world manage to export successfully into the EU without themselves being members of the EU. Incidentally, that includes a considerable volume of goods produced in Japan. These non-EU countries that manage to trade so successfully with the EU have no representatives on EU bodies, no seat at the Council of Ministers and no MEPs. Nor do they have to pay a penny towards the EU budget, nor impose EU regulations on the rest of their economies. (They do, of course, have to meet EU standards on those goods that are exported to the EU.)

Admittedly, it is possible that such rational considerations could prove wide of the mark. It is possible that, post exit, the EU could cut its nose off to spite its face and become extremely nasty in its dealings with the UK. And it is possible that, faced with such treatment, foreign operators in the UK might decide to downgrade their operations there. This danger must be weighed up against other factors in the balance of considerations.

Exaggerated importance?

Yet once again, the British establishment's typical assessment of the extreme importance of the FDI factor is at odds with the evidence. Interestingly, the Single Market as a whole has not been very successful at attracting FDI, compared to both non-EU European countries and countries outside Europe. And between 1993 and 2011, the rate of growth of the UK's stock of FDI was below the median of other Single Market founder members.[26]

But so what? The level of FDI a country receives is not an accurate indicator of the amount of benefit that accrues from it. It is possible to secure more FDI by offering more generous grants and other inducements for firms to locate operations in your country. But in that case, taxpayers' money is being used to subsidize such activity and resources are being drawn away from other sorts of activity. In general, economists think that such interference with the market is not a good idea. Why should FDI be any different? Only if the FDI makes a contribution to the economy over and above what can be captured by the participants in normal market dealings might such interference be justified.

There may well be such benefits through the spillover of enhanced skills and management practices into other parts of the host economy. But this is not inevitable. The case needs to be argued and assessed against the costs, not merely taken for granted.

Given that the UK pays for Single Market membership, directly through the UK budget contribution and indirectly through the cost of the EU's regulations imposed throughout the UK economy, if FDI comes to the UK only because of the UK's Single Market membership, then this FDI has indeed been heavily subsidized. Moreover, to the extent that such subsidy is justified by the benefits that FDI brings, then it might be possible to secure the FDI more cheaply by offering direct subsidies to attract it, funded out of the money saved by not being part of the Single Market.

The bias towards the filmable

FDI is an example of a well-known phenomenon in economics, namely the concentration of the benefits and hence their easy identification, versus the diffusion and opacity of the costs. Suppose that UK withdrawal of the UK from the EU caused a Japanese car manufacturer to close down operations in the UK. It would be easy to identify the losers, most notably all those workers in the Japanese company's UK plants. Television crews can be easily despatched to film the now deserted buildings and the closed-down or boarded-up local shops. Interviews can be held with now redundant car workers, and all those local businesses and their employees that were dependent on the now defunct plant.

Yet that only deals with a fraction of the issue. Workers let go by this car operation will be employed elsewhere. The land and buildings formerly occupied by this plant can be used by another enterprise. And the money saved by the UK's withdrawal could be used to bring benefits elsewhere.

But where exactly is *this* observable? How do you film substitution effects rippling through the economy? Who do you interview? Because of the impossibility of knowing exactly how an economy will adapt to the new opportunities and challenges presented by a business failure or withdrawal, there is a natural tendency to overestimate the importance of the business's survival.

FDI is a serious issue in the debate about EU membership, but I feel sure that its importance tends to be overestimated compared to other factors.

The EU and the City of London

At the opposite end of the spectrum from car manufacturing, a business operating predominantly with tangibles, and clearly, therefore, very much affected by tariffs, lies the financial services industry, which very much deals in intangibles, for which the tariff question is irrelevant. The industry is nevertheless heavily affected by EU regulations and matters of access to European markets. Moreover, just like the car manufacturers, many of the big businesses providing Britain's 'output' in this sector are foreign owned.

There is no doubt that how well the UK might do outside the EU is closely bound up with the fate of its financial services industry, which is often referred to as the City of London, or simply 'the City', even though not all British financial activity takes place there.[27] Hereafter, I will use 'the City' to refer to the whole of the UK's financial services industry, no matter where it is located. The City's interests are a powerful factor to put into the mix of considerations that should form the basis of a decision about whether to stay in, or leave, the EU.

As with so much else that forms the subject matter of this book, however, there is no certainty about magnitudes. It is not uncommon to hear estimates of the financial services industry's contribution to GDP as high as 8–10%. But these figures cover all financial services, including things like mortgages and domestic insurance, as well as the wholesale and international activities that are often bundled together as 'the City'. According to the City of London Corporation,[28] in 2012 the City's contribution to the UK's total national income (gross value added) was 3.7%. My suspicion is that the City is more important than the bare figures make it seem, because of the inter-linkages between City activities and others things that go on in London. Whatever the exact figure, it is clearly very important to get relations between the City and the EU right. But how?

Over the years, a running battle has been fought between the British government and the EU over various attempts to influence or control the City's practices and institutions. Recently this battle has intensified, as major changes to EU financial-sector legislation have been proposed in response to the global financial crisis. In particular, five measures are likely to have a large impact on the City: restrictions on the over-the-counter derivatives market; a ban on 'short selling'; the so-called Basel 3 agreement, which imposes tougher requirements for capital and liquidity; caps on bankers' bonuses; and the proposed financial transactions (Tobin) tax.

From the UK perspective, the danger of such measures is that they might lead to an exodus of business, key personnel and/or financial firms to other financial centres, such as New York and Hong Kong. In fact, although these changes may seem troublesome enough to many in the City, what should concern them more is what measures might be forthcoming in the future. This is the City's nightmare. After all, the story of the EU from the beginning has been that you accept one set of arrangements and then, bit by bit, you are bludgeoned into accepting something much more draconian – something that if you had been presented with in the beginning you would have found unacceptable. It is death by a thousand cuts.

The advantages and disadvantages of staying in

Probably the most serious issue arising from Brexit concerns so-called 'passporting rights'. These enable a financial institution with operations in one EU country to sell into all other EU members without having separate operations there.

A bank can sell from London throughout the EU, for instance, but by contrast, Swiss financial institutions cannot sell directly into the EU; they have to set up subsidiaries in an EU member country. In practice, foreign banks, both Swiss, American and from just about everywhere else, overwhelmingly choose London in which to locate and run their EU operations from. But if the UK left the EU, under the existing rules they would have to set up subsidiaries in a member country – as would British banks wanting to do business in the EU.

At the very least, therefore, British banks as well as foreign ones with operations here would face a substantial increase in costs, and would have to transfer a significant volume of business, together with the attendant jobs, from London to some other EU city, most likely Paris, Frankfurt, Luxembourg or Dublin. In the extreme, they might think that it wasn't worth having two European centres, one in and the other out of the EU. Given the requirement to have one inside the EU, they might plausibly move all their business away and close their London operations altogether, or maintain just a token presence.

How serious is this threat? The UK sells about £20 billion of financial services to the EU per annum and enjoys a surplus with it of about £16 billion. Without passporting rights, it is possible that UK financial services exports to the EU could fall by about half, or roughly £10 billion. This is a very large sum, but it is not overwhelming, being roughly equal to the UK's net contribution to the EU's budget. And not all of that £10 billion would be an outright loss. The resources used in producing that income – principally the skilled labour employed – would be released for employment elsewhere.

But would the loss be even as great as this? There is a spectrum of possible outcomes ranging from complete relocation from London at one end, to setting up a token brass-plate operation on the continent at the other. Where the outcome rests along this spectrum will probably vary between different parts of the financial sector, and will also depend upon the result of negotiations between the UK and the EU.

It seems likely that the fund management industry would not be greatly inconvenienced by the loss of passporting rights since most big fund managers already have established legal entities in other parts of the EU, usually Dublin or Luxembourg.

For banking activities, however, if the UK left, the EU would insist that in order to do business within the Union, banks would need to have a significant subsidiary operation located within it, with dedicated capital and substantial numbers of jobs. Nevertheless, that would still be compatible with a large amount of activity continuing to take place in London.

Indeed, several factors would encourage banks to keep as much as possible of their business in London. For a start, London has a huge web of support facilities, including legal and accountancy services that no other European city can match. Moreover, outside the EU, although the UK would not be a regulatory soft touch, it would be able to rescind various EU regulations and restrictions, including the bonus cap which limits bankers' bonuses to two times salary. When this was first introduced, banks complained vociferously about it and warned that it could lead to the loss of business and jobs outside the EU to Zurich, New York, Dubai or Singapore. Outside the EU, their London-based operations would be shot of it.

Equally, it has been easy to lure European bankers and other professionals to work in London, not only because of the entertainment and lifestyle attractions of this great global city, but also because of a favourable personal tax regime – particularly compared to France. And, more generally, it is widely recognised that financial services are not highly regarded in the EU. The proposed Financial Services Tax is currently stuck somewhere in the EU regulatory long grass. If it were to re-emerge, it could potentially deal a serious blow to financial services businesses. Given all this, would any self-interested investment bank transfer activities wholesale to Paris or Frankfurt? Surely their approach would be to transfer the bare minimum to comply with European regulations.

It is not even as though remaining in the EU means that the EU authorities will welcome and support the City's pre-eminence. Indeed, there is a clear desire on the part of some European officials to see the City cut down to size. In fact, the British government only recently managed to stop an attempt by the ECB to deny euro liquidity to euro clearing operations outside the euro-zone by winning a judgement at the European Court of Justice. The ECB's clear intention was to shift euro-denominated activity to the euro-zone.

The UK government managed to win this particular judgement, but it could not be guaranteed to win the next time such a move is contemplated. Of course, in his 'renegotiation', Mr Cameron has sought to protect the role of the City, but in view of the past record and the evident preferences of the EU authorities one can scarcely be confident that inside the EU the City's interests would be secure.

Looking to the longer term, despite its peculiarities and particular interests, the argument about the City falls within the same scope as all other industries. That is to say, over the long run the EU is going to fall in relative importance. In an ideal world the UK in general, and the City in particular, would not have to choose between doing business with the EU and the rest of the world. But if it comes to a choice, the most important market for the UK's financial services industry is going to be the rest of the world, for which it can surely be the global financial hub. It is essential that nothing prevents London from seizing that prize.

Remaining in the EU, with growing regulatory burdens and dislike for financial services, might well prevent it. Outside the EU, even if the City loses some European business, it can still fulfil that role. Gao Jian, Vice-Governor of the China Development Bank, seems to agree. In relation to the impact of Brexit on China's use of London, in April 2013 he said:

> *It may make a little difference but not much. The City's position as a global financial centre with close connections to Hong Kong would not change. Because of its infrastructure, because of its legal environment, because of its participation in the world, China will definitely use London as a financial hub for many international transactions.*

The EU and jobs

One of the chief arguments of those who are keen to maintain the status quo with regard to the EU is that a huge number of jobs is bound up with the continuation of the UK's membership of the EU, not just in the City but throughout the economy. In the UK, both the present Coalition government and the previous Labour government have said that 3.5 million jobs are linked directly and indirectly to the export of goods and services to the European Union. Several other sources have come up with similar figures.

It is true that very many jobs are connected with trade with the EU. As so often with economics, though, the issue is not the precise number – 3.5 million or 3.9, or 2.8 – but rather the concepts underlying the estimate. The number of jobs concerned with exports to the EU is not the same as the number of jobs that would disappear if EU membership were to end.

As I have argued above, there would be powerful incentives, on both sides, to ensure that considerable UK–EU trade continued after any break. More importantly, as I have argued throughout this book, the economic case for EU exit is that the gamut of economic consequences that flow from EU membership, including the ludicrously intrusive flood of regulations, harm economic growth and prosperity. If this is right, then outside the EU, the UK stands the chance of being more prosperous. More prosperity translates into more jobs – even if they are not exactly the same jobs that exist today.

The issue of trade and employment bedevils the lobbying by various business groups in favour of continued EU membership. Typically some grand, lavishly paid, corporate panjandrum, often bedecked with some gong or other and speaking as the chairman of this, that or some other business organization, opines to the effect that EU membership is vital to their business and, by extension, to the whole of the UK economy. There they are, having been throughout their life immersed in widgets, or insurance or water management, and now in their 60s, given a position of power and prestige, newly able to pronounce on the state of the world beyond the widget.

For instance, in May 2013, a group of prominent and distinguished businesspeople wrote a letter to the British newspaper *The Independent*, accusing eurosceptic MPs of 'putting politics before economics' by calling for Britain's withdrawal from the European Union. The letter said that 'The economic case to stay in the EU is overwhelming' and that EU membership is worth as much as £92 billion a year to Britain. The signatories included the chairmen of

BT, Deloitte and Lloyds, as well as Sir Martin Sorrell and Sir Richard Branson.

We should beware of such wisdom. The economic case for staying in the EU, just like the economic case for coming out, is far from overwhelming. The arguments need to be carefully weighed, leading to a balanced judgement. With a few honourable exceptions, such corporate wizards should go back to their widgets, insurance, water management or whatever and leave the issues of national economic and political management alone. The essential problem is that insofar as they can accurately assess the interests of the current widget-making industry, or their own part of it, they cannot judge how that industry will change, whether or not there will be any need for widgets in five years' time, or whether, if there is, widgets will all come from China. Nor can they speak for the widget manufacturers, still less the manufacturers of widget substitutes, as yet unborn.

Most importantly, they cannot speak for the huge part of the economy, the dominant part, which has nothing whatever to do with making widgets and yet is still profoundly affected by the EU and its various interferences. The essence of economics is substitution and uncertainty. The essence of successful economic policy-making is to fully recognize the latter and to give full rein to the former. This has little relevance to the widget-making processes so well known by Sir Thingummy Whatnot.

In fact, it is possible to find all shades of opinion about the EU among businesspeople, business organizations and lobby groups. Moderate, well-informed business organizations can easily sound as though they come from opposite sides of the debate. In October 2013, John Longworth, Director General of the British Chamber of Commerce (BCC), said:

> *Those calling for the Prime Minister to abandon his efforts to reform and change the UK's relationship with the European Union fail to recognize that the status quo is not an option. The EU is changing and UK politicians must defend our national interests as the future of Europe is decided – not simply accept a blueprint dictated by others.*

On the same day, the Engineering Employers' Federation (EEF) said that Britain must remain part of the EU with no 'ifs or buts'. Terry Scuoler, EEF Chief Executive, said: 'Britain must not gamble on its future in Europe. The stakes are enormous. It is naive to think we can simply pull up the drawbridge and carry on as normal.'

The upside of leaving

There is an alternative scenario to the one conjured up by the danger of a major loss of trade and investment, as discussed above. It needs due emphasis – which it rarely receives. Outside the EU, the UK, without the EU's many interferences and now sensing itself, rather like Singapore some 50 years ago, both up against it and open to the world as a whole, might manage its affairs rather well and prosper accordingly.

To some people that may seem a fanciful prospect. Yet history is littered with examples of countries that have enjoyed a shot in the arm from exposure to adversity. Equally, there are plenty of examples of countries, by contrast, that have suffocated under a blanket of institutional calm and stability. Indeed, the need for periodic upsets to institutions is what underlies the thesis of the celebrated economist Mancur Olson about why some countries succeed and others fail. While there would be nothing inevitable about the UK succeeding outside the EU, at the very least it would be presented not only with challenges, but also with opportunities.

Suppose that the UK rose to the occasion and took a number of steps to deregulate the economy and make it more competitive. In that case, the costs of operating from a UK base might begin to look more favourable. The non-pecuniary benefits of being in the UK would also start to seem more attractive. Those Japanese and German manufacturers that chose to stay in the UK would conclude that they had made a good decision; just as they did when they chose to stay in the UK after it transpired that the UK had not joined, and would not join, the euro. And those that had left might have cause to regret it.

The US view of UK membership

Businesspeople are not the only foreigners to whose views the UK must pay close attention. There is also a major diplomatic aspect, especially concerning America. The US remains Britain's closest ally. At the moment, the US Administration seems to be extremely keen to keep the EU together and to keep the UK in. With the UK clearly contemplating exiting the EU, the US is alarmed. It sees the UK as vital to keeping the EU on the straight and narrow; that is, focused on maintaining close links with America and favouring free markets and open trade against the dirigisme and protectionism that lurk just beneath the surface of the French establishment.

The US Administration probably suspects that Britain is suffering from delusions of grandeur, believing that outside the EU it can strut its stuff on the world stage, or even cuddle up more closely to America. On both these issues it would like to put Britain right.

However, it has got the British completely wrong. Both the UK's politicians and its people usually underestimate, rather than over-estimate, the importance of the UK. Being a medium-sized power, but being independent, is the alternative to the current set-up and one that many British people find attractive – including rather *less* cuddling up to the US.

Of course, America's interests, both politically and economically, are best served by having a prosperous and strong Europe. The issue is whether that would most likely be achieved by a continuation of the EU status quo. In terms of economic dynamism, the EU is a failure. The rapidity of European economic growth in the early decades of the postwar period has blinded many people to the current reality.

As this book has made clear, the EU has severe political problems too. Its institutions do not work; it is profoundly undemocratic; and its leaders are isolated from ordinary citizens. Unless the EU is radically reformed, the US interest would be best served by the Union breaking up. If the UK left the EU, or the EU broke up, the US would soon continue to take a close interest in how the UK fared and would lend its weight to the maintenance of open trade across the world.

Legal red herrings

It is often presumed, particularly by eurosceptics in the UK, that the ability to escape from European human rights legislation, introduced into the UK under its membership of the European Convention on Human Rights

(ECHR) and enforced by the European Court of Human Rights, which is also referred to as the ECHR, is another of the key considerations that should be classed as a gain from the UK leaving the EU. Indeed, there are several human rights cases that have angered the British public. The most inflammatory has probably been the case of Abu Qatada, a radical Islamic cleric, whom the British tried unsuccessfully to deport to Jordan for more than a decade, before finally succeeding in 2013.

It is true that since 2000 the Human Rights Act has made the ECHR enforceable in Britain's courts. However, the ECHR is not part of the EU. In fact, it predates the formation of the EU, having been drafted in 1950 by the Council of Europe. Neither is it directly associated with the European Court of Justice.

Nevertheless, as part of the Lisbon Treaty, the EU itself acceded to the ECHR. Accordingly, it would not be possible for the UK to abolish the Human Rights Act, as Prime Minister Cameron has said that he would consider, without withdrawing from the EU – unless this was agreed by treaty. A former British Lord Chief Justice, the aptly named Lord Judge, said in 2013 that the Human Rights Act should be amended to make it clear that Britain's courts are not inferior to the European Court of Human Rights. Again, as things stand, this cannot be done without the UK withdrawing from the EU. On the other hand, if the UK chose to leave the EU, it could keep its membership of the ECHR – or not, as it so chose.

Weighing up costs and benefits

So where does the balance of the argument lie? I will give my judgement in a moment, but I must emphasize that it is a judgement, rather than the result of a totting-up of sums in the way that an accountant would analyse a firm's performance. Many of the really major issues are intangible, or not readily quantifiable, or contingent on how events turn out.

Given this, it should not be surprising that although many accounting exercises have been carried out, they come to widely different conclusions. This is not because the authors are incompetent or dishonest, but simply because on the major issues the uncertainties are so great that it is readily possible to come up with different numbers.

One particularly tricky area to assess is the cost of EU regulations. A study by the think tank Open Europe, published in October 2013, estimated the cost to the UK economy of the top 100 EU regulations at £27.4 billion a year, or roughly 2% of GDP. Others consider this to be way too high and some too low.

More broadly, it is extremely tricky to assess the net benefit of the Single Market. In July 2013, the UK government produced a study of the Single Market under its Review of Competences research programme. This shed little new light on this difficult issue and on the subject of quantifying the benefits quoted a series of pre-existing studies. These produced estimates of the net benefit of the Single Market ranging between plus 0.3%–0.9% and plus 4.25%–6.5% of GDP. There is an even wider discrepancy between different estimates of the balance of advantage with regard to the broader question of membership of the EU, as described below.

A study by the Institute of Directors (IOD), published in 2000, put the overall cost of the UK's membership of the EU at 1.75% of GDP, which is getting on for one year's normal economic growth. By contrast, a study by the National Institute, published in the same year but updated in 2004, concluded that if the UK left the EU its GDP would be 2¼% *lower*.

A 2004 study by the think tank Civitas put the annual direct cost of EU membership at 4% of GDP. Another by economists Patrick Minford and Vidya Mahambre, published in 2005, put the continuing costs of the UK's membership at 3.2%–3.7% of GDP. Meanwhile, a 2012 study by economist Tim Congdon came up with a much larger estimate – 10% of GDP, or over £5,000 a year per household. This figure is so high mainly because Congdon includes a high figure of 5% for the costs of EU regulation and another 3¼% for the cost of the EU's protectionism.

A 2006 study by Patrick Minford estimated that the EU is costing its citizens, in both the UK and the rest of the Union, in the order of 3% of GDP by protecting its industries from world competition. At the other extreme, a November 2013 report by the Confederation of British Industry (CBI) said that UK membership of the EU adds between £62 billion and £78 billion to the UK economy, amounting to £3,000 per household, or £1,225 per individual. Moreover, a poll of the CBI's members (consisting of a wide selection of British businesses) revealed 78% in favour of the UK remaining in the EU.

In fact, as far as narrow economic factors are concerned, it is possible that the balance of advantage from staying in, or leaving, the EU is comparatively small. Interestingly, this is what many studies concluded immediately before and after the UK's accession in 1973. It is also the conclusion reached by Martin Howe and Brian Hindley in their pamphlet 'Better Off Out?', first published in 1996 and revised in 2001. This contrasts with the fulminations on both sides of the debate to the effect that membership of the EU is either absolutely vital, or completely ruinous.

Wider considerations

So on what basis, if not a narrow totting-up of definable costs and benefits, should a country decide whether to stay in the EU or leave? It should surely be on the basis of the form of governance in the EU and the way that this, and its inter-relation with the economy, is likely to develop. I argued in Chapter 2 that the EU is a fundamentally undemocratic organization and it is difficult to see how it can be otherwise. It is bad at making decisions and its interventions in the economy tend to be damaging. These tendencies will probably only increase, especially if it becomes larger and more diverse. Meanwhile, as I showed in Chapters 3 and 6, its share of world GDP is falling and is set to drop further.

The cost of the UK's EU budget contribution is not huge but, without fundamental reform, it is likely to rise over time; similarly for the cost of complying with the ever-increasing burden of EU regulations. As against these factors, the UK may stand to lose exports to the EU if a reasonable trade agreement is not reached and it possibly stands to lose some FDI.

While assessing the relative weight of these various factors is a difficult business, it seems to me that without fundamental reform, the EU does not sound like an entity to which it is sensible to hitch your wagon. Trying to achieve fundamental reform is a sensible objective. If the UK could secure fundamental reform of the EU, including substantial repatriation of powers, a cast-iron exemption from the objective of ever closer union, an exit from the Single Market and the other changes mentioned in David Cameron's Bloomberg speech, which I analysed in Chapter 7, then it would probably be worth staying in the EU.

However, if such a deal cannot be secured – and that is not the deal on offer – then I believe that the UK's best interests would be served by leaving the EU, standing outside the Single Market, but trying to secure a free trade agreement with the EU, supplemented by cooperation in all areas in which the UK and the EU see joint advantage, including the environment and possibly defence policy.

Mind you, this would not be the pain-free, risk-free arrangement that many eurosceptics imagine. In particular, it runs a major risk that in practice, leading members of the EU would cut up rough and would seek to exact revenge on the UK for, as they might see it, disrupting the workings of the EU and threatening its future. Moreover, as I discuss in the next chapter, this could take place in an unfriendly world in which the open international trading system had collapsed and the US had retreated into an isolationist stance.

These are serious risks but, in my view, if the EU has not been fundamentally reformed, then they are risks well worth taking. The upside is the prospect of being able to run the domestic economy and to trade with the rest of the world, without the various encumbrances that EU membership brings.

The Netherlands dimension

Clearly, the UK is not the only country that might consider leaving the EU, although it is the only one whose government has arranged a referendum on the issue, and if any country leaves, it is the most likely candidate. Nevertheless, many of the factors that figure in an assessment of the UK's position would also be the key issues for any other country to consider. But there are also some key differences that deserve brief consideration here.

As it happens, my firm, Capital Economics, published a study in February 2014 considering the effects of an exit from the EU by the Netherlands.[29] Such an event is widely referred to as NExit, following the use of the term 'Brexit' to refer to an exit by the UK and 'Grexit' to refer to an exit by Greece (whether of the EU or merely of the euro). Two key differences from the UK's position are that the effects on the financial services and car manufacturing industries do not figure as large; nor does the Netherlands have such a large stock of foreign-owned direct investment in its economy.

On the other hand, the Netherlands must take account of some other factors that do not figure for the UK. First of all, it is, of course, a member of the eurozone and if it were to leave the EU it would have to exit from the euro and start its own currency – the 'new guilder'. This gives rise to extra complications because this new currency might rise or fall considerably against the euro and all sorts of assets and liabilities are denominated in euros. Accordingly, for the Netherlands, and indeed for any other euro member country that left the EU, the factors that figure in the discussion of euro break-up or exit that appear in Chapter 4 would be of overriding importance.

Furthermore, the Netherlands is both a much smaller economy than the UK and one that is even more closely intertwined with the EU. Accordingly, getting the right sort of relationship with the EU post-exit would be even more important.

Obviously, as with the issue of a possible UK departure, there are considerable risks and uncertainties surrounding the matter of an exit by the Netherlands, but the Capital Economics study came to the conclusion that the Netherlands would be a net gainer from exit. Like other countries, it would save its contributions to the EU budget and benefit from being able to rescind EU regulations. In addition, outside the euro it would benefit by saving its contributions to euro bailouts of weaker southern members, by being able to operate its own independent fiscal and monetary policy and by developing trade links with rapidly growing countries around the world. In principle, the same sort of considerations would figure in an assessment of a possible EU exit by any other euro member.

Watching your language

The language that is used to describe the options facing a country like the UK or the Netherlands that is considering leaving the EU is instructive. People sometimes talk about the consequences of the UK 'leaving Europe'. But that is a geographical impossibility – as it would be for the Netherlands. The EU is not Europe. It is a particular political association of European countries that happens to involve most of the territory of Europe – at the moment. There have been other associations in the past and they have not endured.

Similarly, one also sometimes hears about the UK 'turning its back on' or 'being shut out of' its main market. This is ridiculous. As I have argued, outside the EU the UK would continue to do a major part of its trade with the countries of the Union.

Yet this is not to say that Europeans, including the British, would all be better off if each country retreated into its own little world. If the UK left the EU, the leading obligation, and the prime opportunity, would be to take part in other institutional structures – or to develop new ones to take the EU's place.

10

Possible Arrangements to Take the EU's Place

Talk of the Commonwealth forming the dynamic, like minded, free trading core of a new British network for prosperity is, to use the technical term, cobblers.

—*The Economist*, 30 October 2011

There is a tendency to see the EU as the only possible form of supra-national association for European countries. In fact, there are many alternatives. These are relevant to both the case of an individual member leaving the Union and that of the whole Union breaking up.

The possible shape of alternative arrangements is the subject of this chapter. I start by discussing how European trade relations could be organized if the EU broke up or was dissolved, including possible political associations between European member states. I then discuss the issue of closer European–US trade links, the dangers of countries being shut out from the world's trading blocs and the difficulties of negotiating with those blocs. Next comes a discussion of the importance of the WTO and an examination of the British options if the UK left the EU, including the attractions of the Commonwealth connection. I conclude with consideration of the current intellectual consensus and a critical assessment of European leaders' vision of the EU.

Trade relations if the EU broke up

Suppose that the EU broke up altogether. Would the former members be able and willing to preserve something like the Common Market from which their association began? Or would they sink back into the bad old ways of trade restrictions?

In thinking about future forms of association, the countries of Europe need to abandon not only the idea of 'ever closer union', but also the idea of a Customs Union; that is, a union that imposes common tariffs on imports from outside itself. This model is becoming increasingly redundant. To take the UK as an example, over 90% of British imports are tariff free and tariffs are charged only on goods, not on services or flows of income, which are especially important for the UK. Indeed, outside the EU, there are no significant customs unions anywhere in the world.[30]

This is a clear example of how the world in which the EU was established bears a diminishing resemblance to the world in which we live. When the EU was conceived, trade flows were dominated by goods. Since then, trade in services has developed rapidly and it will surely continue to grow more in the future. This is particularly true of services that are delivered digitally – something that was, of course, unimaginable when the EEC was formed in 1957.

On a more general point, if the EU were to end, there is no need for Europe to go back to a situation of atomistic states, at war with each other in all but name. As far as economic policy is concerned, the key requirement would be the development of a free trade area. This would not be beyond the wit of man to construct. After all, as argued below, the United States,

Canada and Mexico have successfully established NAFTA without any of the political, legal or integrationist mumbo-jumbo that bedevils the EU, and in Asia ASEAN has achieved something similar.

NAFTA as an example for the EU

The North American Free Trade Association (NAFTA) was formed in 1994 to increase trade between, and hence boost the prosperity of, the United States, Canada and Mexico. This it has done, even though these countries have maintained their own sovereign currencies, whose values have fluctuated considerably. And there has been no move towards forming a political union between these countries.

Admittedly, in a television interview given in September 2007, the former Mexican President Vicente Fox advocated the creation of a currency union between the three countries. He claimed that he had talked to US President George W. Bush about the possibility of a North American currency union. The claim was dismissed by the White House press secretary on the same day, who said, 'There is no plan under way to create such a currency', and no official support for the North American currency union has ever been given by the US or Canadian governments. There are numerous reasons for this, not least that the economic benefits for the US would be very small and the potential political losses large.

In an assessment in 2006, the Canadian Department of Finance was explicit: 'The adoption of a common North American currency is not desirable for Canada.' It added: 'A North American common currency would undoubtedly mean for Canada the adoption of the U.S. dollar and

U.S. monetary policy. Canada would have to give up its control on domestic inflation and interest rates.'[31]

As a free trade area, NAFTA has some similarities with the present EU, but also some key differences. It allows free movement of goods and services, mutual access to government contracts, mutual respect for intellectual property rights and the free movement of capital. However, a key difference from the EU is that it does not involve the free movement of people. Two other key differences are that it does not force members' tariffs or other trade barriers to be the same and it does not have the equivalent of the EU's Single Market.

The ASEAN example

Similar points apply to the Asian trade association known as ASEAN (Association of Southeast Asian Nations), whose members are Brunei, Cambodia, Indonesia, Lao PDR, Malaysia, Myanmar, the Philippines, Singapore, Thailand and Vietnam. In general, discussions about an ASEAN currency union have received much more publicity than those for a currency union for NAFTA, although they too have come to nothing.

Indeed, developments in the eurozone have prompted a number of high-profile officials to dismiss the possibility of an ASEAN currency union in the foreseeable future. Speaking at a press conference in early May 2012, the Chief Economist of the Asian Development Bank, Changyong Rhee, stated:

> *The euro-zone should serve as a guide for Asia. Having a single currency and a large union can create problems. Let's see how they solve their problems*

> *and then let's study whether it is still prudent to have a single currency.*

Speaking in April 2013, the Asian Development Bank President-elect Takehiko Nakao stated that Asia 'is not yet at a stage to think about a currency union'. He also commented: 'No common currency is possible unless countries have a willingness to make fiscal transfers between themselves to deal with financial troubles' and 'It's much more productive for Asian countries to focus their efforts on developing the use of their own currencies.'

At the World Economic Forum in June 2013, Thai Deputy Prime Minister Kittiratt Na-Ranong said that an ASEAN currency was 'impossible'. He also said:

> *ASEAN countries have suffered together from the Asian economic crisis in 1997 and we've seen the benefit of exchange rates, which are an important substance of the capitalism system.*

Overall, it is highly unlikely that an ASEAN currency union will be formed in the foreseeable future. There are currently no Asian policy-makers pushing for further talks on this matter. ASEAN leaders are thoroughly focused on the real sources of prosperity: trade, investment, jobs, innovation, education. Again, the lesson for Europe is that currency union or political union is not required for close cooperation, or even integration, on trade.

A model for Europe

Indeed, interestingly, the institutional structure is already in place for Europe to do something similar to NAFTA or

ASEAN. It is called the European Free Trade Association (EFTA), which has been in existence since 1960. Today, EFTA is a poor relation of the EU, consisting of only Iceland, Liechtenstein, Norway and Switzerland, but it used to be much bigger. When it was established, its membership also included Austria, Denmark, Portugal, Sweden and the UK (see Figure 10.1).

The key change came in 1972 when the UK, accompanied by Denmark, left EFTA to become a member of what we now call the EU. Portugal followed suit in 1985. Finland joined EFTA in 1986, but in 1995 it left to join the EU, accompanied by Austria and Sweden.

The decision by the British government to leave EFTA for the EU was a Category 1 strategic error. At the time, the Economic Community, led by Germany and France, was already a larger economic entity and was set to become larger still. (It was far from being a larger entity territorially, though, as Figure 10.1 shows.) Being left out of the EC seemed like missing the only game in town. But this was before it became clear – in Britain at least – how far the Community's ambitions went to form a full political union and before the full extent of the Community's interventions in national life was evident.

Nevertheless, the EFTA structure offers a viable institutional model for Europe if the EU were to break up. There is no need to reinvent the wheel; just going back to EFTA would be an adequate starting point.

Another body superficially offers something similar: the European Economic Area (EEA), which consists of the EU plus the EFTA members except Switzerland. This entity came into being in 1994, but it effectively extended the European Single Market, with all its obligations and restrictions, to the EFTA countries – which

Figure 10.1 **EFTA and the EEC prior to the UK joining the EEC in 1973**

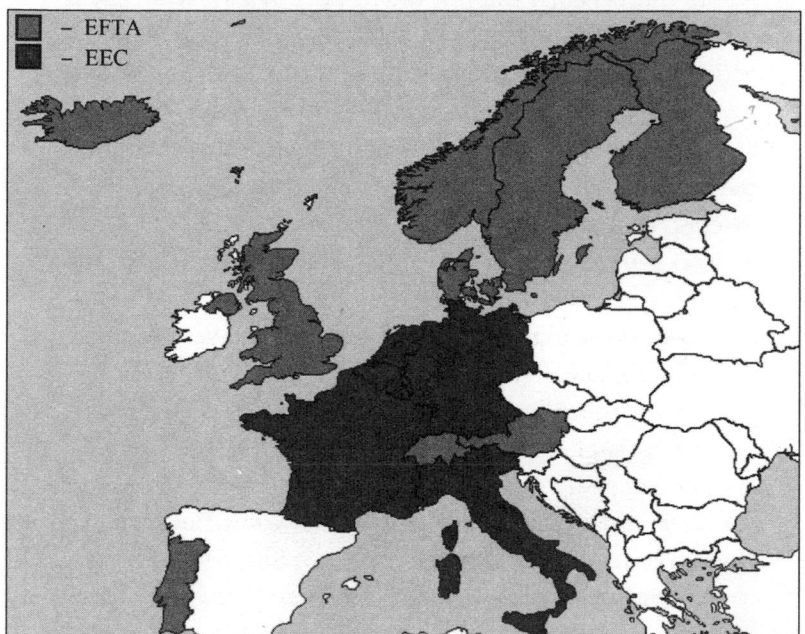

- EFTA
- EEC

Source: www.efta.int, www.europe.eu

is why Switzerland is not a member. If the EU were not to survive, the Single Market, as currently constituted, surely would not survive either. It should not do. It is to free trade that the countries of Europe need to return. Accordingly, it is EFTA, rather than the EEA, that offers a viable framework.

Possible political associations

Within such an arrangement, it would still be perfectly possible for various blocs, or political associations, to develop within Europe. Among the existing members of the eurozone there are two clear groupings of roughly equal numbers of people and one country that could belong to either. Germany plus its like-minded fellow members Austria, Benelux and Finland amounts to about 120 million people. Club Med – that is, Spain, Portugal, Italy and Greece – also amounts to about 120 million people. The remaining country – the pivotal country – is France, with about 60 million people. It could join either group or, if the euro and the EU persist, it could hold the balance of power.

France could easily form a loose association of Latin states with Italy, Spain and Portugal. Nevertheless, it is highly unlikely that it would want a full political union with them – or they with it, or with each other. But why would France need to? Once the objective of 'ever closer union' is discarded, then it is open for countries to make their own individual choices based on different criteria.

Assuming that an EU-wide free trade area exists, there would be no compelling economic reason to make close association with others. The rationale would rather be political, or to do with security. If member states so chose, such an association of states could be loose, involving merely close cooperation and/or Schengen-type open border arrangements. Or it could go all the way to full fiscal and political union.

Belgium is an interesting case. It could perhaps aspire to join the northern core group – if they would have it. But Germany might well resist, not least given Belgium's high debt levels. In that event, Belgium might conceivably try to form a close association with France, or even to join it.

More likely, though, Belgium would break up, as it has threatened to do for years, into two independent small states, or with the southern, French-speaking part combining with France, and perhaps the northern, Flemish-speaking part with the Netherlands. After all, Belgium is a completely artificial country, formed in 1830 at the behest of the British in order to prevent the land, particularly the estuary of the Scheldt and the port of Antwerp, falling into the hands of France. No such considerations would apply today.

Greece and Ireland are outliers. Both could remain solo, integrated into the new European Free Trade Area and whatever other forms of Europe-wide cooperation emerged, but not seeking close association with other member states. In the case of Ireland, however, it would have the option of forging some form of close association with the UK, although this would be fraught with difficulties for obvious historical reasons.

If Europe did coalesce into various groupings, serious questions would be raised over the former Communist countries of central and eastern Europe. Some of them might seek close allegiance with the German-led bloc, if such an entity emerges. Some might form a loose association among themselves and/or some might seek some association with the UK. On the other hand, assuming open trade links within Europe and some sort of pan-European cooperation over matters such as the environment and defence, most or all of these states might prefer to stay on their own.

Clearly, the big worry for these countries if the EU broke up would be falling back into the Russian sphere of influence. All EU members that were formerly members of the Soviet bloc are already members of NATO and if the EU did dissolve, NATO would take on increased importance as a bulwark against a resurgent Russia. In fact, the membership of the EU and NATO is largely overlapping.

Figure 10.2 European membership of NATO and the EU

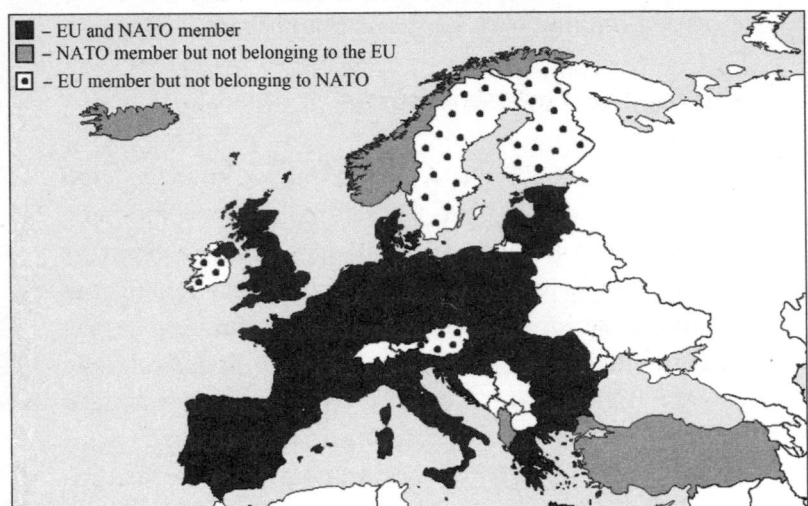

Source: www.nato.int, www.europa.eu

Of NATO's 28 members, only 6 do not belong to the EU: Albania, Canada, Iceland, Norway, Turkey and the US; and of the EU's 28 members, only 6 do not belong to NATO: Austria, Cyprus, Finland, Ireland, Malta and Sweden. (See Figure 10.2, which does not show the US and Canada, which are both members of NATO but not of the EU.)

In many people's eyes, defence against a belligerent Russia is becoming a key reason for the EU's continued existence. This is deeply ironic, because European defence policy has been particularly weak. Indeed, several EU members seem notably reluctant to spend the amounts of money on defence that would be needed to make the EU a credible military force against Russia. For the foreseeable future, the defence of Europe will depend on NATO – which means the US and the two European nation states with strong military capacity and a history of being prepared to use it: the UK and France.

Solving the Turkish problem

One clear benefit of the end of the EU as we know it would be the chance to integrate into its replacement grouping three European countries currently outside it. The first two, Norway and Switzerland, represent only small gains, but the third is seriously big: Turkey. By insisting on forging ahead to ever closer union, now including fiscal and political union, the leaders of the EU have effectively excluded Turkey. The electorates of Europe are never going to stomach having Turkey as a full and equal member of the EU; their leaders know this and are forced to drag their feet on Turkish membership. This has already alienated Turkey and risks pushing it further eastward in outlook and even in the direction of becoming an Islamic state. This is disastrous. For powerful strategic reasons, it is important to have Turkey anchored in the West.

The litmus test for the desirable form of European association of the future is that it must be one in which Turkey can play a full and equal part. As currently constituted, the EU manifestly fails this test. My suggestion of EFTA plus cooperation on the environment and defence (within NATO), coupled with a closer association of those member states that desire it, passes the test.

Even closer US trade links

The ability of each country to do well outside the EU would be greatly helped if the current negotiations between the EU and the US about forming a North Atlantic free trade area, formally known as the Transatlantic Trade and Investment Partnership (TTIP), reach a successful conclusion and, if so, the agreement is carried forward for each individual member, even if it has subsequently left the EU – or to whatever organization or grouping succeeds the EU.

If an agreement can be reached, this would create a trading bloc covering about half of the world's output. The potential gains have been estimated at £100 billion to the EU every year, £80 billion to the US and £85 billion to the rest of the world.

What is at stake is the elimination of a series of practices and duplications that constitute a barrier to trade. For example, in the car industry, manufacturers apparently crash test their vehicles twice in order to pass near-identical but different safety tests. Pharmaceutical companies similarly have to run two separate tests on drugs and medical devices, and cosmetics companies have to produce two separate sets of labels.

The prospect of such a TTIP being successfully completed is often used as a powerful argument for countries, including the UK, staying in the EU. Outside the EU, the Cassandras warn, the UK would be cut off from this huge bloc.

Yet the argument can easily be deployed the other way. If the agreement is reached and then the UK leaves the EU, why would it not be possible for the UK to continue with the agreement that has just been forged? It would be in everyone's interests for this to happen. And if the UK could be part of such an arrangement even though it was outside the EU, what would be the point of its being inside?

Figure 10.3 The world's main trading blocs

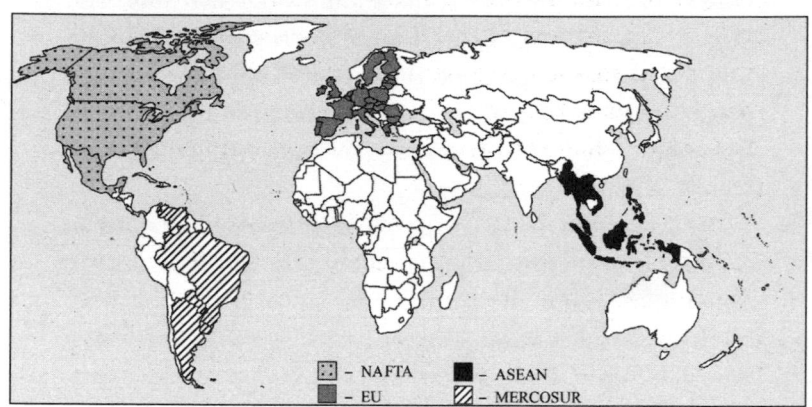

Source: www.europa.eu, www.naftanow.org, www.asean.org, www.mercusor.int

Shut out from the world's trade blocs

More generally and more worryingly, on a superficial inspection the world seems to be moving in the direction of there being several large trading blocs, the EU, NAFTA, ASEAN and MERCOSUR being the leading ones at present (see Figure 10.3). Over and above these blocs, at the end of 2013 talks were progressing on building a 12-nation Pacific Rim trade pact, entitled the Trans-Pacific Partnership (TPP), including the US and Japan. Moreover, Russia was pursuing a plan to develop a Eurasian Economic Union to link former members of the Soviet Union, over and above Belarus and Kazakhstan, which already have a customs union with Russia.

So there is a nightmare vision in which, if the EU broke up, the countries of Europe would find themselves alone in the world, shut out of each other's markets and of markets around the world. This problem of small countries negotiating their way in a world of large trade blocs is greater the smaller the country in question. Even for Britain and France, though, it would hold some worries. It would represent a much worse position than what they endured in the protectionist era between the wars, because then they at least had their far-flung empires to trade with freely. This is the ultimate downside.

Interestingly, in none of these trading blocs, nor to the best of my knowledge anywhere else, have countries opted to abandon or pool national sovereignty. It is only in the EU that national sovereignty is supposedly past its sell-by date. In fact, looking at the last few decades, national sovereignty has been extremely popular. In 1946 the membership of the United Nations was 51 countries; today it is 192.

Still, without the EU, how would individual former member countries negotiate trading agreements with other countries around the world, since their clout would be so much smaller than the EU's? The argument that they would find themselves all at sea has recently been put forward by Kenneth Clarke, then Minister without Portfolio in David Cameron's government and one of Britain's leading europhiles. Referring to negotiations to create a trade bloc between the EU and America, writing in the *Daily Telegraph* on 18 June 2013, he said:

> *Quite simply, the political commitment and dedication [to] the creation of a free market, encompassing over 800 million people, 47 per cent of world GDP and boosting the combined economies of the EU and the US by nearly £180 billion, could only ever be made by the leaders of evenly matched economic blocs.*

In fact this is far from being a clear-cut conclusion. Yes, in principle, being a member of a larger bloc should give a country like the UK more weight, sometimes referred to as 'clout' or 'heft', in negotiating with the rest of the world. But on the other hand, the larger the group of which you are a member, the more difficult it will be for the group to reach agreement on its negotiating stance with the rest of the world, and the less likely that the group's interests will correspond closely with those of an individual member.

This is especially relevant for the UK, since the structure of its economy is so different from most other EU members, particularly in the very large share of services in its exports. In principle, it is perfectly possible for a country like the UK to lose out from having its trade relations with the rest of the world arranged by a much larger negotiating entity of which it is a member. Losses could arise from its being obliged to abide by agreements that are forged against its particular interests, while it is, of course, forbidden to seek similar trade agreements on its own. Or losses could occur because the sheer difficulty of reaching agreement between member countries (28 in the case of the EU) means that some trade agreements prove to be impossible, or possible only after long time lags.

So, once again, this debate comes down to practical experience. Moreover, once again, the evidence runs exactly counter to the widely proclaimed certainties of the pro-EU camp. The fact is that the EU has proved to be particularly bad at negotiating Free Trade Agreements (FTAs).

Recently, the CBI warned of the dangers facing the UK if it took 'the Swiss option [which] would mean the UK negotiating trade deals without the clout of the EU behind it'.[32] As it happens, this comparison with Switzerland is rather amusing. In December 2013, Switzerland had 26 FTAs in force, compared to the EU's 25. On average, the Swiss FTAs were concluded earlier than the EU's.

More importantly, although there are several overlaps, the coverage of these FTAs differs somewhat. The EU has five FTAs in force for which there are no Swiss equivalents: with Syria, San Marino, Algeria, Central America and Andorra. Switzerland has FTAs in force with six countries for which there is, as yet, no EU equivalent: with Singapore, the Southern African Customs Union, Japan, Canada, Ukraine, and China and Hong Kong. It seems as though, without the clout of the EU behind them, the Swiss have been able to secure FTAs with more important trading countries than the EU has managed.

Moreover, as judged by the subsequent growth of their exports, including services, the Swiss FTAs seem to have been more advantageous than the EU's.[33]

Nor is the Swiss experience completely *sui generis*. Plenty of relatively small countries have successfully negotiated deals with other countries and trading blocs, including Costa Rica with China, Jordan with the US and Israel with EFTA. Thus, the idea of being left alone to negotiate trade deals is both unlikely to be realized and less troubling than it sounds.

The importance of the WTO

As matters stand, the defence against countries encountering trade discrimination is the series of trade agreements fostered and supervised by the World Trade Organization (WTO), which was established in 1995 as the successor to the General Agreement on Tariffs and Trade (GATT), set up immediately after the war to bring down tariff and other trade barriers. The WTO has opened up trade through a series of multilateral agreements negotiated in rounds. Until recently, the latest completed round, the eighth, was the so-called Uruguay Round, which was concluded in 1994.

Seven years later in 2001, the ninth instalment, the Doha round (named after Doha, the capital of Qatar in the Persian Gulf), commenced. However, progress was extremely slow, causing disillusion with the WTO and a distinct move towards bilateralism across the world. As it happens, though, at the end of 2013, at a meeting in Bali, world trade representatives struck a deal. So the WTO, if not quite well, is at least alive.

But suppose that the WTO does not last? What then? The key country, of course, is the US. In the decades after the Second World War it was keen to open up world trade, not least to make the countries aligned to it prosperous and thereby to act as a bulwark against Communism. However, now America sees that before long its relative economic decline will cause it to cede economic leadership to China. It is already losing influence and it seems to be in retreat from global engagement. It is already self-sufficient in food (indeed, it is a net exporter) and its prospective achievement of energy self-sufficiency might accentuate any isolationist tendency.

If America did become isolationist, the outside world put up barriers and, following suit, the countries of Europe, whether still adhering to some sort of union or not, did the same, then for a single European country to be outside the union and on its own in the world could be very uncomfortable.

I do not want to play down this risk. It undoubtedly exists and it is possible that we will come to see the post-war world of progressively freer trade as the result of the particular position of the US in the world economy and the international polity of states. While we should regard this as the ultimate worst-case scenario, it is, in my view, not very likely. Even if it were in a more iso-lationist mood, the US would not want to turn its back entirely on Europe and would want to conclude trading agreements with European partners, either collectively or individually. Indeed, even though much of the world has formed into blocs, these are not protectionist in the shape of putting up barriers to trade with other countries, nor do NAFTA, ASEAN or MERCOSUR prevent their mem-bers from making free trade agreements with other coun-tries. Unless something went very wrong with the world, there is no reason to believe that they would be resistant to making trade arrangements with outside countries.

Moreover, the chances are that the countries of Europe would understand that their collective interest lay in hav-ing some sort of free trade agreement. Even though it would be more difficult, it would also surely be possible for them to negotiate umpteen trade agreements on a bilateral basis. And, as argued above, if the EU disinte-grates, it is unlikely that Europe would return to a posi-tion of isolationist nation states; instead, it would form into a series of blocs, within which and between which, it should be relatively easy to organize trade agreements.

The British options

I have made it clear that if the UK were to leave the EU, it would probably secure a favourable and close trading relationship with the EU. I have recognized the risk, however, that this might not be achieved. This raises the fear in many people that the UK would be 'all alone' in the world. The above discussion points to factors that should allay some of those fears. I have explained that the UK would be able to negotiate FTAs with many countries around the world, but in addition, if the UK so desires, there are two particular organizations that could provide the advantages of belonging to a club.

The first of these is NAFTA. Kenneth Clarke went out of his way to rubbish this idea, saying:

> *There has always been something of the romantic in the British soul. We can't fail to be stirred by Charge of the Light Brigade visions of Britain standing alone against the odds. It is the same sentiment behind the idea of exchanging the EU for NAFTA.*

In fact, this is a far from fanciful idea. Senator Phil Gramm of Texas floated the idea of the UK being invited to join NAFTA and it would undoubtedly enjoy considerable support in the US and Canada, as well as in the UK.

The UK cannot join NAFTA while it is a member of the EU, but if it left the EU it could. This presents a favourable scenario for the UK because if it did join, it would have free trade with North America without any imposed restrictions on its economy, while still being able to negotiate FTAs with the EU and other countries or blocs around the world.

The Commonwealth connection

There is another intriguing vista, which does not necessarily cut across British membership of a reformed EU
or the various other forms of association that I have discussed. For the UK is at the centre of a remarkable group
of nations called the Commonwealth (depicted in Figure
10.4).

Although this grouping has faded in the British
national consciousness, the relative size of its collective
GDP has been rising rapidly. The possibilities that it
affords the UK have recently been championed by former Conservative cabinet minister David Howell, in his
book *Old Links and New Ties*. In it he emphasizes that the
Commonwealth is a 'network stretching across 54 independent nations, embracing 16 realms and 38 republics
or other monarchies and somewhere above 2 billion people, just about a third of the human race – and on paper at
least an economic colossus with 20 per cent of the world's
trade and growth prospects that would make European
eyes green with envy'.

It cannot be stressed enough how attractive the growth
prospects of the Commonwealth are – and they are not
restricted to its Asian members. The group includes
many African countries that have recently been growing
strongly. Indeed, many good judges think that the African
economy may be about to take off in just the way the
Asian Tigers did a few decades ago. Interestingly, contrary to expectations, the Commonwealth is not restricted
to former nations of the British Empire. Mozambique
and Rwanda are both members and other countries that
were never part of the Empire have expressed interest in
joining.

Figure 10.4 **The Commonwealth**

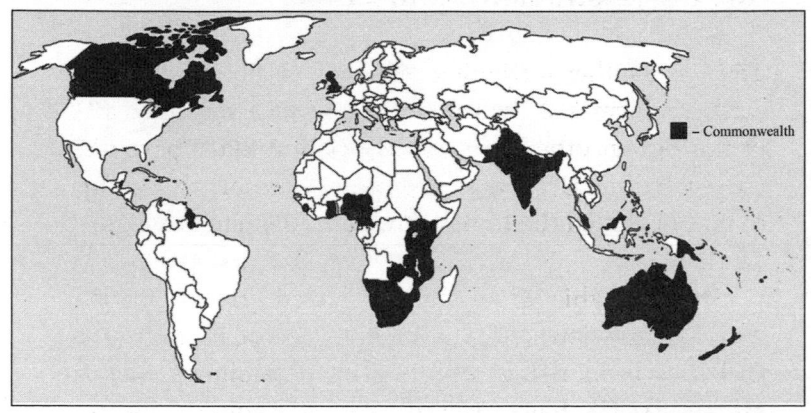

Source: www.thecommonwealth.org

It is important not to overdo the possibilities of the Commonwealth. It is not an economic bloc in the way the EU is. It is not even a free trade area or a customs union. However, that does not make it irrelevant. David Howell emphasizes that in the new digital, networked world, the idea of blocs of countries looks increasingly *passé*. What the Commonwealth offers its members is a set of connections and linkages that facilitate trade. At the heart of it lies the English language and similar institutional and legal structures based on the British model.

There has even been a suggestion of creating a Commonwealth Investment Bank, a Commonwealth business visa and a Commonwealth airport queue. Even though these do not sound like game changers, the possibilities from increased Commonwealth trade should not be lightly dismissed.[34] After all, the EU began with the European Coal and Steel Community.

To summarize the set of arrangements that the UK should seek to put in place following an exit from the EU, these comprise:

- ◆ A free trade agreement with the EU.
- ◆ Membership of NAFTA.
- ◆ Free trade agreements with as many countries as possible around the world, including China.
- ◆ Enhanced ties with Commonwealth countries.

When contemplating such a vision, many British people (and people elsewhere) imagine that the UK would not be able to negotiate FTAs because it is such a small and insignificant country. This is not true. As Figure 10.5 makes clear, the UK is still a rather large country, about the fifth biggest economy in the world, larger than Russia, Brazil or India.

Why shouldn't it be able to negotiate satisfactory trading arrangements? America does. But then the reply is that America is extra large. So what about Singapore? Then the reply is that Singapore is especially small. It seems that the Cassandras believe you either have to be very large or very small and that the UK falls between two stools. It is a sort of reverse Goldilocks scenario: too big to be small, but too small to be big.

This is nonsense. The truth is that as a still significant economy and a large market for others' exports, the UK is well placed to negotiate favourable trading relationships with many countries around the world, just as Switzerland has, as explained above.

What is more, far from fading inexorably in global importance, as most people assume, the UK's position in the world's GDP rankings is set to hold its own, or even to rise somewhat.

The demographic factors that I discussed in Chapter 6 will have a huge impact. Unless substantial immigration completely transforms matters, it looks as though

Figure 10.5 The world's 10 largest economies and selected others in 2015 (GDP at market prices, $USbn)

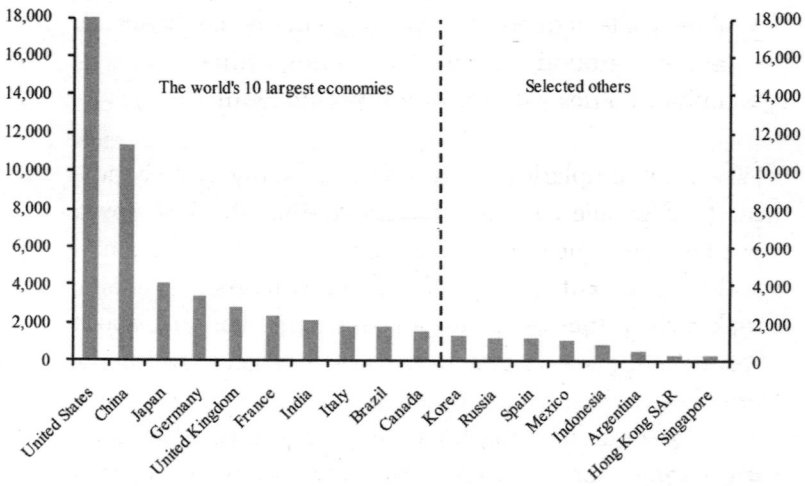

Source: IMF

the populations of Germany, Italy and Spain are set to fall, with France's population rising a little and then stabilizing. Meanwhile, the UK's population is going to rise quite sharply. As I mentioned in Chapter 7, after 2050 it is quite likely that the UK's population will exceed Germany's.

Accordingly, the UK could easily be the largest economy in the EU. Although it would surely, by that point, have been overtaken by Brazil and India, its overtaking of France and Germany would mean that the UK would probably still rank sixth in the world. (These comparisons are made in relation to GDP at market prices. At purchasing power parity the exact rankings might be somewhat different, but the substantive point stands.)

The vision thing

When thinking about the future of the EU, the key concept to grasp is that over the next 20–30 years the world power structure, into which the EU's leaders are so keen to slot the European Union, will have undergone a radical shift. We cannot be sure how things will be, but they are most unlikely to correspond closely to how the EU's founding fathers saw them.

The leaders of the EU have suffered from a fundamental failure of vision. Like generals who have a habit of trying to fight the last war, they are fixated on the idea of a tight economic and political association with countries that are geographically close. Interestingly, this fits with the continental experience up to the First World War of large swathes of territory being united in a contiguous empire. Given what has happened to the world over recent decades, though, this vision is completely out of kilter with modern reality.

Interestingly, it also stands in complete contrast to the seaborne political and economic associations of the past, which were spread over vast distances. Britain, France, Spain, Portugal and the Netherlands all operated huge empires across the seven seas. In the seventeenth century, and even still in the nineteenth and early twentieth centuries, communication between the far-flung parts of these empires was difficult – but it happened.

Of course, the form of political association that sustained these groupings was not something we would find acceptable today; namely, empire. Nevertheless, at the time it was an association that worked. Moreover, some members of the British Empire progressed from the status of colony to dominion, effectively self-governing and equal members of the Empire, tied to the mother country by history, shared legal and political arrangements, a shared language and a shared monarch, even without the benefits of modern communications.

Britain forged and managed such a dispersed empire, the largest the world has ever seen, and made its living (and endured much of its dying) around the world in an age when distance really counted. It is extraordinary that in the age of the internet the UK should believe that it must do the economic and political equivalent of marrying its next-door neighbour. If ever there was a time when matters of language, culture, shared history, law and fellow feeling should trump geography, surely this is it.

What modern communications have done is to transform the possibilities of association. Instant communication across the world means that groupings are not restricted to those who are geographically close. This is clearly recognized in the world of economics and is, after all, what globalization is all about. Firms based somewhere in America often have vital components of their output supplied from China, India, Korea or wherever.

In the world of politics, globalization seems to have made scarcely any impact. Yet there is no good reason now why political, and other close, associations cannot flourish across large distances.

In saying this I am not rejecting the importance of distance altogether. When it comes to environmental and security issues, for instance, it is with countries that are geographically close neighbours that one has most in common. But just as households that are neighbours may form neighbourhood watch groups without plunging their financial or social affairs together, so the countries of Europe could cooperate on security and environmental matters without forming a monetary, fiscal and political union.

The EU pulls off a remarkable feat: it is both too small and too large at the same time. It is too large to make a successful political entity and yet too small to be a self-contained, or even self-centred, economic bloc. In economic affairs, the only entity that it makes sense to belong to is the world. Of that, all the countries in the EU are already members.

Intellectual consensus

Despite the failings and dangers of the integrationist project, there is surely a puzzle as to why so many intellectuals – particularly among the European elites, but also inside the American establishment – have not recognized the issue. (Of course some have and scepticism about the EU is on the rise almost everywhere.) The reason is surely that they see what they want to see. And where they do acknowledge problems, they apply liberal doses of hope for improvement.

Such a systematic tendency towards widespread delusion has a distinguished pedigree. Early in the twentieth century, countless European intellectuals were taken in by Communism and gave enthusiastic support to the Soviet Union. For much of the interwar period many western intellectuals were members of the Communist Party, including the man who was subsequently to become Britain's Chancellor of the Exchequer and Defence Minister, Denis Healey. The list of Soviet supporters also included British writers George Bernard Shaw, H.G. Wells and Walter Duranty; German writers Emil Ludwig, Heinrich Mann and Lion Feuchtwanger;

American writer Theodore Dreiser; and French writers Simone de Beauvoir, Romain Rolland, Anatole France, Henri Barbusse, Louis Aragon and Elsa Triolet. In the 1920s, delegations of these admirers visited the Soviet Union and were impressed with what they saw. It hardly seems to have occurred to them that they were being shown 'Potemkin villages', industrial, agricultural and other scenes specifically constructed for their delectation and approval. (The expression refers to Count Potemkin, Catherine the Great's 'favourite', who was charged with developing the Russian Empire's new territories but showed off to visitors only specially prepared sites, while most of the rest of the country languished in a much more basic, less developed form. I experienced a similar phenomenon when visiting China in the early 1980s, although not with the same effects on my view of the country.)

The essential question is why so many clever and sophisticated people were so readily taken in. The answer is because they were dissatisfied with what they saw in capitalist society and wanted to believe that there was something better. And, as regards Russia, they were well aware of the defects of the Tsarist system that had preceded Communism.

During and after the Second World War, alignment with the Soviet Union became even more attractive since the Soviets stood so bravely against Fascism and were largely responsible for its defeat. This supposedly contrasted with the lily-livered behaviour of the western democracies in appeasing Hitler. This was, to say the least, a rose-tinted view, since it brushed over the facts that Stalin had acceded to the Nazi–Soviet Pact and that the countries that first declared war and fought Hitler were

Britain and France. But why let the facts get in the way of a convenient myth? The myth persisted and it helped to sustain several highly educated Britons who spied for the Soviet Union.

I am not suggesting here that the European Union, or the idea of closer European integration, is to be compared with the evils of Communism. Rather, my point is that it is plainly possible for many intelligent and well-meaning people to be thoroughly misled about the great issue of the day. People can drown in an intellectual consensus. Consensus views take on a life of their own and, once entrenched, are tricky to shift. People can be led to believe what they want to believe, because it gives a comfortable view of the world and its future. Such intellectual bromides are like a drug – and the addiction is very difficult to shake off.

Political delusions

Different countries have different national obsessions that, among other things, affect their attitudes to the EU. In the UK, the policy establishment is in the grip of three serious economic delusions that appear to dictate continued membership of the EU: top table syndrome, sizism and proximity fetishism. Yet the success of the world economy over the last 20 years, and especially the successful development of so many of the emerging markets, stands out against these pretensions to economic wisdom.

If the euro manages to survive, it will surely be because some sort of fiscal and political union is cobbled together to save the currency union, leaving the UK marginalized. This union would tax, harmonize and regulate until the (much subsidized) cows come home. All the indications are that without fundamental reform, such a union would make decisions profoundly inimical to the growth of the EU economy. The formation of the euro, with its awful economic effects, is a ghastly warning of what may be yet to come.

Of course, it would be right to try to reform the EU radically from within and the UK should make a major effort in this regard. Nevertheless, fundamental reform remains a very tall order. The EU would have to shrink back in both power and ambition. In particular, the goal of 'ever closer union' would have to be abandoned. If such fundamental reform cannot be achieved, the UK should be prepared to withdraw from the EU. Far from being an economic catastrophe, this could be the foundation for renewed self-confidence and prosperity. The same goes for other EU members that have reached the limits of their tolerance for integration.

This issue is about more than economics: it is about democracy and the quality of governance. But, as I have argued in this book, economic consequences follow from bad governance. On the basis of experience so far and of the diverse nature of the countries that would need to be forced into some sort of political union, it is surely right to expect the worst from the EU. It has already given us Esperanto money (the euro) and it looks to be about to give us Esperanto government (political union).

Admittedly, the euro is not the sum total of the EU's ills, and even the EU is not the source of everything that has gone wrong in Europe. In that regard, extreme eurosceptics overstate their case. But European leaders have been focused on utterly the wrong things. Their dreams have been about building unity when they should have been about creating excellence, even if that means diversity, which it has throughout most of European history.

Knowing little or nothing of economics, these European elites have acted almost precisely against the interests of Europe, being obsessed with treaties, agreements and restrictions in pursuit of commonality. They little understand that the prosperity of nations is built on the seemingly humdrum actions of ordinary people in factories, shops or service businesses, large and small – if only they are able to pursue their business interests relatively unrestricted by bureaucratic encumbrance.

Meanwhile, in following the integrationist agenda and their social model, Europe's national governments have been pursuing a chimera. These governments are big, but that does not make them effective. On the contrary, they are hopelessly ineffective at doing what governments have traditionally been there to do: defend citizens against internal and external danger. Whether it is immigration or defence, the modern European state is a pathetic failure – big, dithery, expensive, but incompetent. That is the critique from the right. Meanwhile, from the left now comes the complaint that the state is failing in its role as provider of 'social security', under the onslaught of globalization and market pressures.

Both critiques have cogency. But without the EU hanging over them as a mixture of shield, excuse and threat, even European national governments might start to wake up to what needs to be done.

The decline of Europe is the result of the interaction of economics and politics. Economic prosperity has allowed indulgence in self-destructive habits. Degenerate politics have perpetuated the sources of decline, as the politicians have dished out various opiates to the people.

The incessant draw of 'ever closer union' has been a massive diversion from the objective of creating European success.

In the weaker members of the European Union, opposition to the policies of the European elites is tempered by knowledge of the weakness of their own institutions and their own dodgy recent history. They have tolerated for too long the combination of arrogance, incompetence and corruption that wafts out of Brussels.

Dangers and hopes

But this is beginning to change. Across Europe the people are stirring. Will the elites respond? If not, we are going to be faced with something very ugly. The combination of economic stagnation – or, in extreme scenarios, collapse – lack of faith in political institutions, xenophobia and racism could be deadly.

The hope to emerge from this book is that by fundamentally reforming its workings and its nature, the EU will be able to contribute to future European success. If it cannot achieve this, then the hope must be that the EU dissolves, leaving the nation states of Europe, whether singly or as part of some new association, to bring increased European prosperity and enhanced European influence in the world.

11

The Referendum – and Other Existential Challenges

The European Union is at a watershed. The most important of the challenges it faces is the referendum on the UK's membership of the Union. The result will have profound consequences, not just for the UK, but also for the Union as a whole.

The referendum raises issues that go right to the heart of the EU: a mixture of matters economic and political – and these are deeply intertwined. Bad political structures produce bad decisions, and these often have adverse economic consequences. Indeed, the secrets of economic success lie as much in the institutional structure of a country as in its endowments of the factors of production. Equally, bad economic outcomes often produce ugly political consequences. The debate surrounding the UK's referendum is where economics and politics collide.

The road to the referendum

The referendum is being held because of internal pressure within David Cameron's Conservative Party, stemming largely from the rise of UKIP, under its controversial but charismatic leader Nigel Farage, which was riding high in the opinion polls and threatened to take millions of otherwise Conservative votes. In order to minimize the threat to the Conservatives ahead of the forthcoming 2015 general election, Mr Cameron was persuaded to promise that if the Conservatives won the election he would hold an in-out referendum before the end of 2017.

At the time, he probably believed that he would be in no position to redeem that pledge as the chances of an outright Conservative victory were apparently very slim. In the event of the much more likely outcome, namely a hung parliament that would lead to another coalition with the Lib-Dems, they would not be bound by the referendum pledge and would surely refuse to hold one. In that case, Mr Cameron would be released from his promise. But it would have performed a good job in holding the Conservative Party together and maximizing its vote – and would have cost nothing.

Fortunately for Mr Cameron, British voters did not behave according to the script. They returned him with an overall majority; but this victory came with a sting in the tail, and he found himself having to honour what, at first, must have seemed like an empty promise.

Cameron's constraints

Mr Cameron has never been an outright supporter of the EU. Indeed, he has generally been regarded as a eurosceptic. He is both supremely able and deeply pragmatic. In principle, then, it seemed possible that he could endorse either staying in the EU or leaving it – depending upon the detailed arrangements prevailing in the two cases.

But the Prime Minister was not going to accept the status quo as the basis for his decision. Like his predecessor Harold Wilson who, forty years earlier, had agreed to hold a referendum on the UK's membership to keep his own (Labour) Party together, Mr Cameron set out to change those things that the UK did not like about its member-ship – or at least to pretend to change them.

In his Bloomberg speech of January 2013, he went much further than outlining a mere shopping list of UK demands. Rather, as discussed in Chapter 7, he gave a fairly comprehensive analysis of the EU's failings and what needed to be done to put them right. Moreover, the whole thrust of the speech was less about changing the relationship of the UK with the EU than changing the EU itself, for the good of all the people of Europe.

This was such a constructive way of approaching the issue that many people of eurosceptic disposition, includ-ing this author, wondered whether the EU could yet be so reformed that they could lend their support to continued UK membership. At the very least, they would have to see what transpired in any attempt to reform the EU before deciding how to cast their vote – if and when it came to a referendum.

But all this was before the Conservatives' 'shock' victory in May 2015. Afterwards, when faced with having to honour his pledge, Mr Cameron had to grapple with four key constraints:

1. Across the continent there was serious irritation with the UK for putting the EU into yet another crisis – unnecessarily, as they would see it – for the sake of managing Mr Cameron's domestic political difficulties.
2. Profound reform of the EU, even if it were possible and agreed by all parties, would require Treaty changes and there was simply no appetite for that – and no possibility of even contemplating it if the timetable was short.

3. The timetable had indeed to be short since there was due to be a general election in Germany and a presidential election in France in 2017. The EU would be bound to figure prominently in both. The UK's referendum would surely have to be settled well before then.

4. In 2015, a new European crisis emerged with potentially huge implications for the EU and for the UK's vote on continued membership, namely the flow of large numbers of migrants into Europe. Among voters this influx appeared to strengthen the resonance of the border-control argument for leaving the EU. The flow was always going to be stronger over the summer months. Accordingly, there was a good argument for the referendum vote taking place before the full flood to be expected in the summer of 2016, never mind the following summer.

Consequently, far from embarking on a root and branch reform of the EU as a precursor to the decision over whether to stay or leave, Mr Cameron set about making an intensive diplomatic effort to secure the backing of the EU's leaders for a much more limited set of UK requirements, to be agreed as soon as possible.

The negotiating strategy

How much should he ask for? The usual negotiating tactic, immortalized in the haggling scene in *Monty Python's Life of Brian*, is to ask for a lot and then climb down under pressure, finally settling somewhere in the middle of the two protagonists' initial positions. But whatever the merits of this approach, it would necessarily entail failing to achieve several goals. This would inevitably be portrayed in the British press as defeat and would look, again, as though Britain was being dealt with badly by its continental partners, which might serve greatly to increase the 'Out' vote.

So, instead, the strategic choice was made to ask for very little; indeed, to ask only for what, in some sense, could reasonably be expected to be agreed by Britain's partners. Then Mr Cameron could come back with his 'deal', which he would portray to the voters as a great victory and he would be able to campaign to stay in 'a reformed EU'. So it was that Mr Cameron forged a deal that was adopted at a meeting of the European Council in February 2016. He duly settled on 23 June as the date for the referendum, in readiness to campaign – along with most of the government – for the UK to stay in the EU.

In this story of realpolitik, there are two mysteries. First, if he was sincere in his Bloomberg speech, once it had become clear that he was going to be able to secure precious little from his continental partners, what persuaded the apparently eurosceptic and eminently practical Mr Cameron to support continued UK membership come what may?

Second, having made this decision, why did he go public with it before negotiations began, thereby undermining his already weak position with the EU? If you tell your opposite numbers that whatever they concede, or do not concede, you are going to back the deal with the voters anyway, you do not exactly maximize their incentive to make concessions.

If the first mystery may never be solved because the key to it lies deep in Mr Cameron's mind, the second increasingly looks less of a mystery and more of a blunder.

The 'deal'

Mr Cameron asked for five things, a mixture of minor pocketbook issues and overarching matters affecting sovereignty:

1. If an EU migrant's child is living abroad they should receive no child benefit or child tax credit.
2. In order to be able to claim in-work benefits, an EU migrant must have lived in the UK and contributed for a minimum of four years.
3. Exemption for the UK from 'ever closer union'.
4. National parliaments to be able to block unwanted European legislation.
5. Protection for non-euro countries from being dictated to by the euro-zone and, relatedly, protection for the City of London.

He duly secured something on all these points, though decidedly less than he had asked for. Under the deal, migrants with children living abroad will still be able to claim benefits, but they will be indexed to the level of benefits available in the migrant's home country.

Mr Cameron failed on limiting the claims of in-work benefits to those who have lived in the UK for at least four years. However, the agreement provides for an emergency brake on overall migrant numbers where 'exceptional' levels of migration are putting pressure on the social security system or public services. This brake will last for seven years with no option for renewal. States that wish to apply the brake have to submit a request to the European Commission and approval must come from the European Council.

On ever closer union, the agreement says that: 'It is recognised that the United Kingdom ... is not committed to further political integration in the European Union ... References to ever closer union do not apply to the United Kingdom.'

The agreement provides a 'Red Card' system on parliamentary powers, allowing national parliaments to strike down legislation if 55% of them agree.

Nevertheless, these 'victories' were pretty hollow. It is not even certain that the agreement is legally watertight. In particular, aspects of it may be overturned by the ECJ.

The so-called 'Red Card' system is a joke. After all, a majority of countries have to be in favour of the legislation in the first place. Given this, it will be next to impossible to secure backing from 55% of parliaments to oppose a measure. In any case, the original ambition was for individual parliaments to have the ability to check EU legislation. Meanwhile, the restrictions on migrants' ability to claim benefits will do next to nothing to restrain the numbers of migrants moving to the UK. And the time-limited 'brake' on inward migration is under the control of the EU, not the UK.

The recognition that the UK is not committed to 'ever closer union' is worth something. But it stops well short of a cast-iron protection, as does the defence against the euro-zone dictating to non-euro members such as the UK. Moreover, in order to secure these 'victories', Mr Cameron had to make a major concession, namely that the UK would not impede moves towards further integration in the euro-zone. This effectively surrendered the UK's veto on this issue, which was perhaps the strongest card it could play in post-referendum negotiations.

So the net result is that, after the high hopes raised by Mr Cameron's Bloomberg speech in January 2013, the deal he reached in February 2016 comes as a bitter disappointment. He asked for surprisingly little and, remarkably, he got even less. The upshot is that the details of this deal should not, and probably will not, persuade anyone how to cast their vote. That should rest on a careful consideration of the economic and political issues which are largely the same as they were before Mr Cameron embarked on his diplomatic mission.

This book has laid out the arguments and tries to present a reasoned assessment. The conclusion is that the balance of immediate economic advantages and disadvantages is probably pretty close. That does not sound like a dramatic conclusion. What is dramatic, however, and should be emphasized, is that it implies that the economics of the matter should not present any barrier to leaving the EU if that seems desirable on political and other grounds. And the analysis in this book has argued that this does indeed seem desirable as the EU's many political inadequacies are an affront to parliamentary democracy. What's more, from such bad government only bad economic outcomes can be expected in the future. Meanwhile, European societies are set to be torn apart by the EU's cack-handed mismanagement of the migration question.

Nevertheless, there are several key issues that have been left dangling by the analysis that now need to be addressed, starting with the question as to why so many business leaders apparently favour remaining in the EU, if the economic case is indeed finely balanced.

Why big business favours membership

By no means do all business leaders support staying in, but it is true that a preponderance of the leaders of big business, and their lobbying organisations such as the CBI, do favour it (just as they favoured joining the euro). We must presume that they see advantages for their businesses, yet that does not necessarily mean that their perceived self-interest in doing so indicates an overall advantage for the UK, or that the political and constitutional factors favour staying in. On both these issues business leaders are completely unqualified to pass judgement, except in their capacity as ordinary citizens with a vote.

In fact, when interpreting what business leaders say, there are some key structural features of the economic case that need careful attention. Even if the net balance of advantages and disadvantages of Brexit were exactly zero for the country as a whole, there would be distinct gainers and losers; and it is quite understandable that the latter should make it plain that they would rather stay in. The potential losers from Brexit would tend to be those companies with substantial exports to the EU, minimal imports from the rest of the world and comparatively little UK business. Businesses that fall into this category are predominantly large – and well represented in the CBI.

By contrast, the gains from Brexit would be felt disproportionately by consumers, in the form of lower prices, including for food, and perhaps also lower taxes. They, of course, have no representation in business groups. And the corporate gainers would tend to be those who suffer from excessive EU regulation but don't export much to the EU. These businesses tend to be small and not heavily represented in the CBI.

Moreover, there is a category of gain that will not appear directly in the calculations of any business leaders, namely the benefit of the end of the EU regulatory juggernaut in the public and non-profit sectors. Britain's most prolific cancer researcher, Professor Angus Dalgleish, told the journalist Dominic Lawson that the EU's Clinical Trials Directive had increased the cost of experiments more than ten-fold.

The upshot is that although it is important for the voice of business leaders to be heard, we should beware of thinking that they have some special insight into the balance of economic advantages – still less into the all-important political and constitutional issues.

The Scottish question

Few constitutional issues are more important than the Scottish question. Many people believe that if the UK came out of the EU, this would trigger a second referendum on Scotland's membership of the UK which, given recent polling and the likelihood that Scots will have voted to stay in the EU, would lead to Scotland's departure. If this reasoning is sound, it would give many euro-sceptics pause for thought. They may not like one Union, namely the EU, but they tend to approve strongly of the other one: the UK.

In fact, this Scottish argument is less threatening than it looks. The UK government is by no means bound to concede a second referendum whenever the Scottish Nationalist Party thinks it can win one. And there is a marked reluctance at Westminster to do so. The last one is supposed to have settled the matter 'for a generation'.

Moreover, although the opinion polls do not presently dance to this beat, since the referendum in September 2014, economic circumstances have moved sharply against independence. The economic arguments were always tenuous at best, particularly given the tricky question of what currency an independent Scotland would use. But that was in the days of oil prices at $120 per barrel. Now the price is nearer $40 a barrel, an independent Scotland would immediately have to levy huge increases in taxes and/or impose swingeing cuts in public spending.

Furthermore, the situation of the EU has altered profoundly since September 2014. It is in crisis, whether or not the UK leaves. In these circumstances, if Scotland left the UK, where would it find a supportive home? Even if the EU were to survive, it would not be bound to invite Scotland to rejoin. Indeed, various EU leaders have made it clear that it would have to take its place in the queue of other countries wanting to join. And Spain in particular, with its secessionist issue over Catalonia, would be likely to resist any move to admit Scotland.

Security and foreign policy

The fate of Scotland impinges on the UK's security. It is sometimes argued that this security would be imperilled if the UK were to leave the EU, particularly now, given the increasing bellicosity of Putin's Russia and the rise of international terrorism.

This view is incongruous, however, because security is one sphere in which the EU has contributed next to nothing. It is the UK's membership of NATO that gives it protection, and that would continue if it were to leave the EU. Indeed, with the exception of France, other members of the EU adopt a generally unenthusiastic stance with regard to defence issues. Unilateralism and pacifism tend to be strong, and these countries regularly fail to meet the NATO commitment of spending at least 2% of GDP on defence. If we had to rely on other European countries for our defence, then heaven help us.

Meanwhile, in intelligence and counter-terrorism the UK continues to punch well above its weight. It is a member of the so-called 'Five Eyes' group of countries that share intelligence: the US, the UK, Canada, Australia and New Zealand. There are no prizes for noticing the key feature that all these countries have in common.

Equally, although to some countries the UK might seem of diminished importance if it left the EU, it would still remain a key global player. Ironically, if there is an immediate threat to its permanent membership of the UN Security Council, that comes from the EU, which is keen to replace its seat – along with France's – with a seat for itself. As Lord (David) Owen, a former Foreign Secretary, has put it:

> *To pretend that this country is too weak politically, economically and militarily to vote to leave the EU is absurd and deserves to be laughed out of court.*

The effect of Brexit on the EU

The exit of the UK, if it happens, could not occur at a worse time for the EU. It could prompt developments that would lead to the end of the Union. First, there would be the simple matter of the UK's budget contributions, amounting to about £10 billion net. In normal times, sharing out this burden among the other EU members might not be too difficult. But these are not normal times. Which country would line up to take its share of the burden? Germany – again? France? The result would be an unseemly row between members.

Meanwhile, a clamour for a new deal, or a referendum on membership, in several other countries would be likely. The leading candidates are the Czech Republic, Hungary, Poland and the Netherlands. And French eurosceptics are licking their lips at the prospect of Brexit, looking with anticipation to the presidential election in 2017.

But the really major threat from Brexit would come in a few years' time. If the UK were to prosper outside the Union, then that would lead to serious pressure for EU reform – or for departure and dissolution. And we have repeatedly seen how difficult the EU finds it to reform itself. So a break-up of the EU would be a serious possibility.

Should this prospect give British eurosceptics pause for thought? Quite the reverse. I have argued that whatever the EU achieved for Europe in earlier decades, it is now beyond its useful life. Indeed, with its elitism, self-aggrandizement, waste and focus on regulation and harmonization, it has become the major factor holding Europe back. Accordingly, if Brexit were to lead to the end of the EU, then Britain would have done the people of Europe a great service.

The trouble with Europe

This book has identified four main sources of trouble with Europe. Interestingly, each has found new endorsement in the events that have occurred since the first edition.

First is the Union's fundamentally undemocratic nature. The European Commission is unelected. The European Parliament is a much weaker body than equivalent national parliaments and it is meant to be. Meanwhile, the European Court of Justice is above challenge. European integration is a project of the European elites imposed on people below.

Second, largely because of its institutional structure, the EU makes some appallingly bad decisions. Poor decision-making emerges from a peculiar cocktail of characteristics: a dreamlike quality, emanating from the origins of the EU and its ultimate ambition to become a fully fledged state; horse-trading between the individual member states; an over-powerful bureaucracy, disdainful of national differences, with little knowledge of markets and even less respect for them; weak parliamentary supervision, with the Parliament having next to zero connection with the European electorate.

Third, because of its bad decisions, from the macro disaster of the euro-zone to the myriad micro interferences that inhibit business, the EU is a gigantic zone of economic failure. Despite the manifest advantages of its European heritage, the EU is underperforming, not only the emerging markets, but also the other advanced economies of the world. Meanwhile, its labour markets are a disgrace, condemning millions of people – particularly the young – to lives of misery.

Fourth, the EU understands neither what it is, nor its purpose. Its current ambition seems to be to get bigger and bigger. Its negotiations with Ukraine over some form of associate membership played a key role in prompting President Putin's annexation of Crimea and the destabilization of eastern Ukraine. In similar vein, it has now moved a step closer to admitting Turkey as a full member.

With some 80 million Turks having the rights to move, settle and work anywhere in the EU, this would be a recipe for complete disaster. By contrast, this book has argued that Europe needs to include Turkey as a full member of some European association, but that association must not encompass freedom of movement of persons, still less the pursuit of fiscal and political union.

The EU's number is up

When thinking about the EU's future the comparison that frequently comes to my mind is that of the Soviet Union, which lasted just under seventy years. Seventy years after the Treaty of Rome would take us to 2027. I am not at all sure that the EU is going to survive quite that long.

As we all know, the UK did not play a role in how the EU began; but I reckon it is set to play a major role in how it ends. This would be fitting. The people of the UK have made a marvellous contribution to the world, but one that is not evenly spread. Our contribution to popular music is outstanding, yet our contribution to unpopular, i.e. classical, music is not in the same league. Wonderful though our classical composers are, you could not say that their music bears comparison with the greatest from Germany (and Austria). In painting we cannot match the Italians, the Spanish or the French, or perhaps even the Dutch. Our literature is wonderful, but so is the literature of many European countries. Of course, our native cuisine is unique – but not quite in the way we might hope.

Our contribution to the world has been enormous in science and the advance of knowledge. Yet I suspect the area in which the UK has made the greatest overall contribution is not in this exalted sphere but rather at the other end of the spectrum, in the messy business of democratic government. Parliament and the common law are the foundations of freedom – and prosperity.

It is striking that the British genius – or is it the abiding nature of Perfidious Albion – somehow enabled us to avoid the two greatest errors of the EU's ascendancy: the euro and the Schengen passport-free travel zone. Still, these victories are only minor. The EU hurtles towards a truly ghastly end – economically, politically and socially. If British voters elect to stay in the Union, although they will be able to avoid the worst of the coming crisis, they will be unable to avoid the fallout from the gathering disaster across the Channel.

If they elect to take the UK out of the EU, although there will be many painful wrenchings, they may trigger a series of consequences that will save, not just the UK, but Europe. And, in keeping with what the British are best at, they would then be in pole position to help construct a new Europe from the wreckage of the old.

Postscript: History Moves On

In 2012, the year of the euro's existential crisis, I visited Schönbrunn Palace, which lies on the outskirts of Vienna. It is a sort of Mitteleuropean Hampton Court, only grander. From one of its magnificent rooms, next to the desk from which the Habsburg emperors administered their huge territories, you look out onto a majestic park and, in the other direction, down a straight avenue leading to central Vienna.

The place oozes power and prestige. Indeed, for centuries the Habsburg Empire was one of the Great Powers of Europe. On the eve of its dissolution at the end of the First World War, who could have thought that Vienna would shrink back to be only the capital of tiny Austria – all musical heritage and Sachertorte? Yet that is what has happened, with only the wonderful buildings, like Schönbrunn, to remind us of past grandeur.

In some not too distant future, I wonder if tourists will also visit the EU buildings in Brussels and muse on lost power (if not be overcome by the wonder of the marvellous architecture), with the city now shrunken back from being the de facto capital of Europe to what it was not so long before – the crossroads of cultures and the home of wonderful moules-frites.

Glossary

Aggregate demand The overall level of demand for goods and services in the economy.

ASEAN Association of Southeast Asian Nations. Established in 1967, its membership consists of Brunei, Cambodia, Indonesia, Lao PDR, Malaysia, Myanmar, Philippines, Singapore, Thailand and Vietnam. This is a free trade area and not a customs union.

CAP Common Agricultural Policy. This serves to raise the income of European farmers, but thereby keeps the price of agricultural produce artificially high.

Common Market The colloquial name for the EEC, which was established by the Treaty of Rome in 1957.

Competitiveness The position of one country's general price and wage level compared to others when translated at the current market exchange rate. If that price level is high relative to others, the country is said to be uncompetitive.

Customs union A grouping of countries that impose common restrictions on imports from outside the union, but operate free trade, or nearly free trade, between members.

Deflation A period when the general level of prices falls; the opposite of inflation.

Devaluation or depreciation The process of one currency's value falling compared to others. This is a way in which a country can restore its competitiveness without having to undergo falling prices.

ECB European Central Bank. Based in Frankfurt, this is the central bank for the whole eurozone.

ECHR This acronym is used to refer to both the European Court of Human Rights, not to be confused with the ECJ, and the European Convention on Human Rights.

ECJ European Court of Justice. Established in 1952 and located in Luxembourg, it dispenses judgments that have legal force throughout the EU.

Economies of scale The tendency for average unit costs to fall as the volume of output rises.

ECSC European Coal and Steel Community. Established in 1951, this was a forerunner of the EEC.

EEC European Economic Community. Established by the Treaty of Rome in 1957, this later became the European Community (EC) and then the European Union (EU).

EFSF European Financial Stability Facility, a fund for extending financial support to troubled members of the eurozone.

EFTA European Free Trade Association, formed in 1960. This was a sort of rival to the EEC, but when Britain left it in 1972 it lost more members and faded in significance. It still exists, with Iceland, Liechtenstein, Norway and Switzerland as members, and it could become the kernel of some new European trade grouping if the EU were to disintegrate.

EMU European Monetary Union, the system in which the countries of the eurozone have a single currency.

ERM Exchange Rate Mechanism, a forerunner of the euro.

ESM European Support Mechanism, a fund for extending financial support to troubled members of the eurozone.

EU European Union, the present name for the association that first began life as the EEC with the Treaty of Rome in 1957.

European Commission The de facto government of the EU.

European Social Charter Established in 1961, this provides guidelines on working conditions and intervention in the labour market in favour of certain specified groups.

Eurozone The group of countries using the euro as their currency.

Foreign Direct Investment (FDI) The investment by companies in plant, machinery, buildings or other business assets in another country.

Free trade The practice of buying and selling goods and services across countries without the imposition of tariffs, quotas or other restrictions.

GATT General Agreement on Tariffs and Trade, set up in 1947 to negotiate and implement multilateral agreements on the liberalization of trade. It was succeeded in 1995 by the World Trade Organization (WTO).

GDP Gross Domestic Product, the most commonly used measure of national output, or income.

Gold Standard The system of tying currencies to a specified amount of gold into which these currencies would be exchangeable. This had its heyday in the nineteenth century under British leadership, although Britain left it twice, in 1914 and again, having returned to it in 1925, in 1931. The Gold Standard effectively broke down during the late 1930s.

Inflation A process in which prices in general rise; the opposite of deflation.

Internal devaluation The process of falling prices through which a country can restore its competitiveness without changing its exchange rate.

Keynesian Relates to John Maynard Keynes, or Lord Keynes as he later became. He is generally regarded as the greatest economist of the twentieth century and one of the greatest of all time. The adjective 'Keynesian' is often deployed to refer to a policy of boosting aggregate demand, sometimes by running government budget deficits.

Lisbon Agenda A program of objectives to reinvigorate European economic performance. Announced in 2000, it is generally regarded as a flop.

MEP Member of the European Parliament.

Mercosur Mercado Común del Sur (Common Market of the South) is an economic integration project established in 1991. Its membership comprises founding members Argentina, Brazil, Paraguay and Uruguay and associate members Venezuela, Chile and Bolivia.

NAFTA North American Free Trade Association. Established in 1994 between the US, Canada and Mexico, this is a free trade grouping and not a customs union.

NATO North Atlantic Treaty Organization. This commits member countries, which include most of western Europe and the US, to mutual defence.

OECD Organisation for Economic Co-operation and Development.

OMTs Outright Monetary Transactions, the policy of the ECB standing ready to purchase the bonds of troubled members of the eurozone, potentially without limit. The policy was announced in July 2012, but by the end of 2013 it had not yet been implemented.

Open Europe A British-based think tank.

Optimum Currency Area The extent of a group of countries or regions that, according to certain theoretical criteria, can best operate with a single currency rather than each country or area having its own currency.

Productivity The amount of output produced in a given time per unit of inputs. Productivity is often measured in relation to the input of labour, when it means the level of output produced per capita.

Review of Competences A major research initiative announced by the British government in July 2012, consisting of a range of reports on a wide variety of subjects. The full range of reports is planned to be available by autumn 2014.

Schengen The agreement signed in 1995 that allows travel without passport control in various European countries.

Single Market A system that combines both free trade between members and the common imposition of agreed standards and regulations across all member countries. The European Single Market was established in 1992.

Stability and Growth Pact An agreement put in place in 1997 in order to restrain the government budget deficits of members of the eurozone.

Subsidiarity The principle that within the EU decisions should be taken as close to the citizen as possible.

Target 2 Balances The claims on or obligations of one central bank or other central banks within the eurozone under the clearing system known as Target 2. The German Bundesbank has substantial claims on other central banks.

Tariffs A tax on imports levied by the importing country.

Treaty of Rome Signed in 1957, this established the European Economic Community (EEC), which evolved into the European Union.

TTIP Transatlantic Trade and Investment Partnership. This is still under negotiation between the EU and the US, but if successful it would establish a north Atlantic free trade area.

WTD Working Time Directive, which, among other things, lays down maximum daily and weekly working time restrictions.

WTO World Trade Organization, established in 1995 as the successor organization to GATT.

Selected Bibliography

Acemoglu, D., & Robinson, J. (2012) *Why Nations Fail: The Origins of Power, Prosperity and Poverty*, London: Profile.

Alesina, A., & Spolaore, E. (1997) On the number and size of nations, *Quarterly Journal of Economics*, 112(4): 1027–56.

Alesina, A., & Spolaore, E. (2003) *The Size of Nations*, Cambridge, MA: MIT Press.

Alesina, A., Angeloni, I., & Schuknecht, L. (2001) What Does the European Union Do? NBER Working Paper 8647, Cambridge, MA: National Bureau of Economic Research.

Bannerman, D.C. (2013) *Time to Jump: A Positive Vision of an Independent Britain Outside the EU in an EEA Lite Agreement*, Epsom: Bretwalda Books.

Barro, R.J. (1991) Small is beautiful, *Asian Wall Street Journal*, October 11.

Becker, G.S. (2005) Response on small is beautiful, Becker-Posner blog, 22 April, http://www.becker-posner-blog.com/2005/04/response-on-small-is-beautiful-becker.html, viewed on 11 September 2013.

Becker, G.S. (2005) Why small has become beautiful, Becker-Posner blog, 17 April, http://www.becker-posner-blog.com/2005/04/why-small-has-become-beautiful-becker.html, viewed on 11 September 2013.

Becker, G.S., & Mulligan, C.B. (2003) Deadweight costs and the size of the government, *Journal of Law and Economics*, 46(2): 293–340.

Booker, C. (2001) *Britain and Europe: The Culture of Deceit*, London: The Bruges Group.

Booker, C., & North, R. (2003) *The Great Deception: The Secret History of the European Union*, London: Continuum.

Booth, S., & Howarth, C. (2012) *Trading Places: Is EU Membership Still the Best Option for UK Trade?* London: Open Europe.

Buchan, D. (2012) *Outsiders on the Inside: Swiss and Norwegian Lessons for the UK*, London: Centre for European Reform.

Burrage, M. (2014) *Where's the Insider Advantage?* London: Civitas.

Cameron, D. (2013) EU speech at Bloomberg, https://www.gov.
uk/government/speeches/eu-speech-at-bloomberg, visited
31 January 2014.

CBI (2013) *Our Global Future: The Business Vision for a
Reformed EU*, London: Confederation of British Industry.

Charter, D. (2012) *Au Revoir, Europe: What if Britain left the
EU?* London: Biteback Publishing.

Chevènement, J.P. (2013) *1914–2014: L'Europe sortie de
l'histoire?* Paris: Fayard.

Congdon, T. (2004) *Will the EU's Constitution Rescue Its
Currency?* London: The Bruges Group.

Congdon, T. (2009) *The City of London under Threat: The
EU and Its Attack on Britain's Most Successful Industry*,
London: The Bruges Group.

Congdon, T. (2012) *How Much Does the European Union Cost
Britain?* Newton Abbot: UKIP.

Connolly, B. (2012) *The Rotten Heart of Europe*, London: Faber
and Faber.

Dixon, H. (2014) *The In/Out Question*, London: Scampstonian.

Dustmann, C., & Frattini, T. (2014) The fiscal effects of immmi-
gration to the UK, *Economic Journal*, 124(580): F593–F643.

Eichengreen, B., & Boltho, A. (2008) *The Economic Impact of
European Integration*, London: Centre for Economic Policy
Research.

Erickson, J. (2004) Size Matters, review of *The Size of Nations*
by A. Alesina & E. Spolaore, *SAIS Review of International
Affairs*, 24(2).

Fresh Start Project (2013) *Manifesto for Change: A New Vision
for the UK in Europe*, London: Fresh Start Project, http://
www.eufreshstart.org/downloads/manifestoforchange.pdf,
visited 31 January 2014.

Gamble, A. (2003) *Between Europe and America: The Future of
British Politics*, Basingstoke: Palgrave Macmillan.

George, S. (2008) *An Awkward Partner: Britain in the European
Community*, 3rd edn, Oxford: Oxford University Press.

Giannakouris, K. (2008) *Ageing Characterises the Demographic
Perspectives of the European Societies*, Luxembourg:
Eurostat European Communities.

Giddens, A. (2014) *Turbulent and Mighty Continent: What
Future for Europe?* Cambridge: Polity Press.

Grant, C. (2008) *Why Is Britain Eurosceptic?* London: Centre
for European Reform.

Grant, C. (2013) *How to Build a Modern European Union*, London: Centre for European Reform.

Green, D. (2013) *What Have We Done?* London: Civitas.

Green, D. (2014) *The Demise of the Free State*, London: Civitas.

Hannan, D. (2012) Switzerland is a more attractive model than Norway, but Britain could do better than either, *Daily Telegraph*, 15 December.

Harari, D., & Thompson, G. (2013) *The Economic Impact of EU Membership on the UK*, London: House of Commons Library.

Heisbourg, F. (2013) *La fin du rêve européen*, Paris: Stock.

Hewish, T., & Styles, J. (2012) *Common-trade, Common-growth, Common-wealth*, Cheltenham: The Hampden Trust.

Hindley, B., & Howe, M. (2001) *Better Off Out? The Benefits or Costs of EU Membership*, London: Institute of Economic Affairs.

HM Government (2013) *Review of the Balance of Competences between the United Kingdom and the European Union: The Single Market*, July.

HM Treasury (2005) *The Economic Effects of EU Membership for the UK*, https://www.gov.uk/government/uploads/system/uploads/attachment_data/file/220965/foi_eumembership_presentation.pdf, visited 31 January 2014.

Howell, D. (2014) *Old Links and New Ties: Power and Persuasion in an Age of Networks*, London: I.B. Taurus.

Johnson, J. (2012) *Britain Must Defend the Single Market*, London: Centre for European Reform.

King, A., & Crewe, I. (2013) *The Blunders of Our Governments*, London: Oneworld Publications.

Kremer, M., & Parkes, R. (2010) *The British Question: What Explains the EU's New Angloscepticism?* Berlin: Stiftung Wissenschaft und Politik, Berlin.

Lea, R. (n.d.) *Britain's Contributions to the EU: How to Save £5bn, Minimum*, London: The TaxPayers Alliance.

Liddle, R. (2014) *The Europe Dilemma: Britain and the Drama of EU Integraton* (Policy Network), London: I.B. Tauris.

Lindsell, J. (2014) *Softening the Blow: Who Gains from the EU and How They Can Survive Brexit*, London: Civitas.

Llewellyn, J., & Westaway, P. (2011) *Europe will work – But it needs to strengthen its governance, fix its banks, and reform its structural policies*, Nomura Global Economics, March.

Mansfield, I. (2014) *A Blueprint for Britain: Openness not Isolation*, London: IEA.

Marsh, D. (2011) *The Euro: The Battle for the New Global Currency*, New Haven, CT: Yale University Press.

Marsh, D. (2013) *Europe's Deadlock: How the Euro Crisis Could Be Solved – and Why It Won't Happen*, New Haven, CT: Yale University Press.

Milne, I. (2004) *A Cost too Far? An Analysis of the Net Economic Costs and Benefits for the UK of EU Membership*, London: Civitas.

Milne, I. (2007) *Lost Illusions: British Foreign Policy*, London: The Bruges Group.

Milne, I. (2011) *Time to Say No: Alternatives to EU Membership*, London: Civitas.

Milne, I. (2013) The British car market and industry, *Civitas Review*, 10(1).

Minford, P. (1992) *The Cost of Europe*, Manchester: Manchester University Press.

Minford, P. (1999) So what NAFTA then? *Daily Telegraph*, 19 July, www.euro-know.org/europages/telegraph/dt990719.html, viewed on 12 November 2013.

Minford, P. (2006) Measuring the economic costs and benefits of the EU, *Open Economics Review*, 17.

Minford, P., Mahambre, V., & Nowell, E. (2005) *Should Britain Leave the EU? An Economic Analysis of a Troubled Relationship*, Cheltenham: Edward Elgar Publishing.

North, D. (1991) Institutions, *Journal of Economic Perspectives*, 5(1): 97–112.

North, D.C., Wallis, J.J., & Weingast, B.R. (2013) *Violence and Social Orders: A Conceptual Framework for Interpreting Recorded Human History*, New York: Cambridge University Press.

Oliver, T. (2013) *Europe without Britain: Assessing the Impact of the European Union of a British Withdrawal*, Berlin: Stiftung Wissenschaft und Politik.

Olson, M. (1974) *The Logic of Collective Action: Public Goods and the Theory of Groups*, Cambridge, MA: Harvard University Press.

Olson, M. (1984) *The Rise and Decline of Nations: Economic Growth, Stagflation and Social Rigidities*, New Haven, CT: Yale University Press.

Pain, N., & Young, G. (2004) *The Macroeconomic Impact of UK Withdrawal from the EU*, London: National Institute of Economic and Social Research.

Peet, J., & La Guardia, A. (2014) *Unhappy Union: How the Euro Crisis – and Europe – Can Be Fixed*, London: Profile.

Persson, M. (2013) Hey Berlin, this is what an EU without Britain would look like, *Daily Telegraph*, 7 June.

Portes, J. (2013) Commentary: The economic implications for the UK of leaving the European Union, *National Institute Economic Review*, 226.

Posner, R.A. (2005) The size of countries, Becker-Posner blog, 17 April, http://www.becker-posner-blog.com/2005/04/the-size-of-countriesposners-comment.html, viewed on 11 September 2013.

Siedentop, L. (2001) *Democracy in Europe*, New York: Columbia University Press.

Smallwood, C. (2010) *Why the Euro-zone Needs to Break Up*, London: Capital Economics.

Smith, A. (2011) *The Theory of Moral Sentiments*, Seattle, WA: Gutenberg Publishers. (Reprint of 1759 London edition.)

Van Middelaar, J. (2013) *The Passage to Europe: How a Continent Became a Union*, New Haven, CT: Yale University Press.

Vaubel, R. (1995) *The Centralisation of Western Europe: The Common Market, Political Integration and Democracy*, London: Institute of Economic Affairs.

Vaubel, R. (2009) *The European Institutions as an Interest Group: Dynamics of Ever-Closer Union*, London: Institute of Economic Affairs.

Notes

1. Stephen Booth and Christopher Howarth (2012) *Trading Places: Is EU Membership Still the Best Option for UK Trade?* London: Open Europe.

2. Sources: Worldology; Hitler Historical Museum; History Place; Jean-Jacques Arzalier (2000) The campaign of May–June 1940, the losses? in C. Levisse-Touzé (ed.) *La Campagne de 1940*, Paris: Editions Tallandier; and John Ellis (1993) *World War 2: A Statistical Survey*, New York: Facts on File.

3. Charles Moore (2013) *Margaret Thatcher: The Authorised Biography, Vol. One: Not for Turning*, London: Allen Lane.

4. Douglass North (1991) Institutions, *Journal of Economic Perspectives*, 5(1): 97–112.

5. Charles Grant (2013) *How to Build a Modern European Union*, London: Centre for European Reform.

6. I am grateful to Christopher Smallwood for emphasizing this.

7. For a brief guide to the evolution of the English constitution and the gradual rise of parliament, see David Green (2013) *What Have We Done?* London: Civitas.

8. See Anthony King and Ivor Crewe (2013) *The Blunders of Our Governments*, London: Oneworld Publications.

9. World Trade Organisation, *EU Trade Policy Review*.

10. R. Allen, M. Gaiorek and A. Smith (1996) Trade Creation and Trade Diversion Summary, Single Market Review Series, Subseries IV: Impact on Trade and Investment, Luxembourg: European Commission; S. Booth and C. Howarth (2012) *Trading Places: Is EU Membership Still the Best Option for UK Trade?* London: Open Europe; A.M. El Agraa (2011) *The European Union Economics and Policies*, 9th edn, Cambridge: Cambridge University Press; European Commission (2011) *External and Intra-EU Trade: A Statistical Yearbook*, Luxembourg: EuroStat; Y. Kandogan (2005) Trade creation and diversion effects of Europe's regional liberalization agreements, Working Paper No. 746, Ann Arbor, MI: William Davidson Institute.

11. Open Europe Briefing Note, Another 50 Examples of EU Waste, 10 November 2010.

12. According to a report in *The Guardian* on 18 September 2013.
13. See R.J. Barro (1991) Small is beautiful, *Asian Wall Street Journal*, October 11; A. Alesina and E. Spolaore (2003) *The Size of Nations*, Cambridge, MA: MIT Press; J. Erickson (2004) Size matters, review of *The Size of Nations* by A. Alesina & E. Spolaore, *SAIS Review of International Affairs*, 24(2); G.S. Becker (2005) Response on small is beautiful, Becker-Posner blog, 22 April and Why small has become beautiful, Becker-Posner blog, 17 April; A. Alesina, I. Angeloni and L. Schuknecht (2001) What Does the European Union Do? NBER Working Paper 8647, Cambridge, MA: National Bureau of Economic Research.
14. David Gilmour (2012) *The Pursuit of Italy: A History of a Land, Its Regions and Their Peoples*, London: Penguin.
15. *Ibid.*
16. *The Financial Times*, 3 October 2013.
17. *The Daily Telegraph*, 8 October 2013.
18. Reported in *The Financial Times*, 22 June 2013.
19. Fresh Start Project (2013) *Manifesto for Change: A New Vision for the UK in Europe*, London: Fresh Start Project, http://www.eufreshstart.org/downloads/manifesto-forchange.pdf.
20. *The Daily Telegraph*, 3 October 2013.
21. Office for Budget Responsibility and HM Treasury, December 2014.
22. See Global Britain Briefing Note No. 64, The Rotterdam-Antwerp Effect and the Netherlands Distortion, published at www.globalbritain.org.
23. I have taken these figures, and the ones that follow later in this section, from Michael Burrage (2014) *Where's the Insider Advantage*, London: Civitas.
24. Burrage, op. cit.
25. For a succinct and informative short study of the position of both the UK car market and the UK car industry, see Ian Milne (2013) The British car market and industry, *Civitas Review*, 10(1).
26. Burrage, op. cit.
27. The GFCI is a widely quoted ranking of financial centres produced by Z/Yen. It draws on two separate sources of data: responses to an online survey; and instrumental factors (external indices produced by organizations such

as the World Bank, OECD, BIS and numerous private companies).

28. Research conducted semi-annually by Oxford Economics.
29. Capital Economics (2014) *NExit – Assessing the Economic Impact of the Netherlands Leaving the European Union*, London: Capital Economics.
30. See Ian Milne (2011) *Time to Say No*, London: Civitas.
31. Sources: Canadian Ministry of Finance, *Financial Times* and Benjamin Cohen (2006) North American monetary union: A United States perspective, *Current Economics and Politics of Europe*, 17(1).
32. CBI (2013) *Our Global Future*, London: CBI.
33. Burrage, op. cit.
34. See Tim Hewish and James Styles (2012) *Common-trade, Common-growth, Common-wealth*, Cheltenham: The Hampden Trust.

Index